Effective Professional
Development Schools

Agenda for Education in a Democracy
Timothy J. McMannon, Series Editor

Effective Professional Development Schools

Richard W. Clark

Agenda for Education in a Democracy

Volume 3

Jossey-Bass Publishers
San Francisco

Jossey-Bass books and products are available through most bookstores. To contact Jossey-Bass directly, call (888) 378–2537, fax to (800) 605–2665, or visit our website at www.josseybass.com.

Substantial discounts on bulk quantities of Jossey-Bass books are available to corporations, professional associations, and other organizations. For details and discount information, contact the special sales department at Jossey-Bass.

Manufactured in the United States of America on Lyons Falls Turin Book. This paper is acid-free and 100 percent totally chlorine-free.

Library of Congress Cataloging-in-Publication Data

Clark, Richard W.
    Effective professional development schools / Richard W. Clark.
— 1st ed.
        p. cm.—(Agenda for education in a democracy series; v. 3)
    Includes bibliographical references.
    ISBN 0-7879-4562-5 (acid-free paper)
    1. Laboratory schools—United States. 2. College-school cooperation—United States.
3. Teachers—Training of—United States. I. Title. II. Series.
    LB2154.A3 C53 1999
    370'.71—dc21

                                   98–58076

PB Printing 10 9 8 7 6 5 4 3 2 1   FIRST EDITION

Contents

List of Tables and Exhibits

Series Foreword

In 1894, a young Theodore Roosevelt proclaimed, "There are two gospels which should be preached to every reformer. The first is the gospel of morality; the second is the gospel of efficiency."[1] The interplay of efficiency and morality in human institutions, particularly in the educational institutions we call schools, continues to intrigue.[2] On the surface, both morality and efficiency are good; *morality* denotes fairness, virtue, and good conduct, among other things, and *efficiency* bespeaks a high level of achievement or production with a minimal expenditure of effort, money, or time. Ideally, our schools, our governments, our places of employment, even our families would be both moral and efficient in their own ways.

Difficulties arise, however, when we attempt to move beyond generalizations to specifics. What is morality? Who decides? Philosophers far wiser than I have spent lifetimes trying to convince themselves and others that there are or there are not definitive answers to those brief but complex questions. How can efficiency be judged? What are the criteria? Again the questions point to no single, certain answers. Moreover, inefficiencies have frequently been imposed on human institutions in the name of efficiency, and immoralities promulgated in the name of morality. When we advance to another level of specificity and consider morality and efficiency in the schools, the questions not only retain their complexity but also become very personal and deadly serious: Should my child's school teach morality? What exactly would that mean? How efficient is the schooling my child is experiencing? Do my child's grades reflect actual learning? These and similar questions shape debates and decisions about our nation's schools.

Neil Postman argues that we come to understand our lives and ascribe meaning to our actions by placing them in the context of a narrative: "a story . . . that tells of origins and envisions a future, a story that constructs ideals, prescribes rules of conduct, provides a source of authority, and, above all, gives a sense of continuity and purpose."[3] If Postman is right—and I think he is—then our chosen narratives help both to determine and to reveal what we are willing to work for, to live for, perhaps even to die for.

Rarely, if ever, are people called on to give their lives in defense of the institution of the school or the process of education. Some heroic teachers have, of course, given their lives in defense of their students. Clearly, their narratives embraced selflessness and sacrifice. But for most educators, selflessness and sacrifice mean no more than forgoing other more lucrative and respected professions, giving up evenings and weekends to grade papers, or serving on interminable committees. Even these sacrifices represent hardships, however, and they raise questions about educators' narratives. What are teachers willing to work for, to give their lives *to?*

Educators in the sixteen settings of the National Network for Educational Renewal (NNER)—be they school faculty, teacher educators, or arts and sciences professors—have chosen to embrace a morally based narrative for education and schooling. They see schools as places where democracy is learned and practiced, where schooling is far more than job training, where education is a seamless process of self-improvement. To them, teaching must be guided by a four-part mission: enculturating the young in a social and political democracy, providing access to knowledge for all children and youths, practicing a nurturant pedagogy, and ensuring responsible stewardship of the schools. Each part of the mission is based on and permeated by moral dimensions.[4]

Because they perceive all levels of schooling to be interconnected, NNER educators insist that the improvement of the nation's schools and the improvement of its teacher education programs must proceed simultaneously. Having better schools requires having better teachers; preparing better teachers requires having exemplary schools in which to prepare them. And the word *reform* rarely enters NNER educators' vocabularies: that term implies a finite process with corruption at one end and completion at the other. Faculty members at NNER settings prefer to think of educational improvement as a process of *renewal* by which they continuously remake good schools and teacher education programs into better ones through inquiry and hard work. NNER participants work toward the simultaneous renewal of schooling and the education of educators.

Without a plan, simultaneous renewal would be no more than a slogan. In other words, it would be morality without efficiency. The plan, or agenda, by which NNER educators pursue simultaneous renewal has come to be called the Agenda for Education in a Democracy. No creation of momentary inspiration, the Agenda emerged over several years as a product of inquiries into schools and teaching, and it was disseminated by means of several books written or edited by John Goodlad and his associates. Goodlad's *A Place Called School* (1984) began the process of explicating the Agenda, and four books published in 1990—*The Moral Dimensions of Teaching, Places Where Teachers Are Taught, Teachers for Our Nation's Schools,* and *Access to Knowledge*—further developed the essential concepts.[5] These concepts were clarified for implementation as nineteen postulates, which describe conditions that must be established in order to achieve the four-part mission for educators and the schools in which they teach.[6] The postulates guide the efforts of school and university leaders as they work together to establish new organizational structures and processes to advance their institutions on the path of simultaneous renewal.

The books in the Agenda for Education in a Democracy series explore key ideas underlying the Agenda and describe strategies for pursuing the simultaneous renewal of schools and the education of educators.

Richard W. Clark's *Effective Professional Development Schools* explores the myths and realities of these schools. Effective PDSs provide professional development opportunities for practicing and aspiring teachers, serve as sites for research and inquiry into education, and provide excellent schooling for the children and youths who attend them. This book presents not only a theoretical basis for PDSs but also practical guidance for establishing, funding, and evaluating them. With the other volumes in the series, *Effective Professional Development Schools* offers a hopeful narrative of schools and teacher preparation programs as increasingly connected, increasingly moral, and increasingly efficient educational institutions.

TIMOTHY J. McMANNON
Series Editor
Agenda for Education
in a Democracy

Acknowledgments

The subject of partner schools, more commonly referred to as professional development schools (or PDSs), has received much attention from those interested in improving the education of educators and schooling for children. Much of what has been published about them consists of edited collections of stories about PDSs by those who have participated in their creation. Except for the third chapter, which was written by John I. Goodlad, a single author wrote this book. The book grew out of my fourteen years of experience with the creation, development, and evaluation of such schools and out of the efforts of educators throughout the National Network for Educational Renewal (NNER) to make progress in the development of PDSs.

Help with content material in the case studies has come from many educators in the NNER, and financial support came particularly from the Arthur Vining Davis Foundations, which helped with the development of secondary partner schools in the NNER. Cori Mantle-Bromley and others in the Colorado Partnership for Educational Renewal contributed much to my thinking about evaluation of PDSs. Particular appreciation is also due Audrey Kleinsasser of the University of Wyoming and Elizabeth Kozleski and Carol Wilson of the Colorado Partnership for their help in reviewing the manuscript.

A special task force of the NNER that included Richard Barnes, Donna Wiseman, Jane Applegate, Kathy Hughes, Barbara Gottesman, and Marge Plecki provided assistance with the finance material in Chapter Six. The Spencer Foundation and the Claude Worthington Benedum Foundation provided funding for the work on finance. Chapter Seven, on evaluation, owes a particular intellectual debt to Ken Sirotnik of the University of Washington. Marsha Levine and Roberta Trachtman, who have been leading the National Council for Accreditation of Teacher Education's efforts to generate standards for professional development schools, also contributed to underlying ideas in several of the chapters.

Portions of this book have appeared in slightly different forms in a variety of publications. In addition to the citations of such items as they appear, special acknowledgment is made here of the permission to use material from Marsha Levine and Roberta Trachtman (eds.), *Making Professional Development Schools Work: Politics, Practice, and Policy* (New York: Teachers College Press, 1997); Russell T. Osguthorpe, R. Carl Harris, Melanie Fox Harris, and Sharon Black (eds.), *Partner Schools: Centers for Educational Renewal* (San Francisco: Jossey-Bass, 1995); Richard W. Clark, *Professional Development Schools: Policy and Financing, A Guide for Policymakers* (Washington, D.C.: American Association of Colleges for Teacher Education, 1997); Richard W. Clark, *What School Leaders Can Do to Help Change Teacher Education*, 2nd ed. (Washington, D.C.: American Association of Colleges for Teacher Education, 1996); Richard W. Clark, "School-University Relationships: An Interpretive Review," in Kenneth A. Sirotnik and John I. Goodlad (eds.), *School-University Partnerships in Action: Concepts, Cases, and Concerns* (New York: Teachers College Press, 1988); Richard W. Clark, "Professional Development Schools," *Contemporary Education* 67 (Summer 1996): 244–248; Richard W. Clark, *Community-School-University Partnership: Literature Review* (Washington, D.C.: Hamilton Fish National Institute on School and Community Violence, The George Washington University, 1998); and Center for Educational Renewal, College of Education, University of Washington, Occasional Papers and items in the *Center Correspondent*.

I am also grateful for the continuing intellectual stimulation provided by colleagues at the Institute for Educational Inquiry and the Center for Educational Renewal—Gary Fenstermacher, John Goodlad, Timothy McMannon, Wilma Smith, and Roger Soder—and by senior associates of those centers who have worked with me on partner schools, including Mona Bailey, Robert Egbert, Calvin Frazier, Paul Heckman, Donna Hughes, and Carol Wilson.

A special acknowledgment is also due my wife, Rosemary, whose patience has been tried once again as she has waited for the completion of this project.

January 1999   RICHARD W. CLARK

About the Sponsor

The National Network for Educational Renewal (NNER) was established in 1986 to put into practice the belief that the improvement of schooling and the renewal of teacher education must proceed simultaneously. In short, good schools require good teachers, and good teachers learn their profession in good schools.

The NNER presently embraces sixteen member settings in fourteen states: California, Colorado, Connecticut, Hawaii, Maine, Missouri, Nebraska, New Jersey, Ohio, South Carolina, Texas, Utah, Washington, and Wyoming. Member settings work to build collaboration among three main groups that play a vital role in the preparation of new teachers: education faculty in colleges and universities; arts and sciences faculty; and faculty in elementary and secondary schools. All told, there are thirty-three colleges or universities, over one hundred school districts, and about five hundred partner schools in the NNER.

The NNER extends the work of the Center for Educational Renewal (CER), which was founded in 1985 by John I. Goodlad, Kenneth A. Sirotnik, and Roger Soder to study and facilitate "the simultaneous renewal of schooling and the education of educators."

To support the work of the NNER and the CER, Goodlad, Soder, and Sirotnik established the independent, nonprofit Institute for Educational Inquiry (IEI) in Seattle in 1992. The IEI oversees leadership training programs for key personnel from NNER settings, administers grants from philanthropic organizations to the

NNER, conducts research and evaluation studies, and publishes a series of Work in Progress papers. The IEI is the sponsoring agency for the Agenda for Education in a Democracy series.

About the Authors

The Author

Richard W. Clark is a senior associate of the Institute for Educational Inquiry and of the Center for Educational Renewal at the University of Washington. In this role, he has been the "chief worrier" for partner schools in the National Network for Educational Renewal (NNER). He has participated in work with the National Center for Restructuring Education, Schools, and Teaching (NCREST) and the National Council for Accreditation of Teacher Education (NCATE) to build standards for professional development schools. He has served as an evaluator on school reform in Philadelphia for the past ten years, participated as a team leader in the School Change Project of the Coalition of Essential Schools, been an evaluator of the New Standards Project, and evaluated reform efforts in Kentucky. He has written and spoken widely on a variety of topics related to school renewal and the improvement of teacher education. Clark worked as a teacher and administrator in the Bellevue (Washington) School District for thirty years, spending the last twelve of those years as deputy superintendent of schools.

In addition to having written articles, pamphlets, and chapters on professional development schools, Clark is the author of nationally adopted language arts and speech textbooks. His most recent book, with coauthors Patricia Wasley and Robert Hampel, is *Kids and School Reform* (Jossey-Bass, 1997).

The Contributors

John I. Goodlad is president of the Institute for Educational Inquiry and codirector of the Center for Educational Renewal at the University of Washington. Throughout his career, he has been involved in an array of educational renewal programs and projects and has engaged in large-scale studies of educational change, schooling, and teacher education. In addition to advancing a comprehensive program of research and development directed to the simultaneous renewal of schooling and teacher education, he is inquiring into the mission of education in a democratic society.

Timothy J. McMannon is a senior associate of the Institute for Educational Inquiry and of the Center for Educational Renewal at the University of Washington and teaches history at colleges and universities in the Seattle area. His main areas of interest include recent U.S. history, the history of American education, and the public purpose of education and schooling.

Prologue

In one of the most devastating yet charming commentaries ever written about human vanity, gullibility, and mindlessness, Hans Christian Andersen told the story of the emperor who paraded in nonexistent new clothes before a crowd of obsequious subjects. It was, of course, a child who said what none of the others in the kingdom were willing to say for fear of being considered stupid. It was a child who declared that the emperor had no clothes.

Professional development schools (PDSs)—places where teachers are prepared and schooling is improved—may not be emperors, but emperors and their subjects in fairy tales are not the only ones who make deceptive claims. Former president of the American Association of Colleges for Teacher Education (AACTE) Mary Diez observed: "As with many reform proposals, the professional development school movement suffers from a rhetoric that oversimplifies the issues. . . . I am cynical when I hear institutions claim to have PDS relationships when only one faculty member is involved in the schools and no one else knows anything about it. My cynicism increases when the PDS label appears to be just that—a new label on unchanged practice."[1]

Another former AACTE president, John I. Goodlad, echoes this warning in *Educational Renewal: Better Teachers, Better Schools*: "The greatest danger to solid, lasting collaboration of university and school personnel in partner schools is *imagology*—the transformation of both reality and ideology into various images of them. There exists just enough progress to create the image of close connections when, in actuality, there exists as yet little more than symbols."[2]

Whether the question is raised as one of imagology, expressed cynically as a new label on unchanged practice, or debunked by observant children, professional development schools are vulnerable to claims that they are shams. Too often, only the innocent wisdom of children reveals the absence of substance in educational reforms such as those represented by PDSs.

This book has been written for those who are attending to the simultaneous renewal of schools and the education of educators, as Goodlad suggests in Chapter Three, and those who truly pay attention to "what matters most," as the National Commission on Teaching & America's Future has suggested.[3] It has been written to help them tailor school settings and develop teachers whom children can immediately recognize as being better than the ones they have experienced before.

Whether the emperor (the professional development school) has any clothes, or has clothes of the quality claimed, is a hotly debated question. Accordingly, one goal of this book is to describe the attributes of a "well-clothed" PDS by using examples of schools that are at various stages in their own evolution. These examples are set forth so that readers can decide for themselves whether there is enough evidence to say the emperor is well attired in many instances.

Beyond providing examples that help answer the question of the current status of PDSs, this book is primarily concerned with constructive suggestions for creating and sustaining effective professional development schools. In an effort to describe what children and adults should experience in a good PDS, the book proceeds first to an examination of the reasons for creating PDSs and an explanation of what they are. Next, in Chapter Two, it turns to the conditions that must be in place "before the beginning" of a successful PDS. In the third chapter, John Goodlad draws on his nearly half-century of experience in attempting to advance the simultaneous renewal of schools and the education of educators. He describes some of the experiences of the National Network for Educational Renewal (NNER) in pursuing such partnerships. The fourth chapter examines the first layer of clothing—processes some call "threshold conditions," because they need to be achieved before refining a PDS. Chapter Five addresses characteristics of fully operational PDSs, speaking to the style of a garment for the PDS that has become a solid contributor to school and teacher education reform. Supportive conditions—finances and resource allocation—are addressed in Chapter Six, and in Chapter Seven the question of how to evaluate PDSs—how to determine whether the clothes are real—is discussed. The concluding chapter addresses the subject of the leadership required to create and sustain uncommonly good PDSs. Throughout the book, I have incorporated brief case studies and vignettes as examples. These stories about PDSs are drawn from partner schools in the NNER and from other PDSs around the nation.

On with the parade.

Bellevue, Washington   RICHARD W. CLARK
January 1999

1

Introduction

Definition, Description, and Benefits of a Professional Development School (PDS)

Some early readers of the manuscript for this book objected to relating the story of emerging professional development schools to the fable of the emperor's new clothes. One complained that using a children's tale trivialized the importance of these schools; another objected to the implication that PDSs were so important they could be likened to emperors. Another raised the question of the appropriateness of the emperor metaphor because of the emperor's gender. These disparate responses themselves help explain why the metaphor seems so apt. The emperor did not have a clear understanding of who he was—or at least had an inflated opinion of himself. His subjects were not clear about him either; they may have known of his feelings of self-importance but were unwilling to see him in a realistic manner.

True, professional development schools are not emperors, although some may have an exaggerated view of their own worth. However, they are the locus of extremely important work in renewing schools and the education of educators. Moreover, people who work in and study such schools have varying views regarding what they are and are hesitant to examine them critically.

Whether or not the fable of the emperor's new clothes provides an apt metaphor for thinking about PDSs, it is essential to begin consideration of PDSs with a clear definition of what they are, one that can serve as a frame of reference for the remainder of the analysis. Toward that end, this opening chapter addresses four questions:

- Why consider creating professional development schools?

- What are professional development schools?

- What should professional development schools look like?

- What benefits do various studies claim for them (for P–12 students, university students, practicing educators, and knowledge about education and its renewal)?

Why Consider Creating Professional Development Schools?

Ideally, America's elementary and secondary schools ensure that all of the nation's young people learn to think clearly and critically, live honorably and productively, and function effectively in a social and political democracy. But in reality, the schools fall short of the mark. As the National Commission on Teaching & America's Future (NCTAF) noted, "In this knowledge-based society, the United States urgently needs to reaffirm a consensus about the role and purposes of public education in a democracy—and the prime importance of learning in meeting those purposes. The challenge extends far beyond preparing students for the world of work. It includes building an American future that is just and humane as well as productive, that is as socially vibrant and civil in its pluralism as it is competitive."[1]

The nation's educational system is at a critical juncture, with a rare opportunity at hand.[2] During this decade, many teachers will retire or switch careers. Schools will hire two million new teachers to fill these vacancies. How they are prepared, selected, and inducted into teaching will be crucial to the success of school improvement. Likewise, many professors in both education and the liberal arts will retire. Colleges and universities also can further school reform by appointing faculty who will work toward teacher education renewal.

Renewing schools and renewing teacher education must proceed simultaneously. The nation cannot have good schools without good teachers. Conversely, teachers must learn how to teach in good schools. At present, neither the schools nor the teacher education programs are good enough.

Many people offer many solutions to the problems they see with America's schools. But they must realize that the schools will not change until teacher preparation programs change. The NCTAF noted this connection, commenting that, "When it comes to widespread change, we have behaved as though national, state, and district mandates could, like magic wands, transform schools. But all the directives and proclamations are simply so much fairy dust. Successful programs cannot be replicated in schools where staff lack the know-how and resources to bring them to life. Wonderful curriculum ideas fall flat in classrooms where they are not understood or supported by the broader activities of the school. And increased graduation and testing requirements only create greater failure if teachers do not know how to reach students so that they can learn."[3]

If schools are to achieve their promise as institutions of democracy, they must be staffed by teachers who are well educated, who clearly understand their moral and ethical obligations as teachers in a democratic society, who have a solid grounding in the art and science of teaching, and who take seriously their responsibilities as stewards of the schools. If schools are to have such teachers, then teacher education must undergo serious renewal in tandem with the reform of public schools. As the NCTAF asserted:

- What teachers know and can do is the most important influence on what students learn.

- Recruiting, preparing, and retaining good teachers is the central strategy for improving our schools.

- School reform cannot succeed unless it focuses on creating the conditions in which teachers can teach, and teach well.[4]

Furthermore, long-term school renewal depends on having all teachers in a school working together, constantly reviewing and improving the whole. Most teacher preparation programs do not provide systematic training in consensus building or experience in working as a team with administrators and parents to improve the overall school. Preparation programs focus on work in individual classrooms, not on school renewal. Yet school renewal is in trouble unless teachers learn to see beyond the limited horizon of the classroom. In the words of John I. Goodlad, there needs to be "a new way of preparing teachers that necessitates good schools in order to have better teachers so that in turn we can have better schools."[5]

A blueprint for the simultaneous renewal of schools and the education of educators is put forth in Goodlad's *Teachers for Our Nation's Schools* and *Educational Renewal: Better Teachers, Better Schools*.[6] Through surveys, interviews, and visits to representative colleges and universities with teacher education programs, Goodlad and his colleagues gathered a formidable amount of data on the teacher education enterprise. *Teachers for Our Nation's Schools* presents Goodlad's conclusions and summarizes the richness and depth of this five-year study, the largest ever conducted on the subject. *Educational Renewal* provides additional explanation of some of the basic concepts introduced in the first book, focusing on key relationships that need to be built among teacher educators, arts and sciences faculty, and school-based educators.

Goodlad raises serious concerns about such matters as the nation's changing demographics and economics, which are creating new expectations for teachers and schools in a democracy; the inadequate way in which teachers are being prepared; and the neglect that teacher education suffers.

The following conclusions are examples of those that Goodlad presented. They indicate why a tremendous amount of commitment, energy, creativity, and support will be required to revitalize teacher education, and they begin to suggest the kind of new clothes that must be worn by a PDS that does not want to be seen as a sham.

Teachers Do Not Know Enough to Teach about the Responsibilities of Living in a Democracy

The schools have a moral imperative to enculturate the young into a democracy and instill in them the disciplined modes of thought required for effective, satisfying participation in human affairs. Goodlad argues that it is fundamental for all students to learn what a democracy is, how it works, and what their responsibilities are for full participation.

However, traditional teacher education programs pay scant attention to helping prospective teachers develop an understanding of democracy in the broadest sense of the word or what it means to teach students the moral and intellectual responsibilities for living in a democracy. Nor do teacher education programs pay systematic attention to the means by which all students can be provided the intellectual tools for participating broadly in the human conversation.

Colleges and Universities Provide Little Sustained Commitment to Teacher Education

College presidents rarely consider teacher education to be a priority for themselves or their institutions, Goodlad reports. Many teacher education programs are tolerated merely because of economic or political expediency. These programs often have no organizational identity, no faculty with decision-making authority, and no constancy of budget or personnel. A reward structure that values scholarship resulting in publication over scholarly work in the field penalizes faculty for getting involved in the clinical phases of teacher education.

College and university leaders must embrace their social responsibility and strive to fund and support fully, promote actively, and advance vigorously their teacher education programs, according to Goodlad, or quit the business of preparing teachers. The president must establish a clearly identifiable group of academic and clinical faculty, drawn from the college and from elementary and secondary schools, and give this group the authority and responsibility for the teacher education program and its students. Goodlad calls the structure established by this group a *center of pedagogy*.[7]

Because of Teacher Shortages, Some States Allow Teacher Certification through Questionable Shortcut Programs

To meet shortages, state officials are turning to preparation programs that are cheap and quick, but these programs have serious disadvantages. The novices prepared in shortcut programs are the greenest of greenhorns with respect to teaching. Their baccalaureate course work, often completed many years earlier, was just as fragmented as that of teacher education graduates, but they have even less knowledge about how to teach, teaching in a democracy, and working collaboratively to improve the schools. In addition, their student teaching occurs in the very schools that everyone has condemned as ineffective. Those who would make mentoring with experienced teachers the primary basis of professional preparation for beginning teachers are, in effect, reinforcing the status quo.

Goodlad insists that state certification policies must strongly support teacher education programs without unwarranted intrusions. Programs "must be free from curricular specifications by licensing agencies and restrained only by enlightened, professionally driven requirements for accreditation," he writes. In addition, programs "must be protected from the vagaries of supply and demand by state policies that allow neither backdoor 'emergency' programs nor temporary teaching licenses."[8]

The Undergraduate Curriculum Is Inadequate for Prospective Teachers

Teachers should be among the best-educated members of society. In reality, the Study of the Education of Educators revealed that their general education consists of disconnected courses in arts and sciences. (These are the same courses that all other students take and that have been heavily criticized as inadequate in recent years.[9]) These courses are followed by more disconnected courses in an academic specialization, methods courses for teaching, and fieldwork and student teaching in local schools. Usually, these courses bear little relation to one another or to what has preceded or will follow.

Goodlad recommends a new curriculum for prospective teachers, including the following:

- A preeducation sequence, much like premedicine for doctors, that gives students a solid, coherent academic foundation, a sophisticated understanding of democracy, and an introduction to the art and science of teaching what they are learning;

- A professional education sequence for the study of learning, teaching, and schooling; and

- A postgraduate sequence of well-supervised practice in partner schools where ongoing assessment and renewal are standard practices.

The curriculum must be sequenced thoughtfully, with elements deliberately integrated to enable students to see the relationships across disciplines and between academics and teaching.

The curriculum also must address how teachers—working with colleagues, administrators, parents, and community leaders—can continually renew their schools.

The Socialization of New Teachers Tends to Reinforce the Status Quo

During student teaching and their first few years of work, new teachers may be idealistic and committed to making improvements, but they are likely to have little impact. New teachers face the tyranny of the status quo: "We've always done it this way" or "Welcome to the real world" or "Forget all that nonsense they taught you in ed school." The message is to fit in. Discouraged and disillusioned, many teachers quit: half leave the profession within five years. Of those who remain, many become isolated, trying to do the best they can in their individual classrooms.

Goodlad believes that a wide variety of laboratory settings and exemplary schools must be available to teacher education students for observation, hands-on experiences, internships, and residencies. Such arrangements demand close collaboration between the schools and the university and clearly delineated connections between class work and fieldwork. Thus, for Goodlad, the schools commonly referred to as *professional development schools*—or PDSs—should be called *partner schools*. For a school to qualify as a partner school, its teachers and administrators must demonstrate their willingness to engage in constant, critical review and renewal of the school's structure and performance. In addition, Goodlad believes that the number of students admitted as a cohort to the teacher education program must not exceed the number of available positions in the partner schools that serve as clinical settings.

Despite the achievements of the school reform movement, schooling in America is still in serious trouble. Linking school reform with reform of the education of educators in partner schools or PDSs substantially increases the chances for lasting improvements in schooling.

What Are Professional Development Schools?

Major organizations—including Goodlad's National Network for Educational Renewal (NNER); the Holmes Partnership; the National Center for Restructuring Education, Schools, and Teaching (NCREST); and the National Council for Accreditation of Teacher Education (NCATE)—agree that professional development schools must accomplish four basic goals.[10] Although the wording used by each organization varies, they concur that such schools provide a clinical setting for preservice education, engage in professional development for practitioners, promote and conduct inquiry that advances knowledge of schooling, and provide an exemplary education for a segment of P–12 students (preschool through twelfth grade).

How many PDSs are in existence? No one really knows. The NNER includes more than five hundred such schools in its 1997–98 directory, and it does not include many that are part of other important reform initiatives. The PDSs reported are substantially different from one another. The agreement on purpose that is apparent in the national statements is not as clear when actual practices in the schools are examined—a condition that gives rise to questions about the legitimacy of the move toward such schools and to doubts that the emperor has any clothes.

Almost all schools calling themselves professional development schools emphasize some element of preservice education. Only a few focus on retraining practicing teachers or on some other form of staff development. For many, staff development activity is limited to incidental learning by the teachers in the PDS. That is, teachers are said to benefit from their exposure to the preservice candidates and their mentors, but there is no thought about the cumulative effect of such exposures on the individual teachers or the relationship of such exposures to the changes a school may need. Inquiry efforts tend to feature projects carried on by individual professors and school faculty rather than focus on the institution. Occasionally, they exist only as a course in action research taught by a university faculty member and made available to people in the PDS. Whether schooling is—or even should be—exemplary for the children enrolled in the PDS is problematic. Little information exists concerning P–12 educational practices in existing PDSs (although the evidence that is available is positive[11]); instead, most published case studies focus on the training given to preservice candidates. University- and school-based educators often worry about whether preparing preservice students in an "exemplary" setting will leave them unprepared for the "real world" of schools. Those who worry about the feasibility of using exemplary schools too often envision such schools as being inhabited by students from the upper socioeconomic groups. However, they do not think deeply about the characteristics of the schools they want the prospective teachers to experience. (These characteristics are discussed at length in Chapter Five.)

For the present, let us note that these schools should be exemplary in the way they approach the ongoing tasks of school renewal and in the way they seek to serve their populations of students. Preparing teachers in settings that are not at least seeking to be good schools ensures that new teachers enter the profession socialized as educators in settings content to be poor schools, a socialization from which they may never recover.

The gap between advocated purposes and the reality of the schools motivates various groups as they seek to develop standards that will separate the "wannabes" from the real professional development schools. The National Council for Accreditation of Teacher Education is advancing the most ambitious of these standard-setting efforts under the leadership of Marsha Levine. The NCATE project builds on work done earlier by the Holmes Group, NNER, NCREST, the American Federation of Teachers, and the National Education Association, as well as on alternative models of quality review, such as the School Quality Review Process in New York and the private sector's Malcolm Baldrige Awards.[12] As of 1998, twenty schools from various parts of the country have been selected to test the utility of the draft standards.

Thus far, each effort to develop standards has made good progress as long as it remained at the committee level. But when the preliminary work products are brought before the parties who are likely to be measured by the standards, people get defensive, and explanations of why each site must be judged on its own merits abound. This has been vexing for both policymakers and funders who are interested in the issue of what PDSs are accomplishing.

In sum, there are nationally stated purposes that are not always reflected in the practices of individual professional development schools. Also, several groups are at work on national standards for PDSs, but there is resistance to external measurement of progress in relation to those standards—resistance even to external standards' defining the characteristics of local PDSs. (Chapter Seven will say more about standards and evaluating PDSs.)

What Should Professional Development Schools Look Like?

Given this gap between asserted purposes and common practice, how else can we define a PDS? Examples are another means of doing so. The following descriptions of elementary, middle, and high school professional development schools show how various settings around the country have been pursuing the task of dressing their emperor by attaining the four major goals of PDSs. Because these same schools are described anonymously elsewhere, pseudonyms are used in this discussion as well.

Bay Elementary and Northern University

Bay Elementary School is an average-size school in an average-size district, but there is nothing average about the way it functions as a PDS. Bay's work with Northern University has received national recognition.

Purpose 1: Preservice

The heart of Northern's efforts to prepare teachers is its field-based fifth-year program. Students who enroll in this phase of the program earn thirty-three graduate credits. University officials note that among the benefits of this approach is that it allows them to charge higher tuition than if the students were undergraduates.

Northern's full teacher training program also includes an eighteen-credit undergraduate minor and a master of education completion phase—nine credits a year over two years after portfolio review for admission. Although the precertification fifth-year phase of the program uses a PDS as its main site, M.Ed. students complete their work in the schools in which they work as new teachers. During each of their two years of study, they complete a six-course sequence of curriculum and foundations courses. The M.Ed. also includes teacher-as-researcher training and the preparation of portfolios that reflect on the candidates as maturing teachers. This master's program provides good support for beginning teachers—about 30 percent of those enrolled in preservice since the new programs were initiated have finished the minor, and about 50 percent have done the completion phase.

Because we are interested primarily in work associated with the PDS, we will look more thoroughly at the fifth-year program, which has four major components. The first is admissions. University faculty screen prospective students, all of whom must hold a bachelor's degree, through a paper review to verify eligibility. Then, through a portfolio review, a screening committee of school and university faculty examines applicants' prior studies and experiences working with children. Prospective students next have an opportunity to visit Bay and other schools that serve as PDSs for the Northern program. These orientation sessions help them choose the setting in which they will seek placement. Candidates are then interviewed by a team of two school faculty members and one university person. For example, candidates who indicate they would like to be assigned to Bay are interviewed by two educators from that school along with the university faculty member who works as the site leader there. The final step in this phase is the placement process, during which decisions are made that balance assignments among the different PDSs while honoring feedback from the interview teams and the candidates' requests. Such detailed attention to admissions is costly, but the educators at Bay and Northern are convinced that it results in better-quality student teachers and more appropriate assignments than do traditional placement processes.

The second component of Northern and Bay's effort is team building. University and school faculty have selected an Outward Bound experience for their candidates. During this two- or three-day adventure, students and teachers develop self-confidence and reliance on one another and begin to build themes for their work during the year. Various team-building activities, from rope courses to problem-solving simulations, are included. In addition to paying facilitation, travel, and housing costs associated with this experience, Northern enhances team building by paying attention to small details such as purchasing T-shirts for members of the Bay cohort.

Curriculum and instruction constitute the third component of Northern and Bay's work. Seven methods courses for a total of twenty-one credits provide a pedagogical background for the prospective teachers. There are courses in teaching mathematics, social studies, science, technology, and two in literacy: one in reading and one in writing. The seventh course focuses on human development. For Northern, the schedule varies somewhat depending on the PDS. At Bay, and in most instances, the course work begins in August and ends in February. This means that some students may finish course work before actually registering for the class. For the most part, the courses are taught at Bay Elementary by university faculty. A course leader from the Bay faculty sets up actual field assignments.

The internship is the second part of the curriculum and instruction component. It includes a yearlong seminar for which students receive three credits in the fall and three in the spring. They also receive six credits for the fifteen-week internship they finish in the spring. Mentor teachers are assigned to the students at the beginning of the year and are compensated by Northern for work done throughout the year.

The fourth component of the program is the portfolio evaluation process. Mentor teachers and the university- and school-based site supervisors work with the students throughout the year to develop their portfolios. In the spring, the candidates make public presentations of their work, exhibiting their portfolios to their mentors and supervisors and to a person not directly involved with the cohort, such as Northern's dean, Bay's principal, or the district superintendent. Northern and Bay faculty recognize that this activity is a program-selling event as well as an evaluative one.

Purpose 2: Professional Development

In addition to providing a location for clinical experiences for preservice candidates, Bay serves as an in-service professional development site. Bay teachers and other elementary school teachers from the same district take courses alongside preservice students in, for example, math, science, and literacy. Teachers pay through the district to attend these courses. Also, considerable efforts are made to assist teachers by promoting networking within and across schools in the school-university partnership in which Northern and Bay participate. The partnership also conducts conferences for teachers in the area; more than five hundred educators engage annually in the discussions of different approaches to assessing student learning.

Work by school and university faculty to develop inquiry and research skills also aids in their professional growth.

Purpose 3: Inquiry

Bay and other PDSs associated with Northern are investigating using portfolios as a basis for certification. Bay teachers are active partners in determining what preservice portfolios should be, including evaluating different approaches such as using videotaped or digitized portfolios. Teachers assemble their own portfolios to help teacher candidates decide what should be in theirs.

Also through the partnership between Northern and the school district of which Bay is a part, teachers are awarded minigrants to promote experimentation with new and innovative approaches to classroom assessment.

Purpose 4: School Renewal

School renewal activities in the partnership concentrate on learner-centered practice. One approach to this has been through promotion of the School Quality Review Process within the school-university partnership. This process, based on concepts developed in New York and in Great Britain, engages teachers throughout Bay Elementary, including some who are not particularly involved in preservice teacher education.

As another approach to school renewal, Bay faculty pick annual themes—for example, teacher portfolios or a focus on integrated learning and articulation across grade levels. Then, with faculty from Northern, they build special courses and seminars for interns and cooperating teachers around those themes.

The Bay-Northern school-university partnership facilitates a wide variety of school renewal activities in connection with various national reform movements, including Foxfire, Atlas, the Coalition of Essential Schools, and NCREST.

Both Bay and Northern have changed considerably as a result of their collaboration. Preservice teachers no longer take courses isolated from the realities of practice. Their student-teaching experiences are closely related to their academic work. Program graduates are hired in record numbers because school leaders perceive them as ready to engage in the ongoing work of school renewal. Children at Bay experience their education in a setting that has become a true center of inquiry for teachers and students. Parents and students choose between classes that include students of different ages and those restricted to a single age group, taking into consideration different teaching styles and patterns of classroom organization. Even the most severely handicapped children interact regularly with other students in regular classrooms. There are clear performance standards with public criteria for student work. Portfolios, student juries, community panels, and public self-critiques by students are all included as assessment strategies. In short, the school models intellectual engagement, learner-centered practice, and norms of inquiry and reflection.[13]

Platte Middle School

Five hundred seventy middle-school students attend this PDS in a blue-collar suburb of a western city. A College of Education professor from Urban State initiated the relationship, and for ten years it was primarily a setting where he worked with student teachers. However, as the school participated in activities sponsored by the broader school-university partnership, the principal, faculty, and the original university contact applied pressure to generate a more comprehensive PDS.

Now when one enters the school the relationship is immediately evident. As a result of a project initiated by a student teacher in art during the previous year, bright yellow, blue, and red life-size silhouettes of children dress up halls that in other schools are covered with layers of paint to hide graffiti or are decorated with pictures straight from school supply-house catalogs.

Purpose 1: Preservice

During the course of a school year, ninety to one hundred university students will be involved with the school. Not all will have the visible and lasting impact that the art student had, but all will leave their marks on the school.

Two university classes are taught on site, even though the undergraduate teacher-training program serves students who are not traditional undergraduates. As is typical of an urban campus, it is not unusual to find people in their forties or fifties in the classes preparing for second careers. When some of these students were asked what they thought about having their classes at the school site, their first response was a question: "Why would it be any other way?" Forty-three students involved in those classes spend approximately two days a week at the school. There are also four full-time student teachers in the school. Teachers from Platte who serve as site coordinators and some of the clinical faculty (or master teachers) sit in on these university class discussions. At times it is hard for an observer to sort the experienced teachers from novices; on other occasions, the experienced teachers' practical wisdom clearly informs the conversation.

Students and teachers alike talk of the power of the cohort arrangement that has students learning from one another as the group progresses through the program. They tell of a university student who heard an eighth grader talking about suicide, obtained help from the counselor, and later used the experience as a point of departure for discussion within the cohort. They tell of preservice candidates sharing their reactions to different approaches they are seeing in classrooms and how the group then helps them sort out what works under different circumstances.

University students are also assigned to teams where, among other things, they serve as tutors for middle school students. In this role, they expand the amount of adult assistance available for children, increasing the likelihood that the younger children's learning needs will be met.

Purpose 2: Professional Development

Platte is organized around interdisciplinary teams at each grade level. Seven seventh-grade teachers have study sessions with university faculty from arts and sciences during which they talk about appropriate content and activities that will help advance learning of content in legitimate ways as they work with students around such themes as "harmony." Teachers from the unified arts—music, visual arts, theater, industrial arts—join in these conversations, of which some occur at the school and others take place on campus. Ninth-grade language arts and social studies teachers join with arts and sciences faculty, including the dean, to talk about units they can include in their core curriculum. Student teachers and teacher candidates who are enrolled in classes that meet at the school join in both types of conversations. Although core curricula and thematic, interdisciplinary units were "hot ideas" in the 1930s and 1940s, the engagement of university or school faculty with prospective teachers that occurs in this PDS promises to bring new life to these approaches. They are enlivened as a result of the combination of scholarship, practical wisdom, and curiosity that the different members bring to the conversations.

Purpose 3: Inquiry

Inquiry efforts provide answers to questions raised by the teachers in the school, faculty from the university, the local school board, and individuals seeking professional growth.

Early in their work, the educators from this school and faculty from the university did research that indicated that 40 percent of the school's students did not have a significant adult with whom they had a close relationship. They used this information to build strategies to personalize their students' schooling. As noted earlier, one approach was to assign university students to teams, thereby enriching adult-student ratios. Preservice students are quickly worked into the extracurricular activities of the school and perform service-learning projects, which also help establish direct adult-student linkages.

In another inquiry project, in response to questions the school and the district board of directors raised, university students are researching ways to make the most effective use of technology at the school and improve the transition from eighth grade to high school. The school emphasizes that it is particularly concerned with young Hispanic women in this regard, an area of inquiry of particular interest to one university faculty member. The district superintendent emphasizes that the board will eventually arrive at its own answers to these questions. Thanks to the work of the university students and faculty, the board's decisions will be much better informed than school board actions often are.

One of the university faculty members working with the school is pursuing a doctorate, and the school has taken on the task of helping her complete the research required for the degree. At the same time, the research she is doing is helping them answer some questions they have had about their physical education program.

Purpose 4: School Renewal

The enhancement of the curriculum and the better adult-student ratio help the school meet the needs of its diverse student body. University students working as tutors help students who proceed at a different pace than the majority of the class. Still, parents worry about whether their children are being challenged enough, and teachers struggle to address the different needs that today's students present.

Through more than a dozen years of work with the school-university partnership, the faculty and administration of this middle school have developed their capacity to engage in critical inquiry on school renewal. They are used to grappling with questions about tracking, authentic assessment, rigorous curriculum, and teaching methodology. Prospective teachers are pulled into their dialogue, ensuring that they enter the profession having developed the habit of such reflection.

Mitchell High School

We look at this school as it existed in 1997 and 1998. Around twenty-three hundred students fill the halls of Mitchell High School in a blue-collar suburb. Twenty-five percent of them are minority students, the largest group of which is Hispanic.

Purpose 1: Preservice

Mitchell has been a partner school with State University, Western City (SUWC), since 1994, when the high school began to focus on teacher education, particularly in math and science. Now, thirty-three SUWC students are actively engaged with the school in foreign language, history, English, and the fine arts, as well as the original duo of math and science. SUWC students also work with an innovative peer-tutoring program in ESL, serve as coaches, and assist with other parts of the extracurricular program. Three site coordinators are assigned full time to assist with the teacher candidates from SUWC. Their positions are financed by the hiring of interns at a reduced salary.

Purpose 2: Professional Development

Seven of Mitchell's faculty are interns—fully licensed teachers (several of whom completed their student teaching the previous year at Mitchell) who receive lower compensation than a beginning teacher. During their one-year assignments as interns, they receive additional support from the site coordinators, the department heads, and their peers through a state-sponsored mentoring program. Although other first-year teachers may have mentors, the extra assistance provided to these interns helps them gain skill and confidence during this induction year. Interns are willing to accept their reduced compensation because they are aware that previous interns have been sought after by other schools (and by Mitchell) as new teachers with unusually good preparation.

The interns also make it possible for one of Mitchell's senior social studies teachers to serve as a faculty member in residence at SUWC, where he assists in subject-matter methodology classes, does research in his subject field, and works with interns at various schools partnering with SUWC. In addition, five other faculty members from the high school serve as adjunct professors in the university's "silver and gold" program, which takes advantage of their expertise. This program is helping to strengthen what was heretofore a weak link between the school and the arts and sciences faculty at the university. The arts and sciences associate dean who works with the school has also developed enthusiasm at the school for a new project of building a seamless curriculum for grades nine through sixteen built on the new state standards. And members of the university and school faculty who participated in their partnership's retreat around the question of subject-matter standards and democracy are eager to pursue additional ways that arts and sciences professors can be involved with the PDS. Other faculty from the arts and sciences have discovered the availability of quality biology labs late in the day at Mitchell, and they are looking for ways to use these facilities during times when their campus labs are overcrowded.

The funds saved by using interns also help support a part-time sabbatical for a language arts teacher who is using his half-day release to write, in local papers and professional journals, about innovations at Mitchell and elsewhere in education. Through his efforts, some of the innovative work is being documented.

In addition to the students who are part of the graduate-level teacher-preparation program, a cohort of administrative candidates works on administrative credentials at the school with collaborative tutelage from school, district, and university staff.

Purpose 3: Inquiry

Inquiry activities have involved participants at Mitchell in a variety of ways. The high school faculty has worked with the Alliance for Educational Renewal, a group seen as a possible precursor to a center of pedagogy. The group spent a year examining barriers that separate the school of education faculty, arts and sciences faculty, and school-based educators. As the year progressed, those in the group concentrated much of their attention on finding ways to measure the effect of their partnership on student achievement.

At the conclusion of the 1996–97 school year, university and school faculty working with Mitchell prepared a portrait of the progress made during the past year. That portrait was shared with educators from around the country at an annual meeting of AACTE and has been used to orient newcomers who are working in this PDS.

Additional inquiry into their work as it relates to evolving national standards is anticipated by those working with Mitchell as they participate in the test of NCATE draft standards for professional development schools. A feeder middle school and an elementary school that are part of their administrative cluster will be working with them on this project. They have also engaged the local union leadership in this inquiry effort.

As part of an inquiry project, preservice teacher candidates prepared background materials on the school for incoming ninth graders. Some of the high school faculty say they learned about the school from the process.

Purpose 4: School Renewal

A university science professor joined with the College of Education science-education faculty member to bolster the astronomy knowledge of the Mitchell teachers and help them translate some of that knowledge into curriculum for the freshman science class.

As a result of the principal's creative use of resources, money has been freed up to permit staff travel and provide faculty the time to meet either during school or over the summer to work on curriculum. The faculty takes pride in the long tenure of many of its members and describes itself as involved in change without revolution. Among the changes one notices in the school are interactive math programs, Internet-aided biology instruction, peer teaching of students in ESL, writers' workshops, and extensive use of writing across the curriculum. The high school is not the only renewing site in this partnership. Members of the leadership team, which includes representatives concerned about teacher education, professional development, inquiry, and exemplary schooling, tell stories of how they have changed university faculty members' minds about some of the innovations that were being taught in SUWC classes at the same time the teachers at Mitchell acknowledge that the teacher candidates are having a substantial impact on the way they teach. As one talks with the senior teachers, one gets the impression that they are more willing to learn about change as they work one-on-one with teacher candidates (TCs) than when they are listening to professors in staff-development sessions. In addition, teachers, administrators, and students commonly point to the presence of the TCs as an energizing force for faculty. A high school junior tells us of her initial regret at having signed up for a favorite teacher only to discover that he was mentoring a student teacher. But she adds quickly that she now thinks the teacher had begun to fall into a rut and that the student teacher helped him become more energized and less boring.

What Benefits Are Claimed for PDSs?

Thus far, in an effort to create a picture of what a PDS is, we have explored some of the reasons why people are creating them, provided a definition, and given three examples of fairly sophisticated partner efforts. As a final means of providing an initial understanding of these schools, let us look at the benefits claimed for them.

As noted earlier in this chapter, the current model of teacher education and school reform has contributed to the perpetuation of a disjointed and confused system of teacher education and schooling for children. It makes sense, therefore, to seek a new one that will lead to improved P–16 learning. The professional development school has inherent benefits because it integrates the use of resources, focuses on core practices of teaching and learning, provides for quality control and accountability mechanisms, and contains within it provisions for reflective inquiry.

Research and the informed opinions of people who have been working with PDSs point to the following benefits for PDSs. More will be said about these claimed benefits later, but for now they are listed to give an idea why people believe it is worth the effort involved to find new clothes for the emperor. All things being equal (and of course they never are):

- Students enrolled in professional development schools perform better than other students on common measures of student learning in basic subjects such as language arts and mathematics.

- Teachers prepared in professional development schools are better able to elicit student learning than those assigned traditional internships.

- Teachers prepared in professional development schools are more familiar with the practices required in today's schools than those who obtain clinical experiences in other ways.

- Professional development conducted by professional development schools is more closely integrated with preservice education (and vice versa).

- Teachers perceive that professional development obtained through a PDS is more valuable than that obtained in traditional ways.

- Administrators report that they prefer to hire teachers whose clinical training occurred in a professional development school.

- Teacher associations believe that professional development schools contribute to the enhancement of the profession.

- Universities benefit from teachers who are prepared in professional development schools because these teachers help enable students to perform more successfully at the university level.

- Universities benefit from professional development schools because they generate tuition and fees in connection with the preservice and professional development course work completed in the PDS.

- Local school districts benefit from professional development schools because they reduce recruiting costs, retraining costs, legal fees, and professional development needs.

- Local school districts benefit from professional development schools because they are useful sources of research information concerning the quality of new programs.

- Teachers working in PDSs are more likely to pursue graduate study to enhance their skills as teachers and mentors of teachers.

- Students in PDSs experience more hours of adult attention than do similar students in other schools.

- Veteran teachers in PDSs exhibit more reflective practice than do teachers in other schools.

- New teachers prepared in PDSs exhibit more reflective practice than teachers prepared through other kinds of clinical experiences.

- New teachers prepared in PDSs assume leadership roles among their peers more quickly than teachers prepared in other ways.

- The university usually views itself as having a substantial responsibility to the community. Service to P–12 schools discharges part of such responsibility.

- Better teachers make better schools.

- PDSs help business secure better workers, because the students in the schools are better educated thanks to teachers who were prepared in professional development schools.[14]

Leading the parade, the emperor, proudly attired in nothing, smiled to his subjects, who cheered and waved. Similarly, the PDS strides out, boldly seeking to enable the simultaneous renewal of schools and the education of educators, claiming many successes as it goes. What is necessary to ensure that the PDS is more real than the emperor's clothes? What has to happen if we are going to be certain that the PDS of reality matches the ideals expressed by those who advocate its development—that the benefits claimed by these advocates are really obtained? The early stages of development for a PDS are critical to later success. It is to those efforts that we now turn.

2

Cultivating the Fabric
Conditions in Creating a PDS

Fortuitously or disturbingly, words often have several meanings. For example, in its most common usage, *to cultivate* refers to the process of preparing the soil for seeds, but the first synonym provided by an electronic thesaurus suggests that the verb also means *to render civil*. Likewise, the most common usage of *fabric* may be as a synonym for cloth, but it also is used to refer to the *substance of a concept*.

This chapter is about *cultivating fabric*, using both terms in both ways. That is, we are concerned with preparing the cloth from which the new clothes that will make up the professional development school are to be formed, while simultaneously we are concerned with rendering civil the substance on which the PDS is to be formed—in other words, we are also concerned with the philosophical clarity on which PDSs are built. Before one can dress the emperor—before one can put clothes on him—one must have the proper fabric from which to fashion the garments. Likewise, before one can create a PDS, one must cultivate the substance (render the school civil), and that is the subject of this chapter.

This chapter treats two broad questions and the issues and topics associated with answering them:

- What are the antecedents to the creation of professional development schools?

The creation and development of school-university partnerships and centers of pedagogy

The creation of a common philosophical base

- What must exist concurrently with professional development schools?

The role of preprofessional, general education

The role of professional education

The role of the policy environment

What Are the Antecedents to the Creation of Professional Development Schools?

In working documents prepared for an ongoing discussion of PDS standards, Marsha Levine described the first stage in the development of a PDS as a "'Time before the Beginning,' a critical period in which relationships between school and university faculty are formed; trust is built and mutual understandings are developed."[1]

To look more closely at this stage, consider the schools described in Chapter One. Northern began developing its current teacher preparation program when one of its professors and the dean of the College of Education approached six local superintendents about the creation of a school-university partnership modeled after those described by Goodlad in *A Place Called School*.[2] For several years thereafter, faculty at Northern and at schools such as Bay Elementary participated in intensive and thoughtful dialogue about school renewal and the needs of the college for reforming its efforts. Lots of good food was consumed and hours of conversations about teaching and learning took place. Subsequently, the partners developed a new teacher education program built on common understandings between school and university faculty members, and Bay nominated itself to be one of the schools to be engaged as a partner in this effort.

For years, Platte Middle School was committed to renewal work and identified as a PDS, but essentially, as Mary Diez has suggested is often the case, a single professor was using the school as a lab site. What happened to make Platte a more authentic PDS provides some additional clues about what is necessary to begin cultivating the fabric. The superintendent of Platte's district pointed out to the university's provost that the conditions of the agreement negotiated earlier between the school and the university were not being met and that if there was no change his district would seek a relationship with another university that would follow through. At the same time, the overall partnership in which the school participated secured external funding from the state's federally funded Goals 2000 project. The partnership began a process through which university and school faculty gave thoughtful, detailed attention to rubrics developed to indicate a school's potential as a successful partner school. These rubrics were used to point out to the university that this was not a partnership but merely the engagement of a single faculty member. The school principal told his counterparts at the university that unless they were serious about all four functions associated with a PDS, his school would look for a different university partner. In response to Platte (and to other concerns, including questions raised by the partnership), the university changed the leadership of the education program, committed to having classes on the middle school campus, increased the involvement of arts and sciences faculty, and increased the credit given to faculty for fieldwork when considering tenure and promotion decisions. The principal saw reason for hope in breaking down walls between subject matter specialists at Platte when university faculty showed that they were willing to work across subject and departmental barriers. As the university sought a new dean, the principal became a member of the committee interviewing candidates. The fabric was clearly being cultivated.

The experiences at Platte and Bay are very different from what happened at Fillmore High School, which is located in a large East Coast city. At Fillmore there was strong individual commitment among its English and social studies teachers and from a history professor from Temple University.[3] Money was made available: the university dedicated several teaching "lines" to providing staff support, and a private foundation funded large blocks of time for leadership at the school, planning activities during the summer, and professional development. The Lab School Charter at Fillmore was one of three well-funded PDS programs initiated simultaneously in the district. In fact, it was the most successful of the three because of strong commitment and leadership from the initial participants, but it was unable to transcend poorly developed institutional relationships, the absence of initial collaboration in the planning, and a lack of support from the central administration.

Two of the initiators had telling comments as they reviewed the first two years of the Fillmore PDS: "Temple University began planning the reorientation of its teacher education programs in 1987. The university developed a preliminary proposal requesting Carnegie Corporation funding for this initiative in early 1988; that proposal laid out the approach that continues to inform the Temple program today [1994]. Given the complete absence of high school input in the formative stages of this planning process—and the university's uncertain commitment to the new program represented in the continuation of the much larger four-year program—the relative success of the Temple-PDS relationship should be more surprising than the difficulties thus far encountered."[4]

After discussing progress made in developing interdisciplinary programs and creating positive environments for student teachers and existing Fillmore faculty, the two noted:

> The program's connection with Temple's College of Education was perhaps less successful. Temple's students reported uniformly positive experiences in their Lab

School field placements. But the College of Education alternated between paying no attention to Fillmore and demanding that Fillmore (and other PDS) teachers holding university adjunct appointments assume the far-reaching responsibilities on the university campus listed in the original Carnegie proposal. The original proposal did not, of course, foresee the enormous commitment in time and energy that teachers would have to invest in the high school component of the program. It may have been naive to expect too easy an integration of university and high school. It is unfortunately not clear that the College of Education has the flexibility to re-create a program already committed to paper even as that program evolves.[5]

In the first two instances, healthy school-university partnerships had been created and nourished over a period of several years before operational PDSs could evolve. No such structure existed to nurture the creation of PDSs in the third example.

The first two demonstrate why we believe that a viable school-university partnership is one of several conditions that should either be in place before an institution of higher education (IHE) and school district begin to develop partner schools or, if not in place, well on the way to being so.

School-University Partnerships

Much has been written about school-university partnerships. From the literature and the experience of partnerships such as those that have been developed in the National Network for Educational Renewal, it is possible to gain an understanding of them that may be useful to those who seek to create such entities.[6] The first concern for those seeking to build such a partnership should be clarifying how the former relationships among schools and universities in general and the prospective partners in particular may affect their success. During their more than 360-year history, America's colleges and universities have had mixed relationships with their communities. Although some communities are dependent on the local college for their existence, there are also numerous instances of failed consulting and partnership arrangements. The problem lies partly in the difference in cultures between community and university; partly in the perceived mission of the university, which may or may not include close interaction with its community; partly in the lack of rewards to university faculty for partnership work; and partly in the limited ability of community organizations to define the work to be accomplished through such partnerships. Nevertheless, school-university partnerships are being encouraged more strongly than ever as complex problems seem to demand collaboration.

Relationships between higher education and the schools during this century have been characterized by university attempts to control the quality of the students they receive, the influence of professors through placement of key graduate students, the use of the schools as clinical settings, the presence of professors as expert consultants, and an increase in the variety of partnership arrangements.

One confounding situation is that prospective partners often do not have a common understanding of what a partnership is. Three approaches may help build the necessary understanding: constructing a useful definition of such partnerships, developing a typology of partnerships to provide new insights into their characteristics, and looking at the major stages of development that partnerships go through.

A Definition of Partnerships

Although a wide range of practices are being called partnerships, the term is best used to describe a relationship in which different entities serve each other's needs in a manner similar to what biologists refer to as *mutualism*. In other words, as Goodlad notes in Chapter Three, a true school-university partnership is, above all, beneficially symbiotic. In such a partnership there should be channels of communication between the university and school districts including a governance group consisting of the district superintendents and the dean of the school, college, or department of education (SCDE) as well as key leaders from arts and sciences, a coordinating group of university faculty and school district administrators, and interpersonal relationships that support open and frank exchanges of ideas involving teachers at both the university and school level.

A Typology of Partnerships

Assuming that partners take into account the context for their effort, three variables enable construction of a typology: purpose/function, structure, and support mechanisms. Partnerships vary with regard to the breadth, complexity, and quality of each of these elements and the relationships among them. Exhibit 2.1 provides an overview of the specific items associated with each variable.

The four types of partnerships depicted in Table 2.1 are determined by the narrowness or breadth—the strength or weakness—of each of these variables. For example, Type I partnerships have a single, narrow purpose, few participants coming from similar backgrounds, and few support resources. Type II partnerships have moderate purposes, several partners, and modest but sufficient support mechanisms. Type III have broad purposes, many partners, and considerable support. Type IV partnerships are mixed; they have levels of support or structures that differ from the level of their purpose or function. The table offers examples of each type, which are more fully explained in the next section.

Type I Partnerships. An example of a Type I partnership was identified by a professor at the University of Hawaii who talked about her partnership with an English teacher in a nearby high school. This collaboration helped both of them to think about their own teaching fields. It required few resources, had a narrow purpose, and was very informally structured—yet it was very satisfying to the professor and the teacher.

Exhibit 2.1. Variables for a Typology of Partnerships

Purpose and Function

Examples of Purposes

Higher education admissions

Teacher (educator) education

Coordination of services from university

Focus on specific discipline or disciplines

School renewal

Community renewal

Implementation of curriculum or methodology project

Focus on specific issue (school violence, passing a bond issue, and so on)

University operates its own P–12 schools

Combination of one or several of the above

Examples of Functions (Activities)

Conduct seminars and training

Design and implement interventions (neighborhood watches, cleanups, school assemblies, youth counseling sessions, graffiti paint-out parties, athletics, lobbying)

Provide tutors, mentors

Serve as catalyst to join existing actors in policymaking and
implementation

Conduct media campaigns

Facilitate research into activities of one or more of the partners

Structure

By Partnership Member

Higher education variables: Students, faculty, center or institute,
department, school or college, entire institution, system, group of
institutions of higher education

School variables: Students, faculty, department, school, region,
district, districts, state

Community variables: Neighborhood, businesses, nonprofit
organizations, region, city, state

By Partnership Nature

Consulting arrangement

Network

Collaboration or partnership

Support Mechanisms

By Governance Arrangements

Informal

Letter of agreement or contract

Representative governance

Managed by individual with advisory group

By *Funding Source*

Institution of higher education

Grant

Schools or community

Schools, community, and institution of higher education

Institution of higher education and grants

Schools or community and grants

Schools, community, institution of higher education, and grants

State/federal sources, or combination of state/federal and one of above

By *Funding Adequacy*

Sufficient funds for immediate operations

Sufficient funds for long-term objectives

Dependability of funding sources

Table 2.1. Partnership Types

	Purpose/ function	Structure	Support mechanisms	Examples
		Variables		
Type I	Narrow	Narrow	Narrow	University of Hawaii Professor-Teacher
				Mississippi State University and Starkville Schools
Type II	Moderate	Moderate	Moderate	University of Southern Maine Partnership
				Boston University and Chelsea Community
Type III	Broad	Broad	Broad	Educational and Community Change Project
				El Paso Collaborative for Academic Excellence
Type IV	Mixed*	Mixed*	Mixed*	Getty Art Partner Schools
				Coalition of Essential Schools
				West Virginia-Benedum

Mixed: Differing scope and/or strength on different variables. For example, the Getty Art Partner Schools project has narrow purpose, moderate structure, and broad support mechanisms.

Robert Hutchison and his colleagues provide a report of another partnership effort that both confirms the potential of partnerships and demonstrates the wide range of purposes for such efforts—even those classified as Type I.[7] A partnership between Mississippi State University and the Starkville public schools implemented an exemplary program in community marketing and communications. Although multiple activities were associated with the work, success was ultimately measured by the 65 percent favorable vote that the school district obtained for a bond issue. The actual partnering consisted largely of interaction between a professor and a district committee. Activities included surveys, focus groups, a twenty-four-hour call-in line, and two newsletters. Minimal funding was provided through a grant from the university.

Mitzi Lewison and Sue Holliday reported another example of a Type I partnership, concluding from their qualitative study of five years of partnership work at an elementary school that there are four critical elements to building a successful partnership: equalizing the power positions of the members, building trust early on with the principal, fostering individual (not just group) relationships, and insisting on frequent and continuing communication among members. This partnership was narrowly structured (essentially one professor with one school) and worked with limited resources to improve a single school. Although the "formal partnership" ended after one year, the professor continued to interact with the school and to report at the end of five years the fruits of the collaborative efforts.[8]

Type II Partnerships. Barbara Beyerbach and colleagues describe an example of a Type II partnership that they named Kids at Work, a model originally developed with National Science Foundation funding, which links schools, businesses, and universities. Its membership is broader than would be typical of a Type I, and the combination of external funding and continuing business participation is also present. The presence of goals in two domains—student learning and teacher learning—is another characteristic that qualifies this project as a midrange one. The authors report that "evaluation results indicate that the project improves school science instruction by classroom teachers, improves student attitudes toward science, and actively promotes parental involvement in the school science program."[9] These conclusions were based on participant observation of and student interviews on classroom teaching; the administration of the Science/Mathematics Attitude Questionnaire (SMAQ); and the use of the New York State Elementary Science Program 7Evaluation Test. Unlike typical school-business partnerships, which feature guest speakers, career education presentations, field trips and tours, and equipment donations, Kids at Work integrates visits to business partner sites with specific learning activities in math and science. It is this integration that the authors report to be the key to the success of the partnership efforts. The partners are the university people who help train teachers and evaluate the program, the schools, and the various businesses that are visited.

The Policy Research in Action Group (PRAG) appears to be another Type II partnership, although it is self-described as a network. PRAG involves four universities and fifteen community organizations in the Chicago area. At first glance, this collaborative effort appears to be narrowly focused because initially it engaged in supporting research projects by making interns available to participating organizations. However, the university-community collaborations included in these inquiry efforts have considerable breadth. In fact, research projects identified as matters of individual interest by professors—the kinds of projects that some might consider to be Type I partnerships—are not funded as part of PRAG. Early investigations included projects related to community gentrification, the preservation of racially diverse communities, the employment of potential new service industries, and effective strategies in community economic development.[10] Even more than the breadth of the topics investigated, the expanding role played by researchers helped broaden the nature of this collaboration. Philip Nyden and colleagues write of the early attitudes that had to be overcome in the project: "Demonstrating frustration with academics' training to be critical of everything, one community leader talked about how academics are people who do not just walk through the door that has been opened for them, but prefer to come through 'kicking, screaming, and fighting every inch of the way.' On the other hand, university researchers talked of the lack of understanding sometimes demonstrated by community organizations when research protocols are followed or when careful research practices mean that the research cannot be completed quickly."[11]

Such attitudes led to a planning process—supported by adequate private foundation funding—that included preparation of background papers and action plans. This process provided direction and helped build trust among participants. In addition to its early foundation support, PRAG received substantial U.S. Department of Education funding. Structurally, the partnership seeks a middle ground between efficiency and flexibility. One university, Loyola of Chicago, serves as the fiscal agent, and a core group consisting of twenty-four representatives from participating universities and organizations provides policy direction. As is often the case in partnerships when the general governance group becomes large, a smaller executive committee provides direction between the meetings of the larger group. A representative from each of the four universities and four community representatives sit on PRAG's executive committee. From its earlier emphasis on providing interns to engage in research activities, PRAG has expanded its work to include nurturing university-community partnerships, providing an on-line internship clearinghouse, conducting policy breakfasts with relevant local leaders, helping groups access routine research tools, and over its years of work, supporting more than 130 work projects.

Boston University's affiliation with the Chelsea community is another Type II partnership.[12] This partnership began in 1989 as a ten-year effort to restore the capacity of that community to provide for its own schools. For a variety of reasons, Chelsea had experienced a decline in the quality of all of its public services and, in particular, its school system. The goals of the partnership have been "to bring children into schooling ready to learn, to provide them with teachers thoroughly qualified to teach, and to join students and teachers in the study of fine academic and vocational curricula."[13] Although the effort to ensure that students enter school ready to learn broadens the purpose somewhat, basically the partnership intends to provide better schooling for all the young students of a particular city—a midrange purpose.

The nature of the partnership, sometimes referred to as a *takeover*, also makes it an example of a midrange collaboration at most. There was a considerable clash between Boston University and the entrenched teachers' union and other local political officials during the initial efforts of the partnership. But by 1994, partnership members, including many faculty and leaders from the college as well as participants from the local school district, were reporting significant improvements in elementary education, using claims of improved curricula and more highly qualified teachers as their measures. However, despite reducing the dropout rate by 60 percent, participants acknowledged that they were still having significant problems achieving success in secondary schools.

Meanwhile, the state and university made substantial resources available. But the bankruptcy of Chelsea in 1992 and the continuing shortage of money for schooling in the community (compared with other communities in the Boston area) have limited the scope of the partnership work.

A third example of a Type II partnership is the Southern Maine Partnership, one of the original NNER settings.[14] Paul Heckman, a colleague of Goodlad's at UCLA and an early senior associate with the University of Washington's Center for Educational Renewal (CER), initiated this partnership through a series of dialogues with a group of university faculty members and superintendents, principals, and teachers from school districts in the greater Portland, Maine, area.

Presently the setting includes six school districts and thirty-four partner schools. The schools that serve USM's Extended Teacher Education Program (ETEP) include some of the most sophisticated and thoroughly studied professional development schools in the country. They have been examined as part of the work of the National Commission on Teaching & America's Future (NCTAF), part of NCATE's efforts to develop standards for professional development schools, and part of the studies included in books edited by Levine, by Levine and Trachtman, and by Darling-Hammond.

The Southern Maine Partnership has expanded its purpose and functions to the middle range typical of Type II partnerships. After the partnership spent several years discussing fundamental issues associated with school renewal, it turned to the task of renewing teacher education, eliminating its undergraduate program in favor of an extended one. The extended program has three components: an undergraduate minor; a fifth-year, field-based certification program; and a master's degree program to be completed concurrently with the first years of teaching. The new program reduced the total number of students enrolled in preservice preparation, offsetting the costs in part with the higher tuition paid by students for graduate credit.

The partnership continues to work with the school districts in southern Maine. It has affiliated with a number of reform efforts, including the Atlas communities, Foxfire, NCTAF, and the National Education Association's Teacher Education Initiative. This partnership has been particularly adept at borrowing from a wide range of efforts those elements it considers important for its own work. Along with some initial foundation resources, this willingness to affiliate with other initiatives has helped it overcome limited funding from a state that has faced major financial problems during much of the life of the partnership. However, this wide involvement has tended to lead to only superficial understanding among some participants of each movement's agenda.

Type III Partnerships. When knowledgeable individuals are asked about examples of effective partnerships, two efforts almost invariably are mentioned. The first is the El Paso Collaborative for Academic Excellence. As a partnership, it is a complex operation that works in conjunction with another collaborative effort, the El Paso

Interreligious Sponsoring Organization. Together, these initiatives are making headway by bringing the resources of all segments of a border community to bear on problems.[15] Parents, policymakers, the university, and the business community have joined in a partnership begun in the early 1990s. The partnership is a member of the NNER, incorporating Goodlad's principles, and one of the American Association for Higher Education's Community Compacts for Student Success funded by The Pew Charitable Trusts. It is led by the superintendents of three large school districts, the presidents of the University of Texas at El Paso and the local community college, as well as community civic and business leaders, and it has focused on setting and achieving clear learning goals for students. Parents and practicing and preservice teachers are learning how to help their children. Hard-core approaches to leadership training and community activism have helped mobilize a considerable body of previously disenfranchised citizens. In this aspect of its work it is tied in with the Saul Alinksy–inspired Industrial Areas Foundation through the Texas Interfaith Education Fund led by Ernesto Cortes—an initiative with a twenty-year history of organizing work in the community. The partnership draws its success from a strong combination of Goodlad's partnership concepts and Alinsky-Cortes activism.[16] It has also been given a boost by substantial private funding from philanthropies such as The Pew Charitable Trusts and federal funding through NSF grants and others.

The success of Ysleta Elementary has helped generate the general positive image of this partnership effort. The school serves a neighborhood of Hispanic children just across the border from Juarez. In 1992, fewer than 20 percent of its students passed all three sections of the Texas Assessment of Academic Skills (TAAS). By 1997, considerable improvement had been made: more than 70 percent passed the reading section, the math section, and the writing section of the TAAS.[17]

The Educational and Community Change project (ECC) is another frequently mentioned Type III partnership.[18] Centered at the

University of Arizona, it began as a Type I partnership involving a university professor and a single elementary school in Tucson. From this modest beginning, it grew into a Type II partnership involving renewal activities in several schools. Eventually it became a Type III project with multiple purposes, numerous participants, and substantial funding. Students in early project schools were primarily Hispanic and Native American, with 95 percent of them qualifying for free or reduced-price lunches. ECC expanded to include four additional Tucson elementary schools and three elementary schools and one middle school in Santa Monica, California.

Many school renewal partnerships seek to implement predetermined innovations, but the university faculty and the school and community participants in this project have worked to reinvent schooling and improve the community surrounding the schools. From the beginning, weekly critical dialogue sessions took place during which the university professor played a key role. However, although serving as a "critical friend," he was careful to avoid providing the other partners with *the* answer. The instigator of the partnership had been deeply involved in earlier work in California and Maine in affiliation with Goodlad and, in keeping with that work, he insisted that this project operate on the premise that all the partners—not just the university expert—are presumed to have knowledge of what is needed. Funds of knowledge that existed in the neighborhoods surrounding the schools were honored and drawn on to solve problems. The common task of those involved was to discover conditions in the schools that deter or enhance the possibility for change and to change the conditions that are interfering with progress.

Support was obtained early on from the district superintendent and local activists who worked in the school neighborhoods. Eventually a coalition was formed that included the university faculty, parents, community members, city council members, an assistant superintendent of the school district, area businesspeople, and staff members of several activist groups. Although focused on school renewal, the partners recognized a need for broad action. They organized more than a hundred people who succeeded in getting the city to clean up vacant lots and seal off abandoned houses in the school neighborhoods. They sought and obtained the city's help in creating a comprehensive community-development plan. Private foundations provided most of the financial support for the initial seven years of the project. As schools began their process of renewal, goals such as teacher training were added to the project. From this project have come not only improved physical conditions in neighborhoods but also changes in beliefs about how learning takes place, increased engagement in the democratic process by adults, additional services such as child care within these communities, altered organizational patterns for schooling and, most importantly, new and exciting learning experiences for the children of the participating schools.

Type IV Partnerships. Type IV partnerships are narrow in some areas, moderate in others, and broad in still others. The Regional Institutes funded by the Getty Education Institute for the Arts are examples. These institutes were created to advance work on a particular concept of education in the arts: discipline-based arts education (DBAE). Although this is a worthwhile goal, it is a fairly narrow one. Originally, membership in each of the six regional institutes was also narrow—generally a few faculty members in an institution of higher education. However, these faculty were required to establish supporting consortia consisting of individuals from the schools where ideas would be implemented and from other organizations so that—at the least—they became Type II when it came to structure. Meanwhile, the substantial resources of the Getty ensured support that clearly qualified as Type III in its breadth. The results of this endeavor are also broader than the original purpose. As Brent Wilson notes, much was learned about the change process that will be of value to those engaging in other school change initiatives. For example, external evaluators of this project concluded that change initiatives are more likely to succeed when change is systemic, that professional development and curricular and instructional planning must be pursued simultaneously, and that change occurs as a result of continuous processes of evaluation and the provision of time to reflect and act on that evaluation. Other conclusions related more directly to the specifics of the project.[19]

Other examples of Type IV partnerships may be found in national efforts such as the Coalition of Essential Schools,[20] Success for All, the National Alliance for Restructuring Education, the School Development Program,[21] Accelerated Schools, and the League of Professional Schools.[22] Although these efforts have been well funded and include many players, they tend to focus on school renewal rather than broader agendas. Olatokunbo S. Fashola and Robert E. Slavin identify these initiatives as "designed, evaluated, and disseminated,"[23] which does not make them sound like partnerships. However, they then claim that some of them are partnership efforts. For example, they say that the National Alliance for Restructuring Education "is a partnership of states, school districts, and national organizations that is affiliated with the New Standards Project."[24] At best, these efforts come closer to being networks than partnerships that exhibit the full notion of mutuality between the engaged universities and schools.

The Pittsburgh-based Benedum Foundation provided substantial funding to the Type IV West Virginia University PDS Collaborative, which is another example of a partnership with strong funding and relatively narrow purpose. This partnership created a group of professional development schools and revised the university's teacher education program. It also exemplifies a potential problem when funding is ample and purpose is modest. Justifiably, funders in such situations can become impatient to see concrete results. Care needs to be taken from the outset to obtain agreement between the funder and the partnership on what will constitute satisfactory outcomes.

Generalizations. Some generalizations may be reached—or at least hypotheses may be formed—based on this examination of different types of partnerships:

- Purpose or function can be achieved only if structure and support mechanisms of the partnership are of equal or greater breadth; in other words, partnership structures and support mechanisms must provide a scaffold sufficient to support the vision, purpose, and function of the partnership.

- Individuals or small centers operating partnerships must maintain a narrow focus.

- Partnerships that begin as one type can change to a different type but will succeed as they change only if they conform to the first generalization above.

- Ambiguity in any of the three major variables (purpose/function, structure, and support mechanisms) will be harmful to the partnership—particularly if purpose and function are ambiguous.

- A partnership between a school, college, or department of education (SCDE) and an elementary or secondary school whose purposes are not broad enough to encompass renewal of both the school and teacher preparation or that does not engage participants beyond the college of education and the school (such as arts and sciences faculty or central school district administrators) will not have a broad enough base to accomplish the full mission of a professional development school or ensure the necessary support mechanisms for a group of PDSs. In other words, Type I partnerships are too narrow in scope to support a group of professional development schools.

Developmental Stages

Carol Wilson, Paul Heckman, and I generated a five-stage developmental sequence based on our examination of fourteen school-university partnerships from across the country that had been in existence for three to five years.[25] Because several investigators who were trying to understand their own settings have found this developmental sequence useful,[26] a modified version of the original description of the stages follows. The changes from the original description reflect continued observations of partnerships since the original formulation of the stages.

Stage 1: Getting Organized. During this first stage, founders seek to determine who will be involved, ask why the partnership is being formed, draw up rules for operation and governance, and determine what resources will be invested. The tendency to stay at this stage for a long time—permanently, in some cases—seems to be inversely related to the willingness of partnership participants to commit to a common goal based on shared discomfort with existing conditions. If one member of the partnership (school or university) remains dissatisfied, the dialogue about structure persists. Goodlad described this stage when he observed that the delegated institutional representatives often spend a lot of time seeking to uncover the initial purposes before realizing that they must assume the task. It is this realization by the participants that they must shoulder the burden—not recommend what others should do—that is critical to getting beyond the first stage. The length of time spent at this stage and the degree of conflict present also depend strongly on the context in which the partnership is formed, including past partnership efforts in which participants have been involved.

Stage 2: Early Success. Excitement spreads as participants join in conferences and seminars, discover that there are common interests, meet with outsiders who reinforce that they are on the right track, and recognize the really significant challenges that face them. This excitement is often recognizable in the glow that new acquaintances share at the end of a conference after they have discovered common concerns and had extended conversations about these concerns. Conference participants are often heard to say, "We need to do this more often" or "I didn't realize school (university) people were really worrying about the same thing I was" or "This is so much more stimulating than attending a conference or a class where someone lectures to me."

Stage 3: Waiting for Results. As this first blush of success and satisfaction fades, there is a lull while participants struggle to achieve some real results from their labors. Impatient participants bail out. There are doubters. Frequently during this stage, partnership leaders retreat to discuss structure, convene meetings to ask what the real goals are, and assign different people to formal leadership roles.

Stage 4: Major Success and Expansions. Next, when results significant to participants are achieved (sometimes in a separate stage, sometimes as part of this stage), the base of participation expands to include participants from multiple areas of interest. Ethne Erskine-Cullen attributes success in reaching this stage in part to the development of a "critical mass for change," that is, educating a large enough group of persons working on the reform effort to ensure that there is common knowledge and commitment.[27] The need for such an educated group has become more evident during the second iteration of the National Network for Educational Renewal. To develop this critical mass, the NNER initiated the Leadership Associates Program that has now been replicated in most of the current sixteen member settings.[28] The NNER's program includes four weeks of residential learning involving cohorts of practicing educators from P–12 schools, SCDEs, and departments of the arts and sciences, as well as the engagement of participants in cross-setting inquiry. Once they have completed the initial program, associates gather annually to reinforce learning from earlier stages of the program. The growing number of informed participants created by such programs makes it possible during Stage 4 for the initiators of the partnership to discover that success breeds success.

Also during this stage, outside recognition accorded the partnership leads others to seek admission, opens up sources of additional funding, and permits the partnership to penetrate more deeply into all segments of the communities, schools, and universities involved.

Finally, during this stage all participants commit additional resources.

Stage 5: Mature Partnership. Few of the many extant partnerships have reached this stage. During Stage 5, participants provide leadership to other major partnership efforts designed to accomplish similar purposes. They also accomplish their own stated purposes with great skill. Conversation is dominated by critical inquiry into the progress of their partnership. Community members and individuals from schools and the colleges or universities involved are visibly engaged in substantive changes that go beyond tinkering. All the elements of a truly symbiotic relationship are present. Significant resources are committed on a long-term basis. Members of the group inquire together into their present circumstances, try out alternative practices, and share what they continue to learn with one another.

These, then, are the five stages originally posited by Wilson, Heckman, and myself—the ones applied to progress in Toronto and Bozeman and found accurate. However, there is clearly another stage for many partnerships.

Stage 6: The Death of the Partnership. Given the nature of partnerships, it has become increasingly apparent that there is a sixth stage, which is neither a reversion to earlier discussions of structure and purpose nor Trubowitz's "regression stage"[29] but rather a stage of decline, decay, and death. Frequently, this terminal stage corresponds to the cessation of external funding or the departure of a key player. In other instances, personal agendas of individual members may take the partnership in a different direction, as happened with at least one of the partnerships originally in the National Network for Educational Renewal. Unfortunately, there are few careful analyses of failures of university-school-community partnerships from which one can learn about this sixth stage. In an essay for a Festschrift dedicated to John Goodlad, Wilma Smith and I provide brief descriptions of two partnerships that have failed and contrast them with two that remain healthy.[30] One of the healthy partnerships—Southern Maine—was discussed at length earlier in this chapter.

The other, the Brigham Young University (BYU)-Public School Partnership, has a thirteen-year history and has evolved into a mature Stage 5 partnership.[31] It is important to note that the stages of development and the partnership types discussed earlier interact. As is the case with Southern Maine, the BYU partnership is a good example of a Type II partnership. It has maintained a steady focus on the simultaneous renewal of schooling and the education of educators, created a structure that is consistent with that purpose, and has had the resources—mostly from the university—to make good progress.

In contrast, the two partnerships that died reached the fourth stage, then lost sight of their original purpose and failed to develop a clearly articulated new purpose. Moreover, both defunct partnerships had exceptionally high turnover in key participant roles—deans, superintendents, principals, university faculty—and did not have the critical mass of informed people in the membership that is needed to sustain their efforts. In both cases, a lack of resources became an excuse for the dissolution of a partnership that no longer had the glue to bind purpose, function, and structure.

This limited examination of failed partnerships leads to another possible generalization connecting the notion of stages and that of partnership types: partnerships that fail to maintain consistent structure, support mechanisms, and purposes are most likely to reach Stage 6 at some point along the way and dissolve.

Although progress has been made in defining partnerships, clarifying different types, and understanding stages of development, there has been limited progress in assessing the success of partnership efforts. The available studies have a number of limitations because it is difficult to study such complex phenomena and because most studies have been derived from fairly informal inquiry by individuals implementing the partnerships. Responsible parties from private and governmental organizations involved in funding such partnerships express reservations about what they have accomplished and about their future. Despite their concerns, however, everyone seems to be getting into the act of creating partnerships. Whereas relationships among these entities used to be described as "research opportunities" or "consulting agreements," now almost every interaction has become a "collaboration" or "partnership." Many different federal and private funders have been investing in these partnership arrangements largely on the intuitive notion that working together must be a better way of solving complex, interconnected problems than working in isolation.

Despite the limitations of available studies, it is possible to make the following points, which should prove helpful to those who would embark on such efforts. Although these conclusions pertain to the larger partnerships that should be created as antecedents to PDSs, they are also relevant to smaller PDS partnerships.

To have lasting, successful partnerships, participants need to be thoroughly grounded in the context of their work. They need to know the history of such relationships generally and be familiar with relevant experiences within their specific community. They need to build on past successes and use past failures as a guide to what they should avoid.

Mistrust appears to be the "natural state" of relationships involving university, school, and community members. Holding extensive dialogue about substantive matters of mutual concern and accomplishing specific goals are the most successful strategies for changing this climate to one that is more trusting.

Partnerships succeed only when participants have the same clear understanding of the collaboration's purpose and function. This is best achieved by extended conversations among the participants, not by formal agreements drafted by a few and passively accepted by others.

A partnership that has as its purpose only the creation of a partnership—rather than the accomplishment of some ultimate goal—is inevitably doomed to early failure. Continuous, critical examination of the reasons for a partnership is the only prevention for this possible malady.

Clearly understood purpose and function must be supported by the right structure (group and individual membership and organizational arrangements) and adequate support mechanisms (governance arrangements and funding).

If the function of the university participants in a partnership is to play the role of expert evaluators, it may be wiser to call the arrangement a consultancy than to establish in the minds of participants the expectation of mutualism commonly associated with a partnership.

Getting the right people to participate to accomplish the purpose of the partnership is critical. For example, engaging school-based educators without sufficient support from the district administration, civic organization staff without support of their board, city departments without support from the mayor or city manager, or professors without support from the departments and colleges from which they come will work only if the task is limited and of short duration.

Obtaining the right convener or initial leader is a critical factor in the success of partnerships. Ideally, this person will have charismatic leadership qualities and be perceived as a friend (or at least a neutral party) by all participants.

Boundary-spanners or intermediate engineers are necessary to facilitate communication across the cultures of different participating groups. In partnerships that include university, school, and community, these individuals must know and be accepted in each arena.

There must be a sufficient number of individual participants who are thoroughly familiar with the agenda of the partnership in order to achieve the goals and sustain the work in the face of the inevitable turnovers in key positions. This means that a complex partnership must have a training strategy and the resources to implement it.

Individuals engaged in partnership activities must be engaged in authentic ways. Token participation by youths, senior citizens, or any other segment of the population is likely to backfire on organizers of a partnership.

Turnover among key participants is inevitable. Partnerships will continue to progress through various stages of development only if they revisit their basic purpose and work plans periodically to obtain the commitment of current participants.

Partnerships progress through stages of development. To avoid getting hung up at the first stage, participants need to avoid celebrating victory too soon. Early success should be built on, not dwelled on.

Partnerships that move beyond the initial stages tend to have effective mechanisms for evaluating their progress and use these evaluations to help them make corrections. Often an outside agent or critical friend plays an important role in assisting with such formative evaluations.

It is not enough that partnerships facilitate communication. There must be agreement at the school district level and among university faculty on the aims of school renewal, including the need to place a priority on teacher preservice and continuing education. This will come only from sustained dialogue. Therefore, the partnership needs to provide collegial, reflective consideration of reform issues by school district administrators and teachers at the university and school district level.

A Common Philosophical Base for Partners

One of the key functions of a partnership is to nurture a common philosophical base among the potential participants in a professional development school. This extends beyond the nature of school renewal to the heart of teaching and learning. In the Northern University partnership described in Chapter One, several years of in-depth conversation resulted in a shared commitment to understanding constructivist views of teaching and learning.

At Montclair State University, years of working with teachers and schools on the centrality of critical thinking provided the basis on which professional development schools such as the Harold Wilson Middle School could grow. Wheelock College's long-term commitment to fundamental child development theories are shared by its professional development schools, including the Devotion School in Brookline and the Cambridgeport School in Cambridge, Massachusetts. Maryville University and Parkway South High School find congenial views of school renewal and of learning and teaching in the Common Principles of the Coalition of Essential Schools.

But not all partnerships have succeeded in developing common views. For example, at the University of Washington, extensive dialogue concerning school renewal that began in the Puget Sound Educational Consortium in an effort to create the necessary philosophical consensus proved insufficient to overcome the changes wrought by new school and university leaders who had their own philosophical orientation and had not participated in the original conversations. In California, a partnership foundered when school faculty members and administrators who had developed a particular outlook on school reform clashed with a new group of university faculty members who had different values. These school people searched for another university with which they could partner but decided that an apparent match in philosophy did not actually guide the practice of the higher education faculty, and the partnership died without having established effective professional development schools. In Virginia and Massachusetts, university-based initiators of partnerships took for granted that their values were the correct ones and were unable to establish ongoing PDSs because people from the public schools simply saw themselves as being used by their university "partners."

School-university partnerships are necessary preconditions to the establishment of effective PDSs. However, they will reach this goal only if the partnerships are well governed, develop clear communication, and through this communication gain common understanding among all participants regarding school renewal and the fundamentals of teaching and learning.

Centers of Pedagogy

The role of the school-university partnership as a vital antecedent and an ongoing support mechanism for a PDS has been discussed at length in the previous paragraphs. Associated with such a partnership there needs to be what Goodlad has called a *center of pedagogy*.

Elsewhere, a colleague and I have argued the case for such a center as an integral function of a partnership.[32] Here I remind the reader of some essential notions Goodlad has put forth. First, "a center of pedagogy brings together in a single faculty three different groups of actors from three different settings: the schools, the arts and sciences, and the schools, colleges, or departments of education."[33] These actors are responsible for the education of the future teachers. Although they are likely to have other responsibilities as well, their participation in the center ensures that decisions about teacher education are made by the individuals who must implement them.

One purpose of the center is to support and direct partner schools. As Goodlad notes, "A center of pedagogy may require twenty or thirty partner or 'teaching' schools to accommodate its future-teacher student body."[34] PDSs are concerned with more than teacher education, and the broad partnership that supports them should be too. However, the center of pedagogy, which concentrates its attention on teacher education, is a vital partnership within a partnership.

What Must Exist Concurrently with Professional Development Schools?

Some people write and talk about professional development schools as if they exist in a vacuum. The emperor is said to have no clothes because the school alone does not suffice to accomplish all that is needed in either school reform or teacher education. But in reality it is unreasonable to expect that the fabric chosen for the PDS makes up the only garment the emperor wears.

When it comes to teacher education, much of a preservice candidate's general education, professional course work, and educational experiences needs to occur at a location other than the professional development school. Those working at the PDS and those at the other locations need to collaborate closely in their efforts. Although extensive treatment of these topics is not possible here, it is important to make clear that significant issues are related to them. How these issues are resolved will (or should) have an effect on the way in which the PDS is structured and operated.

Just as elements of teacher education do not depend on the PDS, critical aspects of school renewal, inquiry, and the education of children exist concurrently with the life of a PDS and therefore influence it and are influenced by it. Some critics of PDSs complain that these schools will give less attention to basic research, erode scholarly courses and faculty scholarship, or decrease attention to the education of the children because of the presence of other activities. Table 2.2 indicates that PDSs are not intended to replace all other efforts but to be places with particular emphases. At any given PDS, because of differences in schools, institutions of higher education (IHEs), states, and students, the percentages may vary from those suggested, but they most likely will be distributed rather than occur only at a PDS.

General education occupies most of a preservice teacher's time. Although most of it may occur outside a PDS, as suggested in the table, how it is defined and how well it is carried out are vitally important to the success of a professional development school.

Preprofessional General Education

Nearly all of a teacher's general education occurs on campus and is the responsibility of the arts and sciences faculty. It is this phase of a prospective teacher's education that truly provides the foundation on which the remainder is built. Because of its importance—and because of strong differences of opinion within academia regarding how general education should be approached—conflict over the shaping of general education persists at many institutions. Seymour Sarason, offering advice to those who are thinking about teaching as a career, commented on this conflict, noting that "what the reader contemplating a career in teaching probably does not know is that *these issues are not peculiar to a career in teaching in particular and education in general. They are complex, controversy-arousing issues in the*

Table 2.2. Distribution of Concurrent Activities among PDS, Campus, and Other

Function	Arts & Sciences on Campus (percent)	SCDE on Campus (percent)	At Professional Development School (percent)	District & Other (percent)
Preservice				
General education	80	15	5	
Professional education	5	50	45	
Clinical education		10	90	
Professional development for faculty involved with school				
Pedagogy	5	5	75	15
Content	50	15	20	15
Inquiry*				
About teaching and learning	5	75	10	10
Of teaching and learning in the PDS	5	15	60	20
As a means of staff development	25	25	25	25
Education of children enrolled in the PDS				
Schooling of children		2	96	2
School renewal	5	5	75	15

*Inquiry activities reflect those taking place in all the PDSs associated with a particular IHE.

preparation of physicians, lawyers, psychologists, social workers, and others. Whenever and wherever one deals with professional education, the timing and balance between general and professional education become issues, and one encounters differences of opinion, polarizations, and heated *argument.* What would be truly surprising would be if that were not the case. Education is not a special case" [italics in original].[35]

Special case or not, there continue to be different views regarding this important phase of teacher education. In 1963, James B. Conant's *The Education of American Teachers* reported on the most extensive study of teacher education completed to date. Although his recommendations may now appear dated (and politically incorrect) to some, they provide a convenient starting point for this discussion of the proper content of general education. Not surprisingly for a Harvard president, Conant argued for a strong liberal education:

> Assuming sufficient aptitude and an adequate secondary school preparation, what should be the general requirements for the bachelor's degree in a program of teacher education, and on what assumptions would such requirements rest? If I were advising a teacher-education institution, I should argue that the assumptions are neither new nor far to seek. They are: first, that there are certain areas of knowledge with which all future teachers should be acquainted; second, that in these areas of knowledge there are characteristic ways of grasping the subject; third, that in both the knowledge and the ways of understanding them there are basic principles; finally, that properly studied and taught, these subjects and the principles discoverable in them can further the *process* of a liberal education.[36]

Later, Conant elaborated on this general description, noting: "I am arguing for two years in college aimed at developing such a degree of competence in the usual academic areas that the teacher has some confidence in talking with a colleague who is a specialist in one of these areas. Such confidence is important for the elementary teacher as well as for the secondary. . . . General education for future teachers, then, should be a broad *academic* education."[37]

Exhibit 2.2. Conant's Suggested General Education Program for Teachers

Subjects Already Studied in High School	Number of Courses	Equivalent Semester Hours
The English language and composition	2	6
The Western world's literary tradition	2	6
History (at least one-half other than American)	3	9
Art appreciation and music appreciation	2	6
Mathematics	2	6
Science (physical and biological, each studied consecutively)	4	12
Subjects Not Studied in High School		
Introduction to general psychology	1	3
Introduction to sociology and anthropology	1	3
Introduction to the problems of philosophy	1	3
Introduction to economics	1	3
Introduction to political science	1	3
Total	20	60

And finally, becoming very specific, he offered the list of courses in Exhibit 2.2 to illustrate what he thought should be included in a teacher's general education.[38]

The exhibit oversimplifies Conant's careful discussion of each of these requirements, but it indicates the breadth and depth of study he believed teachers need.

Three decades later, as a part of the reports on his extensive study of teacher education, Goodlad returned to the issue of general education for teachers. He commented, "What I am arguing for is a general education undergraduate curriculum that has not been savaged by the aggrandizement of entrepreneurial departments and professional schools—an undergraduate program deliberately designed to produce broadly educated citizens. At a minimum, that is the necessary grounding for teachers."[39]

And he notes elsewhere that "all students would have intellectual encounters with major concepts, principles, and ideas in six knowledge domains: the nature of the human species; social, political, and economic systems (the global village); the world as a physical system; the world as a biological system; evaluative and belief systems; and communicative and expressive systems."[40]

The question of what teachers need to understand and be able to do beyond their professional competence requires more than a disconnected study of the disciplines. Lee Shulman brings together notions of professional education and general education. He identifies what he calls *categories of the knowledge base:*

- content knowledge;
- general pedagogical knowledge, with special reference to those broad principles and strategies of classroom management and organization that appear to transcend subject matter;
- curriculum knowledge, with particular grasp of the materials and programs that serves as "tools of the trade" for teachers;
- pedagogical content knowledge, that special amalgam of content and pedagogy that is uniquely the province of teachers, their own special form of professional understanding;
- knowledge of learners and their characteristics;
- knowledge of educational contexts, ranging from the workings of the group or classroom, the governance and financing of school districts, to the character of communities and cultures; and
- knowledge of educational ends, purposes, and values, and their philosophical and historical grounds.[41]

Within this list, pedagogical content knowledge is of special interest because it refers to the blending of content and pedagogy into an understanding of how particular topics, problems, or issues are organized, represented, adapted to the diverse interests and abilities of learners, and presented for instruction. In short, it is essential that a teacher not only understand a subject but also understand how a subject is learned by different people.

One central issue in general education for teachers is who should make the decisions about it. Conant recommended that "in each of these fields, collegiate faculties should define the levels of knowledge and understanding or skill that should be required as the product of the total *general* education of the future teacher. *I should hope each institution that has serious concern with educating teachers would, through appropriate committees, define such levels, bearing in mind that the entire general education course should not require more than half the student's time during four years*" [italics in original].[42]

Here we see an example of the promise of a center of pedagogy—and an area of potential conflict about such a center. Historically, one of the most important disputes has been the extent to which specialization or breadth should prevail. Another has been the extent to which liberal education dominates vocational or professional study. Should general education take approximately half of the student's time, as Conant recommends? If decisions concerning general education are made (or at least strongly influenced by) the actors represented in the center of pedagogy, the influence of the teacher education field in determining such elements of undergraduate study will increase. Academics are likely to resist such a result; there is a general antipathy toward including professional schools in such a conversation, let alone people outside the academy. However, the different kinds of knowledge that Shulman suggests teachers need may receive more attention if the center of pedagogy is given significant influence over general education.

Professional Education

Although most general education will occur on campus, professional education will be split between the campus and the PDS. Questions arise about the content of professional course work and who should make decisions concerning it.

Countless recommendations have been made in recent years concerning the reform of professional education.[43] Some would eliminate such course work altogether, but most call for either limiting or reforming it. Some suggest that the focus needs to be on outcomes: How the teacher becomes a teacher should not matter, they say; what should matter is what and how the teacher teaches. Unfortunately, those who advocate minimizing professional education fail to recognize that in creating teachers who are essentially the products of the current system they are perpetuating a highly criticized schooling effort and creating workers for it who are not prepared to analyze it critically and improve it.[44]

Although the question of specialization versus depth dominates much of the conversation on general education, issues such as the importance of educational foundations (history and philosophy), the general study of child growth and development, and learning versus specific training in pedagogical skills tend to dominate arguments about professional education. Another focus of attention is whether learning can best occur through course work or clinical experiences. The intent here is not to add another voice to the chorus of opinions on such matters but rather to emphasize that the way in which such issues are resolved has a significant influence on the functioning of a PDS. For example, whether a PDS is to be the locus of professional education or to serve as a site where practical applications are sought for ideas dealt with on campus makes a considerable difference for those creating and operating the school.

Also, as is the case with general education, who makes the decisions regarding professional education is critical to the way in which PDSs are shaped. Goodlad recommends that, through their centers of pedagogy, people at local settings make decisions on the nature of their programs: "There are no substitutes, however sensible and enticing they appear to be, for the institution-based curriculum development process of setting and holding to a mission, determining the nature and needs of the student body, sorting out the most fundamental curricular themes, projecting the necessary array of organizing centers for developing these themes, sorting out faculty commitments and responsibilities, and engaging in formative evaluations and revision of the whole."[45]

Others would place such decisions in the hands of the school, college, or department of education; in national professional bodies; in accrediting groups; or in state or national policy bodies. However, the further from the PDS such decisions are made, the less likely it is that people will have a thorough understanding of what the aims and strategies of their programs are. It is this last point that brings us to our next concern about concurrent conditions influencing a PDS: public policy.

Policy Environment

State policy and policymaking structures that separate higher education from P–12 schooling create problems for the development of PDSs. One such problem is that schools do not always see themselves as having any responsibility for teacher education; nor do universities accept responsibility for the condition of P–12 schooling. And as just noted, problems also arise when decision making occurs at levels too far removed from the people who have to carry out the decisions.

During 1996 and 1997, the National Network for Educational Renewal convened a working group of school leaders, state officials, and university faculty who reviewed the policy environment as it relates to PDSs. This group recognized that the more than five hundred institutions calling themselves professional development schools (or one of the related names, such as partner school, professional development center, or clinical school) are at widely different stages of development and, in many instances, have operationalized the concept in different ways. Such schools exist as part of state and local systems of education and are subject to the decisions of many people concerning their role, how they should operate, and how they should be financed.

Elected state officials and their staffs, university regents, state and local school board members, members of higher education commissions, chief executives of school districts and universities, members of faculty senates, and union leaders—all are among the policymakers whose decisions set directions for and provide resources to professional development schools.

First, let us look at what policies are needed to ensure the establishment of professional development schools.

- *State policymakers should adopt laws and regulations that require preservice candidate preparation to include experiences in professional development schools.* This may be done by requiring such experiences as part of certification requirements, for approval of university programs, or both.

- *State policymakers should adopt laws and regulations that identify teacher education and professional development as a basic responsibility of school districts and universities.* This may be done by adopting requirements for collaborative planning, by indicating that a portion of the funding allocated to both kinds of institutions are to be spent on teacher education, or by establishing accreditation or program approval standards that have to be satisfied by both kinds of institutions.

- *Higher education policymakers should adopt policies that recognize the work of professors in professional development schools as contributing to their meeting standards for promotion and tenure.*

- *State policymakers should consider adopting laws and regulations that encourage the placement of first-year teachers in PDSs.* Making beginning teachers part of a team consisting of master teachers, beginning teachers, and preservice candidates would result in an improved process of entry into the profession.

Second, let us look at the policies needed to finance the development and operation of professional development schools. Schools and universities need more funding to meet the increased demands society makes on them. The following recommendations pertain only to the funding requirements that are peculiar to PDSs:

- *State policymakers need to allocate funds for the development of a sufficient number of professional development schools to ensure that all new teachers can be served.* In addition to funds otherwise available, approximately $50,000 a year will be needed by each PDS for a minimum of two years' developmental efforts.

- *State policymakers should make it clear that money allocated to school districts and universities is to be used to provide support to PDSs.* In some states this may require additional funds, in others it may mean providing direction on how existing funding is to be used. In general, once PDSs have been initiated, it should be possible to operate them for no more than 10 percent over what is spent by schools and universities on teacher education, professional development, inquiry, and P–12 education.

- *School district and university policymakers need to allocate funds to ensure sufficient time for collaborative planning by key individuals from both institutional part-*

ners in the PDS. This may take the form of extended
contracts or provision of additional staffing that will
allow planning to be incorporated into the daily
work of the participants.[46]

Adoption of policies such as those described in the preceding paragraphs would obviously have a considerable impact on PDSs. Meanwhile, state officials and national organizations are developing new
standards for teachers, moving to strengthen accreditation of
teacher preparation, adopting expanded tests of general and professional knowledge for prospective teachers, establishing alternative routes to teacher certification, and expanding requirements for
continuing learning by teachers. For better or for worse, all such
actions help define the nature of a PDS. In the creation and continual renewal of these partner schools, people must be aware of the
potential effects of such actions on PDSs.

Cutting the Cloth

Forging a Common Educational Mission

Introduction

A child saw the naked emperor and knew him for the pompous fool he was because children's thinking is not clouded by misconceptions foisted on them by others. One suspects that Hans Christian Andersen could instead have used a village elder to utter the words "He has no clothes at all." Elders who have given their lives to careful and thoughtful study of important matters can see through socially imposed views to the heart of a matter because, much as innocence serves a child, their experience and study serve them to debunk common myths.

Chapter Two set forth some general principles that must be considered before creating productive partner schools. This chapter, written by John I. Goodlad, reveals some of the wisdom that comes from long study as he draws on better than fifty years of careful attention to educational issues to describe the particular view of partnerships that underlies the Agenda for Education in a Democracy. This perspective is important to understanding the rest of this book, because it serves as the general filter through which partner or professional development schools are viewed.

Simultaneously Renewing Schools and Teacher Education: Perils and Promises

John I. Goodlad

Now the schools, with public support, can respond to this opportunity by developing within our young people the intellectual values and skills the First Amendment was designed to protect. To do so, teachers have to intervene constructively in children's lives, and students must be protected against possible abuses. But unless schools exert enough authority to employ sound educational judgments, little serious education is possible. The courts have not somehow licensed authoritarianism; they have merely recognized that educators, not judges, are best able to determine for children what forms of education will develop mind and character. The courts have finally recognized that the First Amendment is best preserved—is only preserved—when the schools are free to educate.

Bruce C. Hafen and Jonathan O. Hafen.[1]

This quotation came at the end of an analysis of two Supreme Court decisions (1986 and 1988) overturning lower courts that had ruled against two school districts in suits challenging their authority to regulate certain aspects of student expression. Students' freedom of speech was claimed under the First Amendment. Hafen and Hafen summarized the thinking of the Supreme Court as follows: "The vision of Frazier and Hazelwood that schools should teach 'the habits and manners of civility' and other 'shared values of a civilized order' reaffirms the broad state authority and responsibility on which public schools have always drawn to teach both personal autonomy and social responsibility. The judicial breakthrough that began in 1986 and 1988 represents a much-needed

call to restore our original understanding about the duties, responsibilities, and authority of public schools."[2]

These actions of the U.S. Supreme Court and the analysis of the
two legal authorities are loaded with implications for the symbiotic
relationship between P–12 school reform and teacher preparation.
As one who has recommended and worked for years to implement
the concept of symbiotic school-university partnerships, I might be
expected to add to this chapter an enthusiastic subtitle such as "Go
for it!"

But there are caveats that grow out of the distinctive missions
of the two sets of educational institutions, their differing cultures,
and the considerable differences in the symbiotic relationships each
possesses or seeks to establish with the society that supports it. Partnerships between schools and universities (the latter convention-
ally regarded as the major players in teacher education) are not
mere extensions of the popular school-business partnerships or
adopt-a-school corporate initiatives. Because both schools and universities are classified as educational institutions, one might well
view symbiotic connections between the two to be natural. They
are not. Nor is the concept without threat.[3]

Responsibilities of the Schools

Let us analyze the quotations with which this chapter began. The
second quotation begins by affirming a purpose for public schools:
to teach "the habits and manners of civility." The authors assume
state authority to affirm and protect school authority to fulfill this
responsibility. The first quotation takes us to the very heart of
schooling: students and teachers. At least two interpretations of the
sentence about protecting students from abuses are possible. Perhaps the authors mean that students should be protected from
teachers ill prepared to exercise instructional authority in the
domain of students' personal autonomy or social responsibility. Or
perhaps teachers' authority to make judgments in the best interests

of students' education should be protected—that is, they should be "free to educate," in the words of the two authors.

The authority teachers need, according to the quotation, is "to employ sound educational judgments." Without protection from intrusions into this authority that can and do come from both beyond and inside the school, "little serious education is possible." The implications for state and district policies and the education and behavior of school administrators are enormous.

Of profound meaning for school-university collaboration, easily and often passed over, are the words in this sentence regarding the employment of sound educational judgments. How is that best ensured? Surely the proper exercise of teachers' authority to make sound educational judgments involves both protection of the teachers from intrusions and protection of the students from teachers' authority.[4] What is the nature of the relationship between schools and universities that is most likely to enhance these dual freedoms? The primary definition of symbiosis is quite neutral in the matter of benefits: it is the union of two dissimilar organisms. But without a moral component, it becomes apparent that a symbiotic school-university partnership could be in the best or worst interests of one party or both.

There appears to be no end of wisdom to be garnered from the two earlier quotations when it comes to their relevance to the conduct of our schools and the education of their teachers. The second paragraph (actually the last of the piece by Hafen and Hafen) ends with the words, "when the schools are free to educate." Clearly, the two authors are not arguing for freedom and responsibility solely from the perspective of a legal interpretation. They have something more in mind regarding the role of education in ensuring a context that understands, values, and protects the conditions education requires—in short, a context safe for education.[5]

The little piece they wrote (about two printed pages) stops short of defining education, but their exposition of its necessary conditions tempts the reader to make assumptions for which they should not be held responsible. Some of my extrapolations appear to arise quite naturally from their words and phrases; others probably are more a reflection of my own biases. The net result is a vision of school settings in which each student is seen as an autonomous individual engaged in a process of self-transcendence that requires and is nurtured by an environment rich in sensory stimulation that continually expands the universe of guided encounters with physical and social phenomena. This environment is at all times a model of the civilized order we tend to characterize as democratic. In other words, the self-development that is education and is always personal takes place in a context that is at once civil, caring, and continually broadening and deepening the ongoing conversation. The best way to ensure such an environment is to people them with teachers whose own educations have engaged them broadly and deeply in the human conversation, developed in them the necessary pedagogy, and honed the sensitivities moral stewardship of the schools requires.

Such settings are the cherished inventions of societies where civism is regarded as a high moral art. Societies that regard their schools as factories shaping raw materials for economic productivity are in decline. The more these raw materials are shaped today to fit precisely the economic machinery and technology of our confidently predicted tomorrows, the more rapid and irreversible this decline is likely to be. And now, with the foregoing as background, let us look at the promises and perils of a symbiotic relationship between school reform and teacher preparation.

The Link between School Reform and Teacher Preparation

There is a paradox in connections traditionally made between schools and the education of their teachers. During hours spent listening to keynote speakers and panelists at recent conferences, I have been struck by the frequent references to the pivotal role of teachers in carrying out this or that educational improvement initiative and the paucity of references to their education. This is not a new phenomenon. Reports on school reform and teacher education reform from the early 1890s to the mid-1980s make scarce reference to the other's respective domains.[6] Although published only four years apart, the widely acclaimed recommendations of James B. Conant on America's high schools (1959) and on the education of American teachers (1963) are almost entirely absent cross-references.[7]

Given this omission of what appears to be a natural linkage, one might expect teacher education to function free of intrusions from the affairs of schooling. Not so. Any study of state credentialing requirements for teachers over the past half-century would reveal an array of specific insertions intended to address school needs. Most states have stopped short of specifying how reading is to be taught, but they have influenced this area through the work of commissions that have approved materials reflecting alternative methods—materials to which future teachers usually are exposed. State legislatures do not hesitate to pass bills attempting to mesh expectations for teacher education programs with expectations for schools—for example, competencies for future teachers thought to mesh with proficiencies for students in elementary and secondary schools. Yet only during the past decade did commissions on school *reform* introduce in their reports the concept that better-prepared teachers produce better schools.[8]

To pass off these recurring omissions as mere myopia would be a serious mistake. Rather, they arise out of the differing histories and ideologies of two separate domains of formal education. This separation and accompanying isolation are not only characteristic of the relationships between the two institutional cultures but also artifacts of their societal context. The "lower" schools are grounded in an ethos of character development and democracy, albeit one frequently challenged and threatened. "Higher" education, by contrast, is grounded in an ethos of individual accomplishment and meritocracy, an ethos likewise subject to challenge. Both the historic cultural differences and the challenges to their continuation create dissonance—in and between the two institutional domains and in the larger culture that supports them.

Within this context, contemporary proposals to make the institutional relationship seamless appear eminently sensible, as do such innovations as school-university partnerships, professional development or partner schools, and the simultaneous renewal of schooling and the education of its stewards. The accompanying assurance of coherence in the whole is the glue of calibrated common standards and assessments. This rational model always has been part of the backdrop—and frequently the forefront—in the expansion of the American "common school." Until recently, it has been subdued in the rhetoric of expectations for "the academy." However, the growing courtship between business and academe has increased references to the bottom line of accountability in higher education. To the rhetoric of systemic connectedness has been added a common mission for the whole: preparing the young for the workplace.

Standards

The rationalization of school-centered educational improvement into linear cause-and-effect models of expectation stirs opposition based on philosophical grounds. Powerful arguments stem from observations of the repeated failure of recurring models to produce results: behavioral objectives are replaced by student competencies, to be replaced by general outcomes or national goals, all to be assessed by tests of academic achievement. The model is so powerfully appealing that "standards" slide easily into the output slot. Once perceived this way, they become static. The reform initiative becomes a process of formulating, agreeing on, and committing allegiance to a set of standards. Nothing much changes but the appearance of change.

The concept of standards is very compatible with those eminently sound definitions of education that speak to the development of the self. Sound concepts should not be rejected because of their abuse in use. They deserve better treatment. It is a shame, then, that the reification of standards into the building blocks from which the measuring stick of our system of schooling is to be calibrated has so captured the imagination of politicians, corporate executives, school administrators, various educational agencies, and individual educators. The ordering of the building blocks, the calibration of the measuring stick, and the scurrying of educational institutions to conform (or appear to conform) will substitute for the incredibly demanding tasks of ensuring in these institutions the conditions education needs in order to thrive—one more time.[9]

The progression of school reform rhetoric over successive eras to settle in the 1990s on fascination with the power of standards should have carried with it a simple but powerful learning: outcomes, however appealingly described, will lie inert and melt away like snow from the rooftops unless, as inputs, they become an integral component of the educative process. Slogans such as "Better Schools Mean Better Jobs" or goals such as "Leading the World in Math and Science by the Year 2000" have no more chance for success than snow on rooftops has not to melt.

The irony is that standards would have a chance if we understood them as inputs competing for attention with other inputs in the choice-making environments of teaching and learning.[10] Standards are inherent in all learning. They are not static. Their value lies in generative capacity, in enhancement of the human drive to move on to a higher level of performance, be it in writing, music, athletics, or mathematics. Standards can be mischievous and deceptive. Stellar performance in reciting the multiplication tables does not a mathematician make. Standards vary enormously in their transfer value. Good marks for high performance in school subjects tend to predict continuing high marks, but not generosity, compassion, relatedness, caring, or even good work habits later on.

In school as on the street, the standards of successful marketing—whether of athletes or cosmetics—overwhelm those of academic learning. If standards are not to become just one more nostrum promising impossibly healthy schools, they must become powerful nutrients in the school renewal diet. They will not find their way there, nor will more than a smattering of schools become places of renewal, until the knowledge and skills of their stewards are vastly enhanced. And this, in turn, will not occur until schools and institutions of higher education are joined in a mission-oriented, symbiotic partnership of obvious good sense and far-from-obvious complexity.

Caveats

I return to the idea of a tightly coupled system of elementary, secondary, and tertiary schooling with as its mission the preparation of humanpower for the workplace—a scenario of such appealing rationality that voices raised against it are regarded in some quarters as those of the moderately deranged. A speaker at one of the conferences to which I referred became so engaged with this scenario that she found it necessary to pause to acknowledge briefly other possible ends for schooling before plunging on into the dangers of a system otherwise oriented. At another of these conferences addressing the school-standards-for-the-workplace theme, I was gratified by the sigh of relief expressed by most of the educators in the audience when the speaker noted that the needs of the workplace would be well taken care of if the education in schools centered not on shaping for work but on making a life.

One must risk being seen as "out of the loop" when one points out two caveats. First, nothing about the nature of partnerships per se makes them virtuous. When building their financial portfolios, many investors avoid partnerships like the plague. The sorrow surrounding failed marriage partnerships is monumental. One key to positive symbiotic partnerships is that each of the different parties supplements what the other lacks or needs. And each must provide this supplementation or the partnership fails.

However, in education this is not enough. For example, there is little to commend in a school-university partnership that maintains systemics that bar access to one or both sets of institutions because of color. The second caveat pertains, then, to the educational mission to be pursued in tandem. Why should a college committed to providing a comprehensive curriculum of liberal studies join with a school district proclaiming its prime purpose to be that of preparing laborers for the workplace? Is a school district well advised to link with a university that perceives its primary role to be providing leaders to the financial marketplace?

The responses of thoughtful corporate leaders to such questions is that a comprehensive liberal education that develops creativity, cognitive power, the ability to solve problems, and the like is precisely what they want for potential employees; there is no dissonance here. And I agree. But even under the best of circumstances, the ethos of the economic workplace and the making of a life only partially overlap. What flows out beyond the former is all the rest of being human. To set for education any mission other than cultivating individual and community moral arts is to ensure its ultimate corruption. I shall assume in the balance of this chapter that the aim of education is to develop democratic character and that this is the overarching mission of the formal educational system that continues to evolve in the American democracy.

Both institutions of higher education and elementary and secondary schools have been hard-pressed to sustain an educational mission that clearly denotes commitment to both the microinterests of individuals and families and the macrointerests of civic societies. Recent emphasis on the role of schooling in individual economic enhancement has led more and more people to look to the local school for what it can do for them. Many come to resent the use of tax dollars for efforts to ensure equitable funding and equal access. The private purpose of schooling increasingly overshadows the public one. The interests of the state and the bureaucracy that supports them have so intruded into the educational rights of individual citizens that state and school must be separated, says one group of critics.[11] Why would and should institutions of higher education, with their traditions of independent inquiry into their cultural surround and accompanying hard-earned academic freedom, join in partnership with schools so torn by conflicting expectations and shorn of public purpose?

Institutions of higher education always have sought out a public audience in articulating their commitment not only to the pursuit of knowledge for its own sake but also to freedom from interference in defining the conditions necessary to that pursuit. Robert Maynard Hutchins, longtime president of the University of Chicago, saw danger to this commitment in the rise of professional schools, envisioning for his ideal university their relegation to the periphery of campus life as vocational institutes.[12] Today the professional schools—more than the universities of which they are a part—are the magnets pulling students across state lines and from abroad. The primary goal among freshmen in our most prestigious universities overwhelmingly is to become doctors or lawyers. The most rapid growth in the funding of endowed chairs in modern universities is in the business schools. There is a growing uneasiness in segments of the communities outside of universities as well as within them about the degree to which research is driven by business interests in the global economy. Why should and would schools, with their egalitarian roots and longstanding commitment to enculturating the young into our social and political democracy, join hands with institutions increasingly becoming captive of the very forces most in need of the independent criticism only free universities are able to provide?

The Contributions of Partnerships

Answers to the "would" part of the two questions raised in the preceding paragraphs are varied and practical. Schools gain prestige from connections with universities and, often, instructional and curricular resources from such collaborations. Universities improve their public image through outreach activities that connect with schools. Research and development funds from government and private philanthropy often are tied to conditions of partnership with schools. A nationwide, politically driven, and federally funded initiative for a "seamless curriculum," based on academic standards and assessments and geared to state funding for compliance, would push schools and universities quickly (but perhaps not happily) toward alliance. But to what end?

The "should" part of the questions adds the moral dimension. To what end *should* schools and universities join in partnerships? They enjoy tax-free status presumably because they serve the public good. The moral argument for joining, then, is to better serve the public good. Assuming that each already serves the public good, practical reasoning argues that the moral good to be gained must more than offset possible loss in the present good each provides. Positive symbioses must protect self-interests or neither common interest nor the public good is likely to be served. Means must be justified in their own right and not by ends alone, however morally intentioned these ends may be.

Of course we want our educational institutions to serve economic ends, but we do not want these economic ends to be their primary justification. As Neil Postman points out, the guiding narrative of the god of Economic Utility "is incapable of sustaining, with richness, seriousness, and durability, the idea of a public school. . . . According to this god, you *are* what you do for a living—a rather problematic conception of human nature."[13] The coming together of a producer of raw materials and a manufacturer of goods from them meets some requirements of symbiosis. The two differ in characteristics, each has something the other wants, and each must serve its own and the other's interests. The common purpose or mission is to raise the economic bottom line. Their moral justification is capitalism: competition in the marketplace narrows profit margins, improves products, and ensures the public of quality goods at modest cost. In business, the mission is profit (which is taxed). Any resulting common good is a by-product. Moral justification is enhanced through philanthropy, often to educational institutions.

In contrast, in education the mission is the common good—the development of democratic character. Individual and collective economic gain is a by-product, sharing secondary status with a host of other by-products. It is difficult if not impossible to envision business and educational institutions joined in symbiotic partnerships committed to a common *primary* mission without also anticipating one or the other losing its soul. With the loser so predictable and with so much to lose, the readiness of educational institutions to enter into partnerships with business is disquieting. One would hope the reason for this readiness is either innocence or keen awareness of and alertness to the dangers involved.

The most defensible and productive joinings of business and educational institutions are not symbiotic—that is, the two differing entities do not live together or, for that matter, conduct their work together. Significant educational improvement in recent years has been the result of a much different understanding and relationship, one where there are no strings attached. Corporate philanthropy has supported cutting-edge initiatives designed to enhance the educational mission of schools in particular with self-interest confined primarily to satisfaction in doing public good and enhancing public image. Of course, there are tax benefits, but that some of this philanthropy has been anonymous softens considerably the cold and severe image of the passionless god of Economic Utility that Postman describes.

Difficult Details

The joining of schools and institutions of higher education for the simultaneous renewal[14] of schooling and the education of educators constitutes a very special case of symbiotic partnering. Much of the dominance of the rhetoric of endorsement over exemplary accomplishment is best understood in the ideological context of the foregoing discussion. The rest is accounted for in the logistics and the accompanying interplay of personalities—in the details, if you will. The yellow lights of caution for both sides often turn red when half the collaboration is to enhance teacher education. Why?

There are many reasons, not all of them commendable.[15] On the university side there is, for example, the legacy of teaching as a low-paid, low-status occupation and of teacher education attracting primarily women at a time when they were not valued for their intellect. A mark of the transition of normal schools to teachers colleges to state colleges to state universities has been the decline in attention to teacher education at each step along the way.[16] Today, the top-ranked schools of education prepare only a handful of teachers or none. When they do produce in the hundreds each year, most of the teaching is turned over to adjunct and part-time faculty. There is a great deal of status and personal advancement to be gained in securing research grants, publishing, and presenting papers to one's colleagues nationwide. The high demands on instructional time lead many professors out of teacher education just as soon as possible after securing grants and tenure—not a choice some, or perhaps most, would make if the reward system were to be more favorable to the educational nurturing of future teachers.

Also on the side of caution for the university is the degree to which the state penetrates the teacher education component of the college curriculum, a domain traditionally viewed by higher education as its own. The academic departments experience no parallel amount of intrusion, and the other professional schools are much less put upon. Professors of education increase their individual and collective autonomy by using their advancement in seniority to teach advanced classes and seminars where state interest is little higher than it is in other graduate programs. Until very recently, flagship public universities have been very comfortable with state policies emphasizing teacher education as an important responsibility of the second tier of institutions. Much of the current reaching out by universities to the schools emphasizes the knowledge resources to be gained and has little to say about the better teachers to be delivered.

On the school side, there is some understandable uneasiness about the extent to which a symbiotic relationship will bring the probing interest of professors more intimately into school affairs—indeed, into classrooms. District administrators feel the threat of a challenge to existing policies and especially instructional and curricular directives. Teachers feel the threat to their autonomy and comfort with what they do daily. Traditionally, supervisors of student teachers from colleges and universities have confined their attention almost exclusively to the neophytes and have respected ongoing classroom practices even in the face of differing views. The rhetoric of renewal speaks to the need for better schools—often referred to as professional development or partner schools—and carries with it the expectation that both partners will engage in renewing both their own and the other's domain. But the ground rules often are vague.

There is a haunting history, too. It is virtually a given in many schools that university professors are off in some other realm, loosely called *theory*. The classic line is that teachers receiving student teachers into their classrooms tell their new charges to forget what they learned on the university campus; those with experience will now teach the newcomers how to survive. Then there is the fear, not unfounded, that the main interest of professors will be to engage the teachers in their research. And of course, enhancing research opportunities is an argument that some education deans use to persuade faculty members to join in partnership with schools.

What I have described here are just a few of the cultural realities that inescapably will shape, at times disrupt, and perhaps bring to an end even the best-intentioned and best-argued partnerships for improving schools and teacher education programs. They may lie dormant for long periods, but they will not go away. These and other cultural realities loom with the potential power to overcome rational arguments on the benefits to be gained from partnership and even persuasion that reaches for the high ground of "ought" and "should." Even when there is strong motivation to proceed, these realities will present contingencies to be reckoned with, just as the terrain presents contingencies on any journey. Difficulty in predicting the rise and play of contingencies stems less from the contours of the cultural surround than from the ties to particular characteristics already existing or perceived by the human players to exist and have personal value. The devil in the performance of the play lies in the personalities of the actors. But so does the excellence of its execution.

In the "ought" and "should" of all journeys educational, it is the power and appeal of moral mission that guide and drive. For many people, reliance on moral argument suggests fragility and failure. In his writings, William James referred to the "soft and tender" and the "hard and tough" in the warp and woof of the fabric of American character and spoke to the difficulty of *a balanced blending*. It is strange indeed that moral reasoning is so often equated with the soft and tender, when its implementation requires so much strength and struggle. As Timothy McMannon has pointed out, the moral argument for school reform is frequently soon replaced with hard and tough efficiency and accountability.[17]

And so it is today. The rhetoric surrounding the Elementary and Secondary Education Act of 1965 and much of the language of implementation envisioned an educational renaissance that would bring access to all and end violence, poverty, and war. Soft and tender, starry-eyed and visionary? Yes. But how much more uplifting than the tirades of blame—of hard and tough—that have dominated our present era of so-called school reform. And as Postman points out, the mission for schools of the god of Economic Utility conveys a rather problematic conception of human nature. He concludes his little book with a quite different *narrative* (his word) for the conduct and continuation of schooling: "My faith is that school will endure since no one has invented a better way to introduce the young to the world of learning; that the public school will endure since no one has invented a better way to create a public; and that childhood will survive because without it we must lose our sense of what it means to be an adult."[18]

Implied in this simple quotation, I believe, is the mission most of us have in mind for our schools. The relatively high rating parents give the schools their children attend, compared with the comparatively low rating they give to schooling in general, confirms for me both the faith in the schools that people know and the damage that has been done to schooling by those who have savaged the schools in their own self-interest. School "reform," with its language of blame and imagery of delinquent schools, teachers, and children to be reformed, must be replaced with the language and imagery of renewal—of schools as gardens to be cultivated and cared for, teachers as their gardeners, and children as the plants to be nourished.[19] The gardeners are to be prepared not just for the garden that *is* but for the garden that *could be*. This means that the garden in which each aspiring gardener works must itself be engaged in renewal toward this vision, as must the theoretical grounding successful gardening requires. Hence the concept of simultaneous renewal.

Effecting Renewal

What follows is a brief summary of one initiative attempting to connect effort and rhetoric—to "walk the talk." In this effort, however, the talk took on ever more depth and nuances, increasingly embellishing and enriching the walk.

The Center for Educational Renewal (CER) at the University of Washington was created in 1985, shortly after its three founders announced their interest in creating the National Network for Educational Renewal (NNER) to be composed of school-university partnerships engaged in the simultaneous renewal of schools and the education of educators.[20] By April 1986, ten settings, each composed of a university and school districts committed to joining in partnership and to the intent derived from the mission statement,[21] constituted the membership of the NNER.

The founders of the CER were aware—but not adequately—of the contingencies likely to arise out of the differing cultural contexts of the two sets of institutions and, indeed, the ways even the concept of partnership roils the waters of each, especially those of higher education. The initial, sometimes bumpy journey is at least partially described elsewhere.[22] Some good things were accomplished, especially in breaking down longstanding barriers and engaging in conversations that have not commonly characterized the school-university relationship. We learned a great deal—more than anticipated, given considerable prior experiences that connected elements of the two cultures.

Our significant learning was not anticipated. We had come to the NNER with confidence in the sensibility of the proposed symbiotic partnership of school and university. Indeed, my own earlier experience in helping to establish the Brigham Young University-Public School Partnership had helped me see the emergence of an agenda in which the self-interests of five school districts and BYU overlapped in such a way as to reveal the potential mutual benefits from collaboration. But this agenda was the end product of a year-long series of carefully designed preliminary conversations. It became increasingly apparent that similar conversations were not the mode in NNER settings. Although some did occur, the ethos was more that of universities in the traditional role of *noblesse oblige*—bringing succor to the needful schools—than of equal partners in mutual assistance.

Our growing awareness was of an initiative clothed in the best intentions making the usual mistake of assuming that these intentions gave sufficient direction to the process of simultaneous renewal. There is in the excess baggage of democracy the benign and often dysfunctional belief that good intentions accompanied by good will are sufficient to bring about near-miracles. Sometimes they do, but at least as often prolonged inability to agree on an agenda converts good will to ill will. Analysis of even modest success stories almost always reveals initial commitment to a common agenda already put forward, however diverse the means of advancing it might be.[23]

We set out to define and raise to high visibility an agenda of both mission and conditions necessary to its pursuit through a process of inquiry that combined two modes of thought—the empirical inductive and the theoretical deductive. The latter produced a two-part mission for schooling and, with two parts added, a mission for teacher education. In effect, teacher education shares the mission of schools and adds what is required to prepare teachers for advancing it. The mission of schooling embraces both individual and collective well-being: in Postman's words, introducing the young to the world of learning and creating a public; in ours, introducing the young to the human conversation and enculturating them in a political and social democracy. I combine the two into a single mission of developing democratic character. To the mission of teacher education we added the moral stewardship of schools and nurturing pedagogy.

The more empirical mode of inquiry—a comprehensive study of the education of educators—was connected with deductive reasoning on the conditions of support, resources, and policies necessary to robust houses of teacher education. The necessary conditions were then built into a series of nineteen aspirations to which teacher education settings should commit their energies and creativity in moving toward their four-part mission. We refer to these carefully reasoned statements as *postulates* (a deliberately chosen, somewhat archaic word that, we were told, brought down the wrath of the trustees at a philanthropic foundation who then denied us the grant we had requested).

This was the agenda of mission and necessary conditions we put forward for the commitment of potentially new NNER settings and recommitment of the old.[24] It resulted in a shakeout among the membership of the first iteration of the NNER, applications from far more settings than could be accommodated, and considerable renewing outside of the NNER, according to information now coming to us. At the time of this writing, the NNER embraces sixteen settings in fourteen states made up of thirty-three colleges and universities joined with more than a hundred school districts that together share processes of simultaneous renewal in teacher education programs and approximately five hundred partner schools.[25]

An interesting thing has happened on the way to the goal of NNER settings' being able to demonstrate, by the end of the century, excellence in their advancement of the agenda—not in all of its components, perhaps, but in many and, with some settings, in most. During the early months and even years of involvement, the nineteen postulates were the primary focus of attention. Indeed, unpacking these postulates for meaning and implications in discussion groups that were to include personnel from the schools, the departments and colleges of education, and the arts and sciences was a requirement for admission into the NNER. The conditions embedded in the postulates necessitate a fundamental redesign of teacher education programs that includes periods of residency in renewing partner schools for all aspiring teachers. The scope of work stretching into the future is challenging, but the activities it calls for are not unfamiliar to educators. Increasingly, however, interest turned from the tasks at hand to the more abstract, at times chimeric, four-part mission we refer to as the *moral grounding of the agenda*. Apparently, it aroused in our colleagues in the NNER settings a renewed sense of faith in the educational careers they had chosen some years ago and in the worthwhileness of their endeavors.

One of our books provided insights into part of this grounding, stimulating in some readers a vision of teaching with implications for teacher educators rising above the narrow, technical role the workplace tends to foist upon both.[26] Humans are associational. Their education should provide them with a "sense of place in the past, present, and future of the human race,"[27] and stimulate "thirst for new ideas and visions of the yet unknown."[28] We need more, not less, sensitive and caring educative interaction between professional teachers and their students in the endless search for an individual and a collective human identity, a process ever more complicated by the frustrations that accompany technological gains—what Edward Tenner calls "the revenge of unintended consequences." In providing a context for describing the discontent with the kinds of increased human work technology demands, Tenner quotes from poet Paul Valéry: "Life has become, in short, the object of an experiment in which we can say only one thing—that it tends to estrange us more and more from what we were, or what we think we are."[29]

Many of our colleagues appear to see in an educational mission to reach self-transcendence and civil society an antidote to what they perceive as the tearing down of the societal structure we have known. It connotes a conception of human nature sufficient to give direction to both their long-term aspirations and their daily efforts to renew together both schools and the education of their stewards.

4

The First Layer of Clothes

Processes in Creating a PDS

There is a difference between getting the cloth ready—the steps "before the beginning"—and starting to dress the emperor. The proper undergarments are required if the emperor is to look good in his new clothes. The drape of a suit will be wrong if the undergarments are too bulky. Certain materials may be too revealing if they do not have proper undergarments. In other instances, the cut of the undergarments may detract from the appearance and functionality of the outerwear.

In the same way, some developmental processes are more likely than others to produce effective professional development schools, and PDSs require certain foundational conditions. This chapter will consider one main question and two underlying ones:

Assuming the existence of a healthy school-university partnership, what process should be followed to create PDSs?

• What conditions need to be in place to create PDSs?

• Are formal agreements needed?

What Process Should Be Followed to Create PDSs?

Once the conditions described in Chapter Two have been met— or at least there is progress toward meeting them—the members of the school-university partnership can begin the process of selecting specific sites. The following criteria are grounded in experiences in creating such schools throughout the National Network for Educational Renewal (NNER). Consider these potential criteria by testing them through stating the negative. In other words, consider whether a school would be acceptable as a PDS if it were one in which the conditions were the opposite of those suggested. Also keep in mind that the decision makers will be seeking potential partner schools that are making real progress toward these ideals. It is unlikely that the collaborators will find a large number of schools that can be highly rated on all the criteria. If they could, the need for simultaneous renewal of schools and the education of educators would be far lower than it is!

Potential professional development schools should

- Be engaged in collaborative inquiry and innovation regarding school practices and professional education; that is, they should be renewing schools

- Be places where staff members engage in self-analysis and professional development as a matter of course

- Have the full support of staff and district administrators who are committed to involvement in preparation of the next generation of education professionals

- Be willing and able to commit sufficient resources to permit teachers to plan for their dual responsibility of educating their own students and prospective teachers

- Be committed to helping children learn to use their minds well (this criterion is deliberately adopted from Ted Sizer's notions about how schools should function to challenge students[1])

- Allow teachers, parents, and students to share with administrators in making essential decisions concerning the curriculum but also be willing to embrace a role for university faculty and prospective teachers in this decision making

- Be willing to assign prospective teachers to roles as junior faculty members expected to participate in all aspects of the professional life of the schools, not just to apprenticeships under an individual mentor

- Give rigorous attention to multicultural issues; among other things, provide a curriculum that does not diminish the self-worth of any person or group

- Accept responsibility to contribute to the growth of students as citizens in a democratic society, contributors to a healthy economy, and full human beings versed in the arts and ideas that help them realize their individual potentials; in short, be prepared to enculturate the young for participation in a democratic society

- Ensure that parents know about and are supportive of the multiple missions envisioned for partner schools

- Authentically assess student learning

The Colorado Partnership's Benchmarks for Partner Schools

Although these general criteria are helpful, the partners forming a PDS should develop their own criteria to guide their work. The specific set of criteria developed should reflect the values and conditions associated with a particular setting. The following example of such criteria shows those developed in the Colorado Partnership for Educational Renewal as benchmarks related to partner schools.[2]

Benchmarks for Partner Schools

At the District Level

Partner schools are a central strategy for renewal and improvement of all schools in a participating district; as such, districts use their partner schools to assist other schools to improve practice.

- Current reform efforts (Colorado Standards, Goals 2000, school professional licensure standards) are all intertwined with school professional preparation and ongoing development.

- Through formal agreements, school boards identify their district's partner schools as vehicles for professional development and renewal of curriculum.

- The partner school program reflects a strong commitment to collaborative staffing decisions and cross-institutional communication.

- Partner school agreements are supported by district personnel policies and master agreements with certified and classified employee associations.

- The school district supports, through formal agreements, a structure of formative and summative evaluation to measure progress in the development of the partner school.

- Communication occurs in such a way as to create and promote a learning community.

At the Institution of Higher Education (IHE) Level

Partner schools are a central strategy for strengthening the preparation of school professionals and renewing education in local communities.

- School professional preparation programs at IHEs are integrally connected to partner schools through joint resource and full-time equivalency (FTE) commitments on the part of IHEs and school districts.

- Governance structures at both the IHE and the partner school reflect shared decision making through membership on their respective operating committees.

- The retention, promotion, and tenure policies at participating IHEs value, recognize, and support the academic merit of faculty working in partner schools.

- Preparation programs in partner schools ensure that all professional educators develop the pedagogical skills needed to educate all children.

- Communication occurs in such a way as to create and promote a learning community.

At the School Site Level

The school is continually and systemically renewed through collaboration with the teacher education program of the IHE.

- The school as a whole (school accountability teams, school professionals, faculty from IHEs, ad hoc committees, classified staff, and students) recognizes and meaningfully integrates the four functions of partner schools into its annual school improvement planning and implementation cycles.

- The school serves all students in the community in which it is situated, including students with significant disabilities, students who speak other languages, teen parents, and other potentially marginalized populations.

- In the school, regular programs and special initiatives are integrated and coherent.

- The mission of each partner school is revisited frequently and evolves as partner schools come to understand their roles in the changing contexts of their communities.

- The school collaborates with other health and human service agencies, employee associations, community businesses and agencies, and families to meet the needs of its constituents.

- Preparation programs in the school ensure that all professional educators develop the pedagogical skills needed to educate all children.

- A variety of strategies, developed jointly by the partners, ensures that student academic progress is measured and communicated to the school community and subsequently used as a weather-vane for school improvement.

- The school is continuously engaged in inquiry that addresses and solves the difficult problems of practice.

- Curriculum and instruction are grounded in teaching and learning in a social and political democracy.

- Communication occurs in such a way as to create and promote a learning community.

At the Institution of Higher Education Faculty Level

Faculty from all disciplines in the School of Education and the College of Arts and Sciences are actively involved with the partner school.

- An IHE faculty member spends at least one day per week in an assigned partner school with course equivalency or other consideration negotiated with the IHE.

- IHE faculty members collaborate in the development of an annual plan to effectively implement the four functions of a partner school.

- IHE faculty members are collaboratively engaged with their school partners in critical inquiry to improve instruction and curriculum.

- IHE faculty members are fully qualified in their content areas, have experience with K–12 students, are current in their teaching and assessment practices, and are engaged in continued professional renewal.

- IHE faculty members share responsibility for teaching students in partner schools, not only in their discipline expertise but as general problem solvers and as an extra pair of hands.
- Communication occurs in such a way as to create and promote a learning community.

At the School Professional Level

School professionals are actively engaged in the implementation of the four functions of partner schools.

- At least one professional in the school assumes leadership for implementing partner school functions.
- The students, school professionals, families, and faculty from IHEs engage collaboratively in inquiry to improve instruction and curriculum.
- The school professionals are fully qualified in their content areas, have classroom experience, are open to learning, and are continually engaged in individual and collective professional development.
- The school professionals ensure that students are actively engaged in providing feedback about their practices.
- The teachers model, guide, and support students in exploring and practicing democratic ideals in a school committed to being a model of democracy.
- Long-term relationships between school professional candidates and their mentors are established at the beginning of their preparation programs and expanded upon over the course of the preparation so that the experience culminates in a junior faculty relationship.

At the Principal Level

The principal focuses the school staff and community on the implementation of the four functions of partner schools in an atmosphere of collaboration and sharing among all parties involved.

- The principal supports students, school professionals, families, and faculty from IHEs who engage collaboratively in inquiry.

- The principal ensures that the whole school and its community recognize and meaningfully integrate the four functions of a partner school into their school improvement cycles.

- The principal works collaboratively with the staff and the IHE to ensure that student learning is positively affected by partnership activities and in the development and implementation of best instructional practices.

- The principal works toward establishing a faculty that is uniformly knowledgeable and supportive of the functions of a partner school.

- The principal is an active and regular participant in external and internal partner school functions.

At the Student Level

Students at the school consider themselves active participants in the partner school effort.

- A process, collaboratively developed by the partners, is in place at the school to ensure that students are actively engaged in measuring academic progress and developing appropriate strategies to respond to and communicate the findings.

- Student performance and well-being are enhanced by virtue of their participation in the efforts of the partner school relationship.

- Students explore and practice democratic ideals in a school committed to being a model of democracy.

At the Teacher Candidate Level

Teacher candidates from all disciplines at the IHE are actively involved with the partner school.

- Teacher candidates actively participate in a broad variety of the activities of the partner school.

- Teacher candidates communicate positively and effectively with the partners in identifying strategies to enhance their own professional development as well as support the school renewal effort.

- Teacher candidates provide appropriate student instruction in cooperation with their clinical instructors, partner school staff, and the IHE faculty.

- Teacher candidates serve as partners in the school renewal effort by introducing and modeling new and appropriate instructional strategies and technologies.

- Teacher candidates act as positive, caring role models for their students and the student body of the partner school.

- Teacher candidates model, guide, and support students in exploring and practicing democratic ideals in a school committed to being a model of democracy.

Keeping their set of criteria in mind, participants in the Colorado Partnership for Educational Renewal developed a set of rubrics to enable their selection task force to evaluate the status of each potential PDS. These rubrics help demonstrate the range of quality that is possible.

Potential Partner School Evaluation Rubrics

I. Understandings of Partner Schools,   SCORE _____
Capacity to Collaborate

1 Point

- Indicates little understanding of the partner school concept.

- Presents an unclear vision regarding the purpose or functions of a partner school.

- Indicates little understanding of the simultaneous renewal agenda.

- Indicates an interest in only one function of a partner school.

- Excludes any reference to an IHE relationship.

2 Points

- Communicates a minimal understanding of the partner school concept.

- Expresses a vision that indicates a minimal understanding of the purpose or functions of a partner school.

- Expresses a desire to deepen the understanding of partner schools and the simultaneous renewal agenda.

- Indicates an interest in two functions of a partner school but cannot relate them to other work under way.

- Refers minimally to any IHE involvement, or sees it only as a way to receive assistance.

3 Points

- Articulates a reasonable understanding of the partner school concept and the four functions.

- Outlines a vision of a partner school that addresses an understanding of the simultaneous renewal agenda and presents a way in which the school community can contribute to the agenda.

- Presents a strategy for deepening the understanding of a partner school and the simultaneous renewal agenda.

- Indicates an interest in the four functions and has related them to other work under way.

- Expresses a desire to work with an IHE.

- Expresses an understanding of collaboration and reciprocity that includes the IHE.

4 Points

- Articulates a clear understanding of a partner school and addresses all four functions in the response.

- Articulates a vision in which the school is a viable contributor to the simultaneous renewal agenda and presents several ways in which this contribution can be made.

- Outlines a definitive plan consisting of several strategies for deepening the understanding of a partner school and the simultaneous renewal agenda.

- Describes in great detail the interest in and commitment to each of the four functions and has related each function to other work already under way in the school.

- Recognizes that the partner school includes not only the school site but teacher education and the arts and sciences—and expresses a desire to work with both.

- Places collaboration and reciprocity at the center of the IHE relationship.

II. Agreement, Consensus, Support   SCORE _____

1 Point

- No clear evidence is present that indicates that effective leadership exists at the school.

- No clear evidence is present that indicates that there is community involvement in the school or in developing the responses to the Initial Questions (a series of open-ended questions asking leaders at potential partner schools to evaluate their schools' understanding of and commitment to the partner school model).

- No clear evidence is present that indicates faculty consensus to become fully involved as a partner school.

- No clear evidence is present that indicates direct involvement of the school district's central administration in the nomination of this school as a potential partner school site.

- No clear evidence is present that indicates that the school district's governing board and coordinating committee members were involved in the nominating process.

- No clear evidence is present that indicates any recognition of the need to communicate with an IHE regarding interest or faculty commitment.

2 Points

- Some evidence is present that indicates that effective leadership is important in this endeavor, but no indication is present regarding current leadership.

- Some evidence is present of community involvement in developing responses to the Initial Questions.

- Some evidence is present that indicates faculty interest but not consensus.

- No clear evidence is present indicating the central administration's support of this school's nomination or a commitment to having it become a district resource.

- Some evidence is present that indicates that the district's governing board and coordinating committee were involved in nominating this school as a potential partner school site.

- Some evidence is present that indicates recognition of the need for IHE support and commitment.

3 Points

- Strong evidence is present that indicates that effective leadership exists at this school.

- Clear evidence is present that indicates community involvement in this school and some involvement in developing responses to the Initial Questions.

- Strong evidence is present that indicates faculty consensus in becoming fully involved as a partner school.

- Clear evidence is present that indicates that the district's central administration supports this school as a potential partner school site but no evidence is present regarding the commitment to use it as a district resource.

- Strong evidence is present that the district's governing board and coordinating committee were involved in nominating this school as a potential partner school site.

- Clear evidence is present indicating a desire to have IHE faculty consensus and commitment in becoming involved with this school.

4 Points

- Strong evidence is present that indicates that effective leadership exists at the school.

- Strong evidence exists that there is community involvement in the school and in developing responses to the Initial Questions.

- Strong evidence is present that indicates consensus among faculty to be fully involved as a partner school.

- Strong evidence exists that the school district's central administration supports this school as a potential partner school site and is committed to using it as a district resource.

- Strong evidence exists that the school district's governing board and coordinating committee members were involved in the nomination of this potential partner school site.

- Strong evidence is present that indicates a need for consensus from an IHE faculty to be fully involved in the partner school or a promise of such involvement has been received.

III. School and IHE Needs/Capacity   SCORE _____

1 Point

- Interests, programs, capacity, and needs are unclear.
- School is not large enough to accommodate a reasonable number of teacher candidates and IHE faculty.

2 Points

- Interests, programs, capacity, and needs are somewhat clear but no match exists with an IHE.
- School seems large enough to accommodate a reasonable number of teacher candidates and IHE faculty but commitment to a reasonable number is unclear.

3 Points

- Interests, programs, capacity, and needs are very clear but a possible IHE match is limited.
- School is large enough to accommodate a reasonable number of teacher candidates and IHE faculty and there is a clear commitment to do so.

4 Points

- Interests, programs, capacity, and needs are very clear and match with one or more IHEs.
- School is large enough to accommodate a reasonable number of teachers and IHE faculty, and there is a strong commitment to do so.[3]

As the selection process moves forward, other practical issues, such as creating rubrics of the type Colorado used, have to be dealt with. For example, the collaborating group will need to agree on such issues as the following: Should selected professional development schools have different staffing procedures than other schools? How long should a school commit to being a partner school? How long should the university commit to working with the school? What procedures would be used if either party wants to terminate the relationship?

What should be the minimum resource commitment by the school, the district, and the university? What should be the form of the agreement among the various parties?

What would be the selection process, including the time line, for people to be involved in making the decision about the creation of partner schools?

Using the Criteria in a Selection Process

The partnership created along the lines described in Chapters Two and Three should solicit school districts that are willing to invest substantial resources in support of partner schools and in identifying individual schools that want to be informed about what becoming a PDS really would entail. Schools that want to learn more about such involvement should then be asked to make a written proposal to the partnership selection committee (or, in the case of a fully operational center of pedagogy, to that entity) explaining why they believe they meet the criteria and why they want to take on the additional commitments involved.

Schools should then be selected as *potential* partner schools. During the year following selection, teachers and administrators from the school and university should engage in an intensive process leading to final decisions by both parties. Schools responsible for preparing people for democracy should be able to make such decisions democratically. During the year, the following should occur.

First, faculty from the potential partner school and the university should engage in a series of seminars on at least a monthly basis. These sessions should be designed as a joint inquiry into the purposes of education and schooling, pedagogy, issues related to school restructuring, and practices for educating new and continuing educators. From such discussions, the partners should forge a common vision of a school committed to enculturating their students as citizens in a democracy.

Next, portraits of each school should be prepared by a team of university and school participants trained in this methodology. These portraits should then be discussed in seminars involving school and university people, and they should be considered by each prospective partner school's decision-making group.

Specific plans for restructuring work at the schools should then be shared, as should plans for continuing education activities facilitated by members of the school's faculty and by professionals outside of the school. Next, written commitments should be made concerning resources by each potential participant.

Finally, in the spring of the study year, the school and university people should be asked to indicate the extent of their commitment and the progress being made toward realizing the ideals of partner schools. The selection committee should then make its final decision regarding participants to be designated officially as professional development schools.

This is an elaborate, time-consuming, and potentially expensive process. However, if universities and school districts really believe in the idea of PDSs, it is an essential process. Ultimately, there is nothing more time consuming or expensive than having to undo a poor initial selection and begin again to create the environment needed to enhance the quality of both the schooling for our children and the education of educators.

The Colorado rubrics and benchmarks were part of an ongoing process by that partnership to develop exemplary professional development schools. Before this process was initiated, a few PDSs had been created, but the necessity of making decisions about which prospective schools were to receive external funding created a need for a much more sophisticated approach. With funding available from Goals 2000 and Eisenhower grants, the partnership sought nominations from district administrators, schools, and IHEs. Written applications were then submitted to the partnership. A team trained in the use of the rubrics reviewed the applications. Representatives from the partnership visited a smaller group before completing the rating scales and making the selections.

Participants in the selection of the PDSs generally agreed that the dialogue they had carried out in creating the criteria and the rubrics, and the application of these rubrics to specific schools, furthered their shared understanding of PDSs more than any previous activity. A lesson to be learned from this experience is that, although the criteria and processes used by others may be helpful to a setting, they should never be considered as substitutes for the hard work of the participants in a given setting designing and implementing their own processes. In short, the criteria and processes reported in this chapter should not simply be adopted but rather used to help a group to develop its own set of guidelines.

In South Carolina, for example, a group of educators—teachers convinced that there had to be "a better way" and university professors and school district administrators who were willing to risk trying truly different approaches—brought about the establishment of the Center of Inquiry. This group based its elementary school PDS on earlier University of South Carolina (USC) faculty conversations about Holmes Group and NNER principles and on reflections by public school teachers, some of whom were enrolled as graduate students. These groups considered criteria such as those outlined in the Colorado example. Moreover, the university had initiated processes whereby faculty from a prospective PDS could spend time in study and reflection before their school was formally identified as a PDS. However, South Carolina's newly created PDS was more a product of its founders' determination to generate a different kind of experience for both children and preservice candidates than a simple identification of a school that could receive some financial help.

Therefore, the participants decided that what they needed was a new setting, one they could shape from the beginning. They started by gaining administrative support from the university and a school district to enable the two institutions to realize their vision. They used political processes that included committed educators' persuading key power brokers rather than dialogue among prospective partners about the creation of the PDS. The superintendent, school board members, PTA leaders, and principals of schools that might be affected through loss of students needed to be convinced. Deans, provosts, university personnel, and business officials needed to be assured that the proposed jointly operated school was in their best interests. Of course, lawyers for both institutions had to be satisfied that there was appropriate legal authority for the venture and that the risks associated with the new endeavor were manageable. More than a course of action that others can follow, what this process demonstrates is that the selection or creation process has to be carefully tailored to the unique needs of each PDS. One approach will not fit all any more than the emperor could be assured that one size of clothes would fit him and all the members of his court.

What Conditions Need to Be in Place in Creating a PDS?

The National Council for Accreditation of Teacher Education (NCATE), in its exploratory project related to standards for PDSs, identified this stage as that of *threshold conditions*. In its draft standards issued in September 1997, the accrediting agency described this stage as including the following:

1. An agreement which commits school, school district, union/professional organization, and the university to the basic mission of a PDS;

2. A commitment by the partners to the critical attributes of a PDS;

3. A positive working relationship and a basis for trust between partners;

4. The achievement of quality standards by partner institutions as evidenced by regional, state, national, or other review;

5. An institutional commitment of resources to the PDS from school and university.[4]

Those PDSs that have progressed beyond the threshold stage are expected to have a tangible commitment from each partner to (1) the support of a learning community for adults and children; (2) collaboration; (3) accountability and quality assurance; (4) organization, roles, and structure; and (5) equity as it affects students and teachers.[5] The commitment of resources identified in the threshold conditions could take many forms, including faculty participation, time commitment, financial support, and organization to support mission.

As indicated in the preceding chapter, of the five threshold conditions, the third needs to occur during the prior development of a school-university partnership. The fourth—achieving national or regional accreditation—is likely something schools and universities will seek whether or not they are PDSs. This would seem to leave as foundational items whether the school, district, and university are committed to the mission and basic characteristics of a PDS and whether they provide the necessary resources. The issue of resources is addressed at some length in Chapter Six. Meanwhile, the issue of commitments takes us directly to the question of whether there should be formal agreements, and if so, what such documents should contain.

Formal Agreements: To Have or Not to Have?

In today's legalistic society, the many reasons for having formal agreements may seem so obvious that their potential downside may be overlooked. At early stages of relationships, formalizing commitments in a legal agreement may lead to heightened mistrust rather than alleviating it as participants in the process begin to think of all the protections that need to be built into the document. Worries about abuse of personal time, compensation for extra effort, clear authority of some personnel over others, and so on may begin to dominate conversations as the agreement is negotiated. Small problems may become large when given heightened visibility. Another downside to the early establishment of formal written agreements for a PDS is that they tend to create rigid conditions—to fix practices concerning such matters as assignment of preservice interns, roles of cooperating teachers, practices for grading student teachers, and length of time spent by preservice teachers in solo practice—at the very stage in the development when experimentation regarding the best approaches to these items should be going on. Still another problem with formal agreements is that the task of writing them "just right" drains considerable energy from the parties involved. Instead of helping the parties become clearer on their commitments (the intent), this process can cause the writers of the document to get bogged down in petty semantic wars that advance neither their understanding nor the larger cause: the creation of the PDS.

Although there are drawbacks to the formalization of arrangements for a PDS, there are also some real advantages. One of the biggest problems PDSs experience is leadership turnover. When principals, superintendents, deans, university presidents, and school board members change as frequently as they do today, it is hard to sustain any initiative. Pragmatically, an effort such as a PDS has a better chance of surviving a leadership change if there is a formal written agreement that has been ratified by several layers of the hierarchies of all parties. Furthermore, because financial resources from several organizations may be mixed in a PDS, clear agreement regarding financing and accounting becomes more important than in some less complex collaborative arrangements. Similarly, personnel working under different union agreements and personnel policies will be mixed together in PDSs, and clarity is essential concerning which work rules will prevail.

However, the most important matter—the shared commitment among partners to mission and to the critical attributes of a PDS—may not be something that can be obtained through a written agreement. On the one hand, it seems reasonable that if the parties spell out in writing what they are agreeing to accomplish and how they plan to go about it, then their commitments will be strengthened. But on the other hand, in too many instances words become meaningless, the people who write the agreement are not fully empowered to speak for the people who have to carry out the agreement, or a philosophical statement in an agreement is treated as "fluff," not a genuinely binding matter. If an agreement truly reflects philosophical positions that have been hammered out by the essential parties and if the agreement is written in such a way that it permits continuing growth in shared understandings, then it may be useful in recording commitments.

If an agreement is developed, it should include the following major components:[6]

Outline of Agreement

1. Preamble
   1.1.   Statement of purpose and overarching goals
   1.2.   General specification of responsibilities of partners

2. Main body of the agreement
   2.1.   Specification of the parties to the agreement
   2.2.   Detailing of specific goals
   2.3.   Specification of responsibilities of partners
           2.3.1.   Regarding accomplishment of the goals of the partnership
           2.3.2.   Regarding governance of the partnership
           2.3.3.   Regarding financing of the partnership
           2.3.4.   Regarding research and evaluation to be conducted by or in relation to the partnership
   2.4.   Term of the agreement
   2.5.   Signatures of the parties to the agreement and date of signing

A Sample Agreement

The following example is offered as an indicator of how one partnership solved the dilemma of whether to have an agreement and answered questions of what should be contained in it. The importance of tailoring any agreement to the particular circumstances of a particular setting cannot be overemphasized—if the parties decide that such a formal document is in their mutual interest.

Preface to Agreement

**KANSAS ALLIANCE OF PROFESSIONAL
DEVELOPMENT SCHOOLS**

PROPOSED PARTNERSHIP AGREEMENT

_____ Public Schools

and

The University of Kansas School of Education

Purpose

The Kansas Alliance of Professional Development Schools (KAPDS) is a collaboration among professionals in the public schools, university faculty, business community and KU students designed to enhance education. The intent of the KAPDS is to move beyond a traditional university-school-business relationship toward a site dedicated to improvement within schools and in the preparation of professionals.

University and school personnel will work together to identify educational needs and propose solutions. Dialogue on all levels, research on current educational practice, and continual questioning and reflection will form the basis for this Professional Development School. Additionally, the Professional Development School will allow for supervised experiences for the preparation of prospective teachers and other educational professionals. The Professional Development School will be an environment where research-based instructional practices and programs can be observed and experienced by those preparing for professional careers in education.

We seek to achieve the following goals:

- To collaboratively initiate, design and implement a professional development school that endorses mutual trust and common interests

- To provide the best possible environment for student academic learning and professional self-fulfillment

- To provide opportunities for preservice preparation and career-long professional development of teachers and administrators

- To collaboratively provide access to knowledge and talent related to student learning and development

- To conduct collaborative research and development projects to advance theory, research, and practice in public education

- To collaboratively agree upon research agendas, publishing rights, and dissemination of results

The School of Education may provide some of the following:

1. In-school supervision and coordination of field-based and student teaching experiences, practicums, and internships

2. Research and development assistance on topics agreed upon by teachers, administrators, and university faculty

3. Assistance or leadership in grant writing for collaborative projects

4. Workshops and seminars related to selected educational topics

5. Consultant services and technical assistance in a variety of educational activities

6. Internships or practicums in administration, counseling, school psychology, and social welfare

7. Selected on-site course offerings

8. University staff to serve on school-site committees

9. Initiation and development of research projects of mutual interest

The school site may provide some of the following:

1. Placement for University of Kansas students in practicums, clinics, student teaching, and internships

2. Flexible field experiences with access to a wide range of grade levels

3. Access to curriculum materials and instructional technology

4. Access, with necessary approval, to student programs and school records for inquiry and instructional purposes

5. Opportunities for school faculty to participate in the evaluation of KU programs

6. Use of office equipment and materials as needed for instruction

7. Initiation and development of research projects of mutual interest

8. Teachers may be asked to lead, teach, or participate in field-based experiences, seminars and research projects

Partnership Agreement

_____ and the University of Kansas School of Education

THIS AGREEMENT made this _____ day of 199_, between the UNIVERSITY OF KANSAS SCHOOL OF EDUCATION (hereinafter KU) and the School of _____, a municipal corporation, acting through its BOARD OF EDUCATION (hereinafter _____).

The University of Kansas School of Education desires to provide practical educational instruction for University of Kansas education students through the Professional Development School located in the _____ school district. This Professional Development School will be established to provide an educational experience of up-to-date instructional practice in an environment to better prepare students for a professional career in education. The partnership is to be a collaboration between KU and _____ to achieve the following goals:

(A) Provide a high quality learning environment that promotes students and staff with academic learning and professional development

(B) Provide an opportunity for _____ teachers to obtain in-service and career professional learning and development

(C) Provide _____ teachers and KU education students access to the most up-to-date information, and qualified KU and _____ instructional personnel to promote maximum learning and development

THEREFORE, the parties do hereby agree as follows:

(1) KU shall assign and _____ shall accept a mutually agreed-upon number of KU Education students per academic year to be assigned with a school-site certified classroom teacher. (For example, KU may provide interns in school administration, school development, school psychology, social welfare and special education as part of the Professional Development School programs.)

(2) The school shall provide a mutually agreed-upon number of certified classroom teachers per year willing to participate in the Professional Development initiatives.

(3) All teaching areas will be open for Professional Development School activities, except personnel files.

(4) The school shall provide all curriculum and instructional materials and facilities for K-12 school activities.

(5) KU shall provide all curriculum and instructional materials for the instruction of KU Education students and assigned school-site teaching staff.

(6) The school shall provide, consistent with the rights of students' privacy, statistical and evaluative information needed to develop new and/or improved teaching programs or techniques, or any other research needs.

(7) KU shall provide for participation by the teaching staff in the admission of students to KU teacher education programs and the evaluation of the Professional Development School at this school.

(8) KU shall provide participating teachers the opportunity to volunteer to lead, teach, participate and/or attend field-based experiences and seminars.

(9) KU shall provide mutually agreed-upon research and development assistance and consultant and technical assistance in program and staff development.

(10) KU will make available staff for technical advice to committees and to assist in writing of grant proposals to enhance the Professional Development School and other programs.

(11) Both parties will have a written agreement for a governance structure for decisions being made at the professional development site.

(12) Both parties will have a written agreement as to the fiscal agent of any or all funding sources for the operation of the professional development site.

(13) The school shall designate a liaison at the Professional Development School.

(14) KU shall designate a liaison for the Professional Development School site.

(15) Both parties shall have a written record that their governing bodies accept the terms of this agreement.

THIS AGREEMENT may be for a provisional one-year arrangement. At the end of the first year, if both parties agree to continue the partnership, a contract of three years, with annual review, will be signed and forwarded to their respective governing bodies.

IN WITNESS WHEREOF, the parties have signed their names this_____ day of _____ 199_.

_____   _____
President, School Board   Executive Vice-Chancellor

_____   _____
Superintendent   Dean, School of Education

_____   _____
Principal   Chair, KAPDS Executive Council

Approved by the Executive Council Jan. 15, 1993[7]

Not unlike a prenuptial agreement, the written agreement entered into by partners constructing a PDS may speak clearly to all of the routine matters anticipated in the partnership but not address the essential commitment that the parties are making to each other. This may be the case with the Kansas example. One knows that the partnership is being constructed to prepare teachers using "best-practice" strategies, but it is not at all clear that the parties share the same view of what a teacher is or does. It is this shared understanding that—as is the case in a marriage—may not be something that can be achieved through a written agreement. As has been suggested previously, it is something that grows out of and is nourished by long and sustained dialogue between the partners. In spite of this limitation, the preceding sample addresses most of the essential issues that need to be treated in an agreement if the parties choose to have a written agreement.

If the emperor is going to look good in his new clothes, those who are dressing him must prepare carefully. So, too, must those who would create a PDS. For them, the preparation period is likely to be quite time consuming. Close attention must be paid to the criteria describing the kind of a school being sought and to the process used for selection. The concern for process may lead the partners to establish a written agreement, but if they do so they need to take care that the agreement does not get in the way of their collaboration.

5

Style, Not Fad

Essential Qualities of an Effective PDS

Not just any old suit will do for a real emperor. Some new clothes are classically stylish and show off the wearer's strengths, others are faddish. Some people make the best-dressed list every year, others the worst.

Similarly, some PDSs are nothing more than institutions trying to keep up with the latest fad, whereas others are truly uncommon, stylish places. This chapter discusses why tailoring a school to attend to the Agenda for Education in a Democracy and to include the vital connections necessary to renewing schools is essential to creating an effective PDS. Two questions are addressed, followed by extended descriptions of two PDSs:

- What is the relationship between effective PDSs and the Agenda for Education in a Democracy, and how do these schools fulfill their responsibility to the public purposes of education?

- In what ways are effective PDSs renewing schools; that is, how are they making a difference for children and developing students who know how to use their minds well?

Effective PDSs, the Agenda for Education in a Democracy, and the Public Purposes of Education

We first need to be clear about the central purpose for schools in a democratic society and how well we believe our schools are doing in satisfying that central purpose. Schools are intended to serve society by *teaching young people their moral and intellectual responsibilities for living and working in a social and political democracy.* In accomplishing this mission they must fulfill responsibilities for development of children as individuals and as members of a community.[1] Unfortunately, schools are not uniformly successful in this mission. As schools and teacher education programs presently exist, too often they are not oriented toward producing graduates prepared to live or teach in a political democracy. Several conditions in the schools demonstrate this.

First, as noted in Chapter One, undergraduate education generally does not provide prospective teachers with substantial inquiry into what it means to be a citizen in our country. The general education provided to all undergraduates is unlikely to give them sufficient understanding of our nation's history or our political and social systems.

Second, academia tends to be elitist. The function of our universities increasingly is to separate out the cream—to sort rather than to educate. Although the United States is a world leader in the number of students entering college, many of those who enter it leave well short of graduation, having been judged of lower quality. Periodically, universities assert their responsibility for serving only the able as they eliminate remedial course work. For example, in 1998 the City University of New York (CUNY) system took this approach to emphasize its high academic standards and protect its role within the sorting mechanism.[2]

Third, we have created an environment in which teachers (whether in universities or in P–12 institutions) are accustomed to being in authority, to not being questioned. In that regard, the late Erma Bombeck wrote in 1998:

People still seem to believe teachers. A teacher travels under the Cronkite aura. His or her words are copied down on notepads, memorized, recited, paraphrased, regurgitated, quoted, recycled, and returned intact and on time.

A teacher is omnipotent, all-seeing, all-wise, and never questioned. Knowing this, a wise teacher in Toledo, Ohio, tried to warn his students against a blanket acceptance of facts. To get their attention, he made up a story about how this country was converting to the metric system. He spun horror stories of how his students would have to send their watches and calendars to the state capital to be converted. To compensate for the time differences, clock faces would be changed so that an hour would be 100 minutes long.

His students didn't blink. They continued to take notes in silence.

He told them that summer vacations under the new system would be 20 days, and those born in July and August would have their birthdays canceled. Not one hand went up. Not one question was raised. There was no discussion. There were no raised eyebrows. There was obviously some talk in their homes, as a couple of parents called to ask when metric time would take effect.[3]

Humorous as Bombeck's story may be, it only slightly masks the truth that students are seldom encouraged to question a teacher's authority in the classroom.

Fourth, consistent with the notion of the teacher as academic authority, schools are preoccupied with controlling their students' lives. We see that preoccupation from the beginning, as preservice teachers demand to know how to manage classrooms. We see it in the walkie-talkies used by principals as they and their security guards patrol the halls of the high schools. Seymour Sarason describes the situation graphically in his book *The Predictable Failure of Educational*

Reform as he talks about the power relationships within the school and how they affect student learning.[4] When educators in these schools justify their authoritative roles by claiming they are trying to create a safe environment or one that is conducive to learning for all students, they trample essential freedoms rather than teach students how to live and learn together in a healthy community.

Fifth, in this culture where authority over ideas is seldom questioned and control is rationalized as a necessary means to ensure student safety, people are inclined to do what they are told. Principals do what the superintendent tells them, teachers do what the principal tells them, students do what they are told or they are pushed out of school—particularly if they happen to be people of color. Doing what you are told is a good qualification for being a member of a military unit or a subject of an authoritarian state; it is not necessarily the best qualification for being a citizen in a democracy.

Sixth, the way we introduce democratic practices to students tends to convey the notion that such practices are inauthentic. We teach bad attitudes toward democracy by the experiences we provide students. For example, student elections in elementary schools teach children that getting elected is a matter of putting up signs, being popular, and perhaps even finding some way to buy a vote. Having established this notion in the very young, we then provide high school students with self-governance experiences that generally allow them to make decisions of no significance. We also censor student speeches and publications, thus letting them know that the First Amendment has no meaning for them, and exclude controversial issues from their consideration in a way that is calculated to leave them ill prepared to deal with different points of view when they complete their schooling.

Seventh, and perhaps most importantly, schools are often settings in which students are not treated as equals. Instead, schools are primarily places that are, in Joel Spring's words, "sorting machines."[5] The best students are singled out for recognition and rewards; the rest are eliminated from pursuit of advanced studies and challenging opportunities.

It is imperative that PDSs be more proficient in enculturating the young to live in a democratic society than are present schools, which employ such practices. PDSs develop means of ensuring that their school and university educators work together to construct common understandings about the PDS's mission in a political democracy. This is a fundamental consideration of the partnerships described in the preceding chapters. Whatever other steps we take, discussions aimed at such an understanding must occur. The PDSs that grow out of this kind of deliberation provide clinical experiences that are a fully integrated part of a center of pedagogy that is created specifically to ensure that clinical and academic faculty have decision-making authority about the education of educators. They model democratic decision making as they take seriously their responsibility to enculturate the young as members of a democratic society.

Instead of perpetuating the antidemocratic learning experiences too often characteristic of our educational system, PDSs become places where civic life is learned. In other words, they offer an answer to Mary Ann Glendon's challenging questions: "Where do citizens acquire the capacity to care about the common good? Where do people learn to view others with respect and concern, rather than to regard them as objects, means, or obstacles? Where does a boy or girl develop the healthy independence of mind and self-confidence that enable men and women to participate effectively in government and to exercise responsible leadership?"[6]

To achieve these ends, professional development schools emphasize critical thinking. Preservice teachers and P–12 students are introduced to formal systems of logic and problem solving and are challenged by opportunities to apply their skills. Such opportunities often come during community service, when problem-solving abilities develop along with attitudes toward others that are consistent with the aims of a democratic society. Instead of engaging students inauthentically in student government, students fill legitimate decision-making roles within the school community.

An answer to the second question of this chapter allows for elaboration on the characteristics of PDSs that are making positive contributions to the Agenda for Education in a Democracy.

In What Ways Are PDSs Renewing Schools?

Successful PDSs are often active participants in important agenda-driven renewal efforts, such as Carl Glickman's League of Professional Schools, Hank Levin's Accelerated Schools, or Ted Sizer's Coalition of Essential Schools (CES).[7] In many ways, the agendas for these reform efforts, such as the Common Principles of the CES,[8] serve as a good answer to the question of what a renewing PDS should look like. This is true particularly if one avoids the oversimplifications of the aphorisms that sometimes substitute for the full statement of the CES principles. The following reflections are offered as additions to such principles, not as replacements for them.

In an effective PDS, preservice and continuing teachers learn with one another, connected to the daily life of schools and communities. Moreover, in the best of these schools the other connections necessary to creating essential schools for students are also evident.

A recently completed longitudinal study of five high schools (three of them identified as PDSs) with reputations as leaders in school renewal reveals that there are essential connections to be made if students are to benefit. Students learned best, the study showed, when the schools succeeded in connecting caring and high expectations; rigor and innovation; routines and repertoire; and small scale and civil discourse.[9]

The last pair of connections is particularly important for a PDS. There is civil discourse when mutual respect is evident among the participants and group decisions are made in the best interests of the civic good of the entire community. When educators engage in civil discourse in order to participate effectively in school renewal, they serve as stewards of their schools and show that they understand the role of schools in a democratic society. The following story told by a principal of a new high school reveals the importance of civil discourse. Her school is a PDS that opened after two years of planning, with one of its goals being to exemplify the principles of the Coalition of Essential Schools. Interviewed during the first year of the school's operation, the principal lamented that much of the extensive preliminary planning for the school was being undone by the teachers' inability to work collaboratively. She complained that the problem originated in part because teachers had worked in isolation during training and in positions they held before coming to the new school. Consequently, although they had agreed during the planning stages that teams and small learning communities were important, when they began to implement their plans they found working together to be very difficult.

My colleagues and I have observed prospective teachers in other settings during their extended clinical experiences. At one school, teams of graduate students assigned to the school as preservice teachers engaged in useful projects that simultaneously developed their skills and helped them learn about the regularities of school life. For example, one cohort of preservice teachers developed and implemented an orientation program for ninth graders. Another group interviewed teachers, administrators, and community members and then prepared a videotape about the school's approach to school-based management (a tape that the principal used when she was called on to explain governance at her school to various audiences). With careful guidance from university and school faculty, those who received their initial training at this school became much-sought-after teachers who, from the beginning of their careers, could provide leadership to the school community.

University student interns at another school participated in whole-school faculty discussions. On one occasion, an intern helped craft a compromise plan for a block schedule that won acceptance by the faculty. On another occasion, an intern served successfully as a cofacilitator during a contentious meeting. Such opportunities allowed these interns to develop their capacity for civil discourse early in their careers.

As we observed such incidents, it became increasingly clear that teachers, administrators, and other members of the school community must exhibit the ability to carry on civil discourse. Moreover, we recognized that the basic organizing unit for students must be small in order to establish the context necessary for civil discourse and other essential connections. For instance, small scale appears to be essential to permitting sufficient opportunities for discussion. In successful PDSs, the people in the school community (preservice candidates, continuing teachers, and P–12 students) arrange time so that reflective behavior required for civil discourse can take place. Having set aside the time, they process information skillfully. Along the way to building consensus, successful PDSs—those whose clothes are real—encourage the examination of all sides of an issue. They know that substituting clever shortcuts for in-depth thought will not produce lasting change. Thus, these communities are wary of processes designed to help them reach decisions quickly because they know that in using them they may avoid examining important, differing points of view. If the basic work unit is a large school, however, it is very difficult to construct a conversation that involves thoughtful participation by the parties necessary to a decision.

PDSs successfully engaging in civil discourse have skillful, risk-taking, values-driven leadership. This leadership does not rest in a single individual but rather is distributed throughout the school community. There are a substantial number of teacher, parent, and student leaders as well as administrative leaders. The school community becomes a "community of leaders," as Scott Peck calls it in *The Different Drum*.[10]

A climate of trust develops in PDSs where civil discourse is evident. This trust extends throughout the community—among teachers, students, parents, and administrators. Without it, one or the other group will inevitably derail the change effort. The starting point for earning trust is the willingness of parties to disclose information honestly. Thus, principals in successful PDSs share financial and other information. Parents are candid when speaking of their children. Teachers are honest in their appraisal of their students' progress. Students are accurate when they share information about events at the school.

Several authors have reported on the benefits of small school communities. Because of the huge investment Americans have made in large school facilities, efforts to create smaller learning communities have often focused on dividing larger schools into subunits. Both Philadelphia and Chicago have experimented heavily with this approach and have had some success. In other instances, notably in the founding of new schools in New York, local communities have determined that children are best served when facilities are created from the beginning as small schools.[11] In any event, socializing and training new teachers in large, impersonal institutions produces negative images of schools as places where control is most important and where creativity is undermined by an emphasis on safe activities that support the management of numbers of people—hardly the clothes one wants on the emperor.

Parents we talked with in South Carolina explained to us that they preferred that their children attend a small PDS rather than the large, well-equipped elementary school they had attended the previous year. They assured us that the previous school had been a good one by traditional standards but reported that in the PDS the teachers always seemed to find ways to challenge their children. The large school had become "somewhat of a bore because the children were less well known by adults." As one parent put it, "Last year my son often said he did not want to go to school. I have not heard that once this year." Such stories are common in small settings where all members of the community feel that they are "known."

Civil discourse and small scale need to be part of the way of operating, not add-on projects. PDSs that succeed find ways to eliminate old ways of doing business as they adopt new practices. In large schools, new organizational structures—such as small learning communities or subschools—create the small scale necessary to improving instructional settings. However, this approach works only when the old structures are dismantled and new ones are specifically designed to support smaller units. For example, schools cannot create subschools and simultaneously put equal emphasis on preexisting grade-level organization. Similarly, new approaches are also needed to facilitate civil discourse. New governance processes, such as school-centered decision making, lead to more authentic involvement of the school community, but they will not work as long as the traditional top-down, authoritarian governance processes remain in place.

Moreover, small scale and civil discourse are useful only when the PDS emphasizes the other three sets of connections as well. In well-tailored settings, teachers really have high expectations for students and employ a nurturing pedagogy that causes students to know that they are cared for. Some teachers in other kinds of schools place too much emphasis on the caring element of this connection. For example, if they become aware that a child is upset, they may leave the child alone or reduce requirements, thinking that that is the best way to show their empathy. Instead, what is needed is action: the teacher should help students who are experiencing difficulty to overcome their problems and succeed academically. Although such strategies are important in any school, they are even more important in a PDS where the preservice candidate learns from the modeling behavior of the classroom teacher and applies those strategies in future teaching situations. Full-service schools such as Lake Agassiz (described later in this chapter) get assistance from other agencies concerned with providing caring services to children in order to strengthen this dimension of their work. Instead of limiting their awareness of the breadth of services available for students to campus-classroom sessions, these full-service schools enable preservice candidates to work directly with social workers, drug and alcohol prevention specialists, and health care providers.

Rigor is combined with innovation so students not only engage in different activities than are found in traditional school settings but also engage in activities that challenge them. Teachers who commonly make this connection reflect continuously about the innovations they attempt. Again, this modeling of trying new techniques or investigating new subject content with students is vital for both the preservice candidates and the students in the school. In an elementary PDS, a group of experienced teachers asked for an outsider to provide them with feedback on their science instruction. When they looked at the data the observer gave them, they realized that they were failing to engage the students fully in inquiry during the science activity, tending to give students answers instead of requiring them to investigate a phenomenon more thoroughly. They discovered that their students were answering many of the questions with "yes" or "no" instead of with explanations of why they believed something was happening. Because neither condition was desirable in their new science program, the teachers made plans for changing the approaches they were taking and for watching and critiquing each other as they tried these adjustments. Preservice candidates who participated in these discussions were thus being socialized into a reflective model of teaching. They were learning at this early stage of their careers that it was good to be innovative but that considerable work was required to implement innovations in a rigorous fashion. They are less likely than teachers who are educated under different conditions to attend workshops where they are introduced to new ideas, try them once to demonstrate they are up to date with the latest fads, and then discard them.

Routines are coupled with teachers' broad repertoires to enable students to stick to tasks, build skills, and learn a range of applications for those skills. At one high school PDS, an experienced math teacher used fourteen different specific teaching techniques during a two-hour block. In an English class, a teacher engaged the students in four very different types of activities during a time period of similar length. At another PDS, an English teacher engaged the students in a heated discussion about the role of women in one of Shakespeare's plays and then, at the height of the discussion, with everyone clamoring for attention, adroitly shifted the activity as she commanded, "Stop. Now write!" The students were well aware of this routine and immediately turned to the task of fleshing out their oral arguments. The change of pace made possible by well-established routine, like the activities in the other classrooms, are exemplary instances of combining routine and repertoire.

Teachers do not develop successful repertoires accidentally. In good PDSs they are carefully cultivated. They come from teachers who model behaviors such as those just described. They also come from reflective seminars. At the University of South Carolina's Center for Inquiry, teachers, the principal, and student teachers get together for brief coaching sessions after the school day is over. At this time, teachers help student teachers find the strengths of their performance and offer ideas to improve their work. For example, a teacher might follow up praise of an aspiring teacher's reading lesson with a copy of another book he thinks would help her extend the learning begun that day, while another teacher might suggest an additional learning activity that the preservice candidate could use. And the coaching is not limited to experienced teachers helping beginners. During one such session we observed, members of the faculty also provided feedback on the activities of the day to the university professor who served as the principal for the school, and student teachers provided feedback to experienced ones. We witnessed similar processes at an elementary school PDS affiliated with BYU, where the student teacher was critiqued by a principal, teacher, and university professor, who then each took turns teaching children and being critiqued by the other three.

The best teachers in PDSs are *artisans*. In other words, they resemble sculptors, gardeners, and chefs more than electrical engineers, tax attorneys, or statisticians. In their teaching, a knack for surprise, variety, proportion, and beauty prevails over dispassionate application of technical methods. Energy, extra effort, and total commitment to link what less earnest colleagues are willing to leave unconnected characterize these successful teachers' performance. As others have observed about the best teachers, these professionals have a passion, a fervor for excellence, that enables them to help their students learn much more than students taught by less committed individuals.[12]

However, as essential as passion is, like other artisans, teachers must learn their trade and, because they trade in ideas, good teachers are initially well-educated persons who continue learning throughout their careers. Because they seek to develop students' thinking, attitudes, and skills as well as their knowledge of subject matter, these teachers possess insights into a wide range of human behaviors in various settings. In an effective PDS, preservice and continuing teachers experience learning with one another, connected to the daily life of schools and communities. In the best of these schools, preservice, continuing education, and school renewal are connected. Furthermore, the connections necessary to creating essential schools for students are also evident.

A PDS is not an island. It is inevitably part of a larger system, and that system must be healthy and supportive if it is to achieve lasting success. The system immediately surrounding the school is usually the school district. Districts involved with successful PDSs are structured so that their work supports and enables rather than controls. Such districts secure the resources that schools need, protect the school from destructive interest groups, and ensure that the norms of the broader community are clearly communicated as expectations to the school. Supportive districts serve as mediating links between schools and the broader environments of the state and the nation. They help by transmitting common values necessary to the continuation of our political democracy. Thus, they insist on common, high expectations for all students at the same time they promote the strengths of the different cultural and ethnic groups attending their schools. Supportive districts also serve as a buffer against transient policies that would distract PDSs from their missions of developing in students those habits that enable them to use their minds well. Thus, when the legislature or other policymaking or policy-influencing body seeks to implement some short-term panacea for a social problem—be it drunk driving or bad dental hygiene practices—districts acknowledge the importance of the issue and deal with it so as not to interfere with the school's primary mission.[13]

A PDS is also part of a broader professional community whose norms are monitored through processes such as accreditation. The National Council for Accreditation of Teacher Education's (NCATE) draft list of critical attributes for quality standards offers another way of looking at a "stylish" PDS. NCATE sets forth five attributes and provides indicators for them in its draft standards for PDSs. First, a PDS should be a community that supports children's and adults' learning. Second, in a PDS, school and university faculty should collaborate to implement the mission of the school. Third, the PDS should be accountable to the public and the profession for upholding professional standards and preparing teachers in accordance with those standards. Fourth, NCATE specifies that a PDS should use resources and time to support continuous improvement of its functions. Finally, a PDS should support equity and learning by all students and adults.[14]

Other than supporting the concept of equity, these standards tend to be relatively value-free. Absent are expectations regarding the purposes of education or the philosophical grounding that is appropriate for schools. At least in their present form, a PDS could demonstrate that it meets these quality indicators and still be very different in its approach to instruction from another PDS. Conceivably, it could train teachers to be highly authoritarian, prepare students who comply with a set of legislated values and, as long as resources are plentiful and the school and university faculty are cooperating, produce children and adult graduates who are highly undemocratic in their outlook on life. Nevertheless, NCATE's quality indicators provide a number of practical reminders about desirable operational conditions. They are undergoing testing that will lead to their refinement.

The following questions draw together ideas discussed in this chapter with the attributes advocated by NCATE and provide a framework for analyzing the cases that follow:

1. In what ways does the PDS enculturate children and adults in a social and political democracy?

2. In what ways does the PDS demonstrate that it is accomplishing its four purposes (to provide a clinical setting for preservice education, to engage in professional development for teachers, to promote and conduct inquiry, and to provide exemplary education for P–12 students)?

3. How is time made available to support adults functioning as an effective learning community?

4. What evidence is there that sufficient resources are available to support the ongoing work of the PDS?

5. Is the PDS organized so that the basic work unit for both teachers and students is a small learning community?

6. In what ways do adults and children in the school practice civil discourse?

7. What are examples of teachers exhibiting caring and high expectations?

8. What evidence is there that rigor and innovation combined in the instruction and curriculum of the school?

9. How are routines and a varied repertoire evident in teachers' work?

10. What evidence is there of ongoing assessment of the efficacy of the PDS?

Two Examples of "Stylish" PDSs

The following examples, one real and one constructed from examples of several different PDSs, should be considered in terms of these ten questions for signs that they include the characteristics of well-planned, "stylish" schools that have been described thus far.

University of North Dakota and Lake Agassiz Elementary School

The University of North Dakota (UND) elementary education faculty and the Lake Agassiz faculty began tailoring this professional development school in 1990. It grew out of a long history of close relationships between the two institutions, using Holmes Group principles as a guide and support from the Knight Foundation's Excellence in Education program. Located on the edge of the UND campus, Lake Agassiz shares the progressive tradition of the teacher education program at the university and has a history of interaction with educators such as Patricia Carini from the North Dakota Study Group on Evaluation.

The university introduces its summary of the design for the elementary teacher education curriculum as follows: "Programs for the preparation of teachers at UND reflect the tradition of progressive education. The progressive vision includes individualized, developmentally appropriate, and constructivist curriculum; student-centered teaming; interdisciplinary approaches to solving real problems; use of primary resources and direct experiences of learners; commitment to community involvement and to the school as a model of democracy; valuing of diversity; and commitment to humane and holistic understandings of learning, teaching, and evaluation."[15]

This statement, developed in part through conversations with students in the preservice preparation program, continues by specifying nine goals for the students, their learning environment, curriculum, instruction, assessment, and the underlying democratic values that guide the program.

Over a three-year period and through a series of summer work-shops followed by engagement of all the educators at the school, faculty from UND and Lake Agassiz developed a complementary set of goals for the elementary school. The educators agreed on cur-ricular outcomes related to "habits of mind," "cognitive outcomes," "social outcomes," and "citizenship goals." For example, under the category of citizenship goals, they agreed that their students should be "able to act for the common welfare" and "responsible for [their] own destiny." Goals for cognitive outcomes included helping each student to be "able to think critically and evaluatively" and a "com-petent reader, writer, speaker, and listener."[16]

What is important here is that the two institutions took time to think themselves clear on the purposes of education and the philo-sophical grounding for their work. From this foundation, they tai-lored their PDS to include a collaborative leadership structure. The school principal chairs the oversight body for the PDS, which is known as the Lake Agassiz Professional Development Steering Committee. Naturally, the committee includes both school and uni-versity faculty. Also, a Lake Agassiz faculty member is a voting member of the elementary teacher education faculty at UND. Var-ious task forces and councils, some chaired by university faculty and some by teachers from the school, carry out specific tasks for the steering committee.

The leaders of the school were careful to ensure that it served each of the primary purposes of a professional development school. This concern shows clearly in the following programmatic descrip-tion, which was prepared by Mary McDonnell Harris, JoNell Bakke, and Sandy Johnson, three educators who helped to create and oper-ate the PDS at Lake Agassiz.

Support to Preservice Teachers
At the undergraduate level, UND's commitment is to develop teachers who are learners, who take an active

role in the learning of students, and who envision alternative approaches to the dilemmas posed by practice. Lake Agassiz supports the preservice program by accepting an average of twelve sixteen-week students per year, an average of twenty students per year in semester-long field experiences, and as many as eighteen students per semester in several brief experiences that accompany the introductory course. The goal of the PDS in work with preservice teachers is to design program features that support deeper learning about teaching and have potential for replication in other schools. Initiatives at Lake Agassiz undertaken to support the preservice program include teacher-led seminars for preservice teachers, welcoming and farewell orientations and receptions, a placement matching program, school location of university classes and visits from classes to the school, and a handbook for field experience students.

Resident Teacher Program

In 1992, Lake Agassiz and UND started a resident teacher program at the PDS. It enables three certified teachers who have never taught under contract to practice full-time in elementary classrooms while earning master's degrees in elementary education. The resident teachers qualify for admission to the UND Graduate School and its M.Ed. program and are selected jointly by school and university personnel. The school district pays the salaries of the residents through a subcontract with the university. UND employs them as twelve-month Graduate Service Assistants, a title that carries with it health benefits and a waiver of tuition. Resident teachers are offered substantial support by a full-time resident supervisor. As of 1998, nineteen resident teachers had completed the program and many were employed by the Grand Forks schools.

Curriculum and Assessment

In 1993, the partnership began an exploration of the development of interdisciplinary curriculum and authentic assessment in both the elementary school program and the elementary teacher education program with the support of the Knight Foundation's Excellence in Education program. Over several years, Lake Agassiz and university faculty have developed and participated in weekly seminars and study groups, visits to other schools, and annual summer workshops that explored approaches to curriculum integration and uses of portfolios in assessment of learning. Faculty members explored these same themes with preservice teachers enrolled in TEAM (Teacher Education through Applied Methods). Combining this project with explorations of extended day and scheduling alternatives, Lake Agassiz found ways to provide time for classroom teachers and content specialists to plan together. Summer workshops provided opportunities to establish and review program-wide goals, which are being linked to assessment practices that draw both on student portfolios and on group demonstrations of learning. Changes in assessment practices have enhanced the constructive involvement of parents in the work of children and of experienced teachers in the work of preservice teachers.

Full-Service School

In 1995, the partnership began to develop Lake Agassiz as a full-service school. This project was partially motivated by the addition of the Department of Social Work and Counseling to the College of Education and Human Development. A full-time social worker, a part-time nurse, and a counseling intern to supplement the work of the part-time school counselor were added in 1998. The partnership has also created a large council of local health and human service agencies that share its interest in providing more holistic services to children and their families. Across the street from the school, UND has built a child-care and student family community center. The school district located its parent resource center, alternative high school, and adult learning center across another street. In 1995, a new wing was added to Lake Agassiz to house the district's Head Start programs. All of these events have enabled the creation of facilities that bring together intergenerational and interprofessional resources for the families and children of the nearby community.[17]

The richness of the educational program at this PDS can be seen in several initiatives. Foundation support made it possible for the Lake Agassiz music teacher to work with the sixth-grade teachers on a project devised by the Metropolitan Opera that involves students' writing and performing an original opera. The project also enabled the music specialists to plan with classroom teachers at each grade level as they converted traditional performances into demonstrations of learning showcasing interdisciplinary outcomes. This activity has been joined by monthly "family learning nights," special reading programs, a schoolwide multicultural program, authors' and illustrators' interacting with students and faculty to enhance the writing program, and invitations to community groups such as the chamber of commerce to early morning breakfasts where they can learn about the accomplishments of the students.[18]

Much of the work at Lake Agassiz has been built around strengthening assessment of student progress. To make progress in this area, outside experts such as Grant Wiggins have provided assistance in addition to the expertise provided locally by UND and the Grand Forks school district. Portfolios play an important part in assessment for both elementary and preservice students at the school.

Agnes Hamerlik, a veteran Lake Agassiz teacher, summarizes her feelings about the PDS with an enthusiasm for the project that is shared by many: "Personally, it has been a realization of how staff development, resource utilization and allocation, positive leadership, collaboration and cooperation, heightened expectations, and all other expanded educational opportunities can contribute to the educational and personal growth of a teacher."[19]

Brook State University and Fairbrook High School

Unlike other PDSs described in this book—which are real even though some have been given pseudonyms—the story of Brook State University and Fairbrook High School is a hybrid of components found in various PDSs around the nation.[20] Quotations included are from such real PDSs. Examine the description that follows to see the extent to which the partnership reflects the preceding discussion of the characteristics of a stylish PDS.

Fairbrook serves twelve hundred students in grades nine through twelve. Located in an urbanizing area near a large city, Fairbrook serves a socioeconomically and racially diverse community. It has recently become a PDS for Brook State University, a regional member of the state university system with a newly revised teacher education program. Fairbrook funding comes from the state, student tuition, and several regional private foundations that have been helping with start-up costs as it has been developing as a PDS.

Five-Year Preservice Program

The new program at Brook State graduates about a hundred students a year and requires that they complete thirty-six credit hours of work. Students participate as members of cohorts over a two-year period (generally their fourth and fifth years at Brook State). To ensure diversity within each cohort, the university and school district have established a recruiting and scholarship program that identifies middle school students who are interested in teaching and provides a series of support activities for them until they officially enter the teacher education program as seniors at the university. Throughout high school and their first three years of college, these prospective teachers meet with a cadre of retired teachers who acquaint them with the profession and help them think about their academic experiences from the perspective of a teacher.

The academic and clinical faculty responsible for its implementation plans the details of the preservice, professional program. Extended contracts for school- and university-based faculty make such collaborative planning feasible. For two weeks each summer and for added days during the academic year, responsible university faculty inquire together with clinical faculty from the schools.

During the first year of preservice professional studies, students earn three credits for field experiences that are associated with other seminars. The credits are awarded upon successful completion of one hundred hours of work in PDSs such as Fairbrook. Such work generally takes place over two semesters, and it may include time spent in schools when the university is not in session. During this experience, students are supervised by a team that includes a tenure-track university professor and field-service clinical faculty who have full-time public school teaching assignments augmented by twenty-day-per-year extended contracts.

Also during the first year, students take part in foundation seminars focusing on issues of enculturating the young in a social and political democracy, access to knowledge, and stewardship of schools.[21] During these seminars, students begin to develop an understanding of the role of schools and teachers in a democratic society. They are introduced to the notion of the teacher as a steward of a school. Specific efforts are made to strengthen their commitment to access to knowledge for all students and to other moral imperatives for members of the teaching profession. Understanding how to assist students from diverse cultures is emphasized here, as it is throughout the program. Students are required to examine a wide range of texts and to use experiences from their ongoing work in this PDS and observations in other schools as a basis for the dialogue that is a feature of the seminars. On the team that facilitates these seminars there are tenure-track professors from the arts and sciences and the Brook State College of Education.

During the first year of professional studies, students also complete pedagogy seminars. Students begin by developing an understanding of learning theory and developmental psychology and proceed to become acquainted with a wide range of instructional strategies that facilitate student learning in developmentally appropriate ways. Concepts of pedagogical content knowledge are introduced. Teams of professors and field-service clinical teachers whose classrooms serve as the laboratory facilitate the seminars. Students work in teams as they become acquainted with a variety of teaching techniques and how to match techniques to student learning needs and the requirements of the content being learned. During this first year, students participate in the equivalent of two three-hour seminars. In addition to laboratory experiences, they engage in a variety of simulations and microteaching exercises. Most of these seminars take place at Fairbrook.

The second year of professional studies focuses on clinical experiences. During their internships, preservice students work full time at Fairbrook for two semesters and earn nine credits per semester. They are assigned as junior members of a hierarchical teaching team. They begin their work with the opening of the PDS's academic year and end it with its closing. Their work as team members includes guided practical experiences at applying different pedagogical strategies, including assessing student knowledge. A tenure-track professor and a practicum clinical faculty member head the team that mentors the preservice students. Each clinical faculty member is released 20 percent time from her or his regular teaching duties and has a twenty-day extended contract. The clinical faculty member is responsible for the final evaluation (grade) of the intern but, because the faculty member is playing a lead role in an instructional team, other school and university members of the team contribute to the assessment of the intern's performance. The interns are considered part of the professional staff of the school.

Students participate in a three-credit seminar each semester. During these seminars, they reflect on their intern experiences to help them build their knowledge of educational foundations and of pedagogy. A tenure-track professor facilitates the seminars. The students' own words provide evidence of the intensity of their experiences:

"Did Dr. Hansen come in your class today? He was in mine along with Dr. Wentworth and Mr. Jensen. That's real pressure."

"No, I didn't see him today. I met with three other student teachers who are having problems with kids sluffing. It was good to talk it over. They had some good ideas I can try. One of the regular math teachers met with us for about thirty minutes to give us some background on all of the things that have been tried in this school. At least I feel better knowing this isn't a problem just in my class."

"The supervisor visit wasn't bad; it just made me nervous. But I think it will help because we talked about some things I can do to make the cooperative learning groups work better. They all had ideas that might help, so I picked the one I liked best and we planned a lesson for tomorrow. Mr. Gillespie is going to help me teach it."

"Let me know how it works. The last time I did groups, I wasn't too happy with them. But my cooperating teacher was thrilled! She said she didn't have much experience with grouping, so we were kind of learning together. It's comforting to know teachers continue to learn."[22]

A mathematics faculty member from Brook who has been working with Fairbrook observed recently: "The difference between the preparation of math teachers before the partnership and after is phenomenal. Previously, I worked with students in a Brook classroom studying the theory of teaching, simulating class experiences, and requiring students to practice on each other. Now Brook students participate in seminars jointly led by me and Fairbrook's staff, learn about the theory, see it implemented by model teachers, and practice it themselves under the mentoring of caring master teachers."[23]

Professional Development

In addition to being a clinical setting for preservice teachers, Fairbrook serves as a professional development setting for the Fair School District.

The work at Fairbrook assumes that school renewal best occurs one school at a time—that the school is the center of change. Therefore, Fairbrook's responsibility is to assist other schools in their renewal efforts, not to provide directly for the training of all employees. As a PDS, it provides assistance in three ways:

- Conducting workshops and follow-up support services to assist practicing teachers to expand their teaching repertoires

- Creating and sharing model structures, decision-making processes, curriculum, teaching, and assessment practices, which are also made available for observation by faculty from other schools

- Offering opportunities for individuals to inquire into issues of pedagogical content knowledge related to various disciplines

For PDSs to provide for professional development, they need to have academic and clinical faculty members available who are committed to and capable of providing the necessary services—and who have the time to do so.

The specific emphasis (and the number of people required) at Fairbrook varies from time to time. Programs are defined collaboratively by the partners, which for this purpose include Fairbrook and the other district schools to be served.

During a typical year, workshops are the most common component of a professional development program. Fairbrook and the schools it serves jointly determine the specific topics for the workshops. Each semester, four are related to teaching and instruction. These workshops serve teams of as many as sixty participants from between four and twenty other schools. Each workshop meets twelve times for two-hour sessions. In addition, each workshop participant is visited by clinical faculty six times for approximately one hour each visit as a follow-up to workshop sessions.

Although workshops make important contributions to professional growth, preservice and regular faculty also engage in other activities that help them develop. A new teacher at Fairbrook who recently completed his training at that school remembers his interactions with a teaching team:

> One method the team utilized for professional growth was team journal sharing. Every Monday a topic would be generated and on Friday we read our individual responses. Some journal entries would evoke laughter, some silent understanding, and some would create tears. Now that I am a regular teacher, I can look back on my student teaching days and see the benefit of this journal activity to the students, to teachers, and to myself. For example, I recall an entry I made after I talked with Heather, another intern, about a student I thought was not being given a fair shake. In that entry I wrote: "I shared my thoughts during a team meeting when we were discussing how students can be mirrors (to either ourselves in the past or now). As a team, we realized that everyone will connect with different students. I realized a valuable asset of the team is that through individual

teachers, individual students will be better understood and no one will be lost in the cracks."[24]

Inquiry

Fairbrook serves five practicing professional educators each year as the primary setting for the advancement of pedagogical content inquiry. These scholars are released from one-third of their normal assignments to pursue their study. The district, university, and individual scholars collaboratively plan the inquiry.

More attention to inquiry is built into the development of pedagogy that emphasizes reflection by both high school and preservice students. Preservice students learn to use action research to help them analyze their own work. During their final year, each one is required to complete a significant inquiry project. In recent years, such projects have included a study of the language needs of Puerto Rican students in the school, an examination of computer-aided instruction in math skills labs, and an examination of the roles of aides working with students who have emotional disturbances. The high school students develop skills as inquirers in science and social science classes, often tying their community service work in with the development of these skills.

A Fairbrook teacher commenting on the value of the PDS, and particularly on its emphasis on research and inquiry, said: "I think it [the partnership] is a positive one. I know there are other people that don't think that [it] was—usually those that are in the retirement club and they have old ways of thinking. . . . That's the greatest thing about the partnership—it keeps us on our toes. . . . And I'm hoping that some of the teachers here also get this bug about researching and getting into that, or at least being reflective about what they do."[25]

School Renewal

Although the professional development activities have a school-wide focus and inquiry projects include discussion of data concerning student learning, school renewal focuses on the school's performance, decisions concerning next steps, action on those planning decisions, and evaluation of progress. To help accomplish this, all members of the Fairbrook faculty have five days of extended contracts beyond those provided other teachers in the district and beyond the extended time provided clinical faculty. In addition, one university faculty member is paid for an extra five days to work with Fairbrook on such renewal planning and evaluation.

Last year, Fairbrook concentrated its renewal activities on examining access to knowledge within the school. Preservice students, high school students, parents, and university faculty joined the high school faculty in an examination of the literature concerning tracking. They studied practices at Fairbrook in light of this literature and discovered that there were many students who could be offered much more challenging course work than was the case. For the current year, Fairbrook has strengthened its course requirements for all students and provided help to teachers in dealing with the more diverse student population that they will have in their classes.

During the past eight years, the school has become a more caring place as graduate students at Brook have coordinated the work of nearly a hundred undergraduate tutors. A national insurance company headquartered nearby has provided financial help to acquire materials and offset travel costs to the high school by the tutors. Several local fast food restaurants provide snacks and coupons that the tutors use as rewards for high school students who follow through on assigned work. Some of the college undergraduates have shifted their career plans to teaching as a result of their engagement with the Fairbrook students. During the past year, additional tutors have joined the effort. Included now are employees from the insurance company, personnel from the local army base, and a group of retired citizens. The graduate students from Brook have created and pilot-tested a training manual to help ensure quality in these tutorial experiences.

In 1990, teachers from Fairbrook decided that they wanted all classes to be taught by teams. They started with teams for ninth-

and tenth-grade students that made strong use of university student tutors. By 1994, all teachers were teaching in teams, and the faculty decision-making council decided that the larger school should be subdivided into four houses, with each house having teams that worked at grades nine, ten, eleven, and twelve. The houses provide educational experiences that enable all graduating students to meet common entrance requirements for higher education. As much as possible, students select their own houses. One element considered in making the selection is that, in addition to the general education requirements, each house has a different career focus. Because of the long-term presence of the university students, the house focusing on teaching as a career has been popular. Many of the preservice students are assigned to this house.

In another renewal effort, a Fairbrook High School math teacher joined with a Brook faculty member from the Department of Curriculum and Instruction and a faculty member from the university's mathematics department to renew instructional practices in the high school's math department. The education faculty member and the high school teacher cotaught a class for two years. During this time, the math professor helped them as they sought to use a constructivist approach engaging high school students in projects and, by introducing applications from technology, linking the math instruction with science. The teaching team produced a journal article as one outgrowth of this work. Further exploration of the possibilities of subject matter integration also emerged from this initiative.

Neither of the PDSs described here fully satisfies all the indicators of "high style" suggested in this chapter. However, both have many good qualities. Certainly, if we consider the ten questions listed before the descriptions of these PDSs as well as the suggestions from previous chapters, we understand that in many ways these two PDSs are well tailored. In these instances, the emperor's clothes are real—

the children and the rest of us would be quick to praise them. Ask these questions about PDSs you know. Having done so, you will gain a much clearer idea of how well tailored those PDSs are.

The discussion to this point has suggested that the resources available to support a PDS contribute significantly to its success. The next chapter examines questions of costs and financing in greater detail.

6

Keeping the Britches Up

PDS Costs and Financing

E ven if the emperor had worn a real set of fancy new clothes, the child's reaction probably would have been similar (and the adults would have tried to look the other way) if, as he paraded before his subjects, his new trousers had fallen down for lack of support. Similarly, good intentions and plans in the establishment of professional development schools may also fail if there is insufficient support.

This chapter suggests that, just as trousers need a belt or suspenders, a PDS needs adequate financing if it is to be effective.[1] While exploring this issue, we will expand on the previous discussions of the characteristics of such schools and offer two more extended case examples.

This chapter addresses three primary questions:

- What are the national trends related to reform and funding?

- How much do professional development schools cost?

- In what ways can PDSs be financed?

Trends in Funding and Reform

Some perspective on the overall state of reform and funding of education provides helpful context for the subject of PDS costs and financing. Education in the United States—for young children through graduate school students—is directed by a complex web of policymakers and funded through an equally complex set of national, state, local, and private funders. When decisions need to be made about which approaches to reform should be attempted or how those approaches will be funded, different parties advocate different solutions.[2] It comes as no surprise, therefore, that it is impossible to say with certainty which recent reform strategies have had real impact on schools; nor is it possible to describe precisely how the various reform efforts have been funded. Still, policymakers who determine funding levels and priorities rightfully seek guidance on the costs of various reforms and the sources of funding for them. This chapter, mindful of policymakers' needs and aware of the complexity of the questions, provides some useful ways of thinking about these matters related to funding PDSs.

Although it would seem logical that budgets should be instrumental to the implementation of reforms, individuals concerned with financial reforms occasionally seem to listen to their own drummer rather than consider the policy aims of the programs that need funding. That is, financial experts become concerned with perfecting technical aspects of funding as if funding were an end unto itself rather than a means to another end. It is also true that universities have been guilty of addressing various aspects of school reform in a manner that is not viewed as helpful by educators in public schools.[3]

Such problems notwithstanding, reforms for P–12 schools and institutions of higher education seem to parallel reforms in educational finance in three ways. Since 1983, when the frequently referenced A Nation at Risk[4] was issued, efforts have been made to add more (resources, personnel, time, or whatever seems to help), to address issues of equity, and either to centralize or to decentralize decision making.

Adding More

Less than three years after the release of the landmark national report *A Nation at Risk,* and in the midst of an avalanche of reports that followed close on its heels, Allan Odden noted: "All the states have expanded their school improvement programs, nearly all have increased high school graduation requirements, most have stiffened college admission requirements, many are deepening the content of course offerings, and many are enacting a variety of polices to strengthen the teaching profession."[5]

Subsequent to this first wave of reform, educational initiatives put new emphasis on staff development, teaching methods, and teacher empowerment, and there were calls for higher levels of student performance to catch up with other nations. During the decade following the report, special services were added to address problems of violence in schools, respond to a growing crisis of drug abuse, and react to health problems such as AIDS. Younger children were included, and as a result the common reference to schools as "K–12" began to give way to "P–12," in recognition of the growing prevalence of preschools.

As the 1990s progressed, reform efforts shifted to focus on creating standards and developing high-stakes tests to measure progress toward those standards. Thus far there has been little recognition of the magnitude of the effort that would be required to meet the wide-ranging standards that have emerged from various national and state groups. However, if students were really to meet all of these standards, children would have to spend much more time in school, and other additions to the schooling enterprise would certainly have to be made. Indeed, by 1998 "adding more" had gained favor again as states such as California moved to reduce class size and Congress approved President Clinton's initiative to add a hundred thousand teachers nationwide as means to achieve higher educational standards.

A new emphasis on privatization and alternatives to traditional public education that do not have to meet the standards being created for existing schools has paralleled and seemingly conflicted with the development of standards. But even in this effort one can recognize the principle of adding more. There is little doubt that one consequence of the privatization drive will be to provide public funding for students now enrolled in private schools, creating an added financial burden for the public.

Meanwhile, there have also been additions in teacher education. Various members of the Holmes Group began experimenting with five-year and graduate-level initial certification programs. Commonly, students were expected to complete a major in a traditional academic discipline rather than in education. Some states, including Washington, passed legislation requiring master's degrees for initial certification. Other states, among them Minnesota, began to add to their teacher preparation requirements a yearlong residency after initial certification. Many of the institutions that persisted in claiming that their preparation programs were undergraduate programs developed such extensive requirements that students frequently could not complete the work in four years.[6]

Still, with the exception of the new standards and assessment initiatives and the experimentation with privatization, within ten years of the release of A Nation at Risk there was dissatisfaction with such add-on solutions as increasing requirements for P–12 students. Perhaps people had begun to recognize that doing more of the same wrong thing was unproductive. Darling-Hammond and McLaughlin make this case well for both public school and university-based teacher development.[7] As the second and third waves of reform moved forward, educators focused more on school renewal and staff development as necessary means of improving students' performance. As they did so, they began to recognize that these efforts needed to be closely linked.

For many of the same reasons that "adding more" began to lose favor in P–12 schooling, it began to be rejected as a solution in reforming teacher education. In Washington State, before the requirement for a master's degree was fully implemented, new legislation was passed repealing it.[8] Behind the rejection of the adding-on solution at both P–12 and higher education levels were concerns about the high costs of trying to make reforms in this manner.[9] The possibility of renewing the schools and improving education for educators more efficiently became one of the primary drivers of interest in PDSs.

"Adding more" also has a long history as a strategy of reform for educational finance. There were substantial increases in P–12 funding beyond those needed to meet inflation or educate additional pupils during the decade of the 1980s. Odden reports that "real dollars per pupil for the schools rose by 48 percent" for that period. He also notes that the increase for the ten-year period ending in 1993–94 still reflects a 47 percent increase.[10] During this same time, private and business foundations began to invest in public school and teacher education reform efforts. Foundations such as Annenberg, The Pew Charitable Trusts, the DeWitt-Wallace Reader's Digest Fund, Casey, MacArthur, Carnegie, Exxon, and Rockefeller have invested in a variety of P–12 and higher education reform efforts, making added funds available. In some instances, these organizations also began to influence reform policy in ways beyond simply giving money.[11]

Funding for higher education has also increased greatly. USA Today described this trend in a feature story in 1997, observing that "there's an economic principle well-known in higher education budget offices: universities raise all the money they can and spend all the money they raise" and that "the appetite for revenue in higher education is limitless."[12]

As of this writing, it appears that adding more funds is not likely to be a long-term solution for either P–12 or higher education. The 1994 elections promised reductions in spending at both the state and federal levels.[13] Odden noted that state shares of school budgets had begun to decline as of 1992 and that a revolt was brewing against raising local taxes.[14] In fact, several states have placed strict controls on the right of local communities to generate tax revenue. What new revenues were created at the state level seemed to be going to close gaps between income and expenditures, build prisons, offset

federal reductions in areas such as health care, or reduce the tax burden on individuals in the state. With the exception of some efforts
to reduce class size, during the flush economic times of the late
1990s, which saw budget surpluses in most states, states tended to
make small reductions in taxes or set aside money in a "rainy-day"
fund rather than make substantial, fundamental changes to support
for education.[15] In addition to taxpayer resistance, colleges increasingly faced objections to tuition increases. USA Today quoted a dean
of admissions as saying, "Colleges are recognizing that they're push-
ing the very edge of the envelope. . . . We've absolutely reached the
end of the family's ability—and perhaps even more importantly, a
family's willingness—to pay what we cost."[16]

However, tuition costs continue to increase. Education Week
reported in March 1998 that "College costs are a major public concern. . . . Tuition at public and private universities is rising at about
6 percent each year, or at about twice the rate of inflation. . . . At the
same time, student-loan debt has exploded, with more students—53
percent of all college graduates in 1997—owing more money—a total
debt burden of $36 billion in federally guaranteed student loans last
year—than ever."[17] In response to such increases, parents and college
students push legislators and other policymakers to reduce the costs
of higher education.

As publicly funded higher education ran into the same taxpayer
resistance that P–12 schools faced, private schools also found that
their clients rejected continuing increases in tuition and fees.

In short, it appears that any approach to reform of P–12 or
teacher education that is to be attempted in the near future should
not count on adding more as a solution to either program reform
needs or funding. Instead, the focus will need to be on finding ways
to reallocate existing resources so they can bring a better return.

Seeking Equity

The second area in which funding and reform parallel each other is
equity. In the name of equity, courts and legislatures have mandated

substantial reforms of school district structures and, occasionally, of specific practices within school districts and schools. Equity concerns have been fundamental in court decisions and legislation concerning special attention for P–12 students for whom English is not the primary language, for those with special learning needs, and for those who are discriminated against because of race, religion, or gender. Such actions have affected higher education as well, with colleges and universities experiencing the need to expand significantly the enrollment of students from underrepresented ethnic groups.

Equity issues have long dominated reform efforts in educational finance. Most recently the courts have become major players in this field. Between 1971 and 1998, state supreme courts issued more than thirty rulings on the constitutionality of state school finance systems; in sixteen instances, courts found the inequities to be great enough to overturn extant funding laws.[18] The most extensive of such suits led to total overhauls of educational systems in Kentucky and other states.[19] But in some states, courts have continued to disclaim their responsibility. In Pennsylvania, for example, the judiciary stated that it was the legislature's duty to define and fund the thorough and efficient schools called for in its state constitution.

Equity issues have not been resolved. Real differences persist, particularly in schools located in areas—both rural and urban—with low socioeconomic rankings. However, in keeping with the generally conservative political trend of the early 1990s, legislatures, courts, and the public (through referenda) have been narrowing the gap, not by advancing the causes of underrepresented parties but by lowering the expectations for equity that earlier laws and rulings had established. In California and Washington, for example, affirmative action programs have been voided, and in California bilingual education has been outlawed at the ballot box. Also, in many urban areas, longstanding court orders for busing have given way. Thus, at the same time funding efforts fail to provide adequate financial support for all public schools, the likelihood of substantial programmatic or financial support to obtain equity has declined.[20]

Centralizing-Decentralizing

In a reform mode that is curiously typical of education in the United States, both centralizing and decentralizing reforms have advanced since the publication of *A Nation at Risk*.

Early in reform efforts, state initiatives often mandated reductions in class size and specified changes in educational requirements. Governors and the president led the way as state and national goals were adopted and professional groups worked to develop "world-class" standards in various disciplines. Increasingly, as the reform wave moved forward, dissatisfaction with the bureaucracies at the state and local level led to attempts to bypass these agencies in favor of site-based management and market-driven privatizing initiatives such as vouchers and charter schools.

While such changes were occurring in P–12 schools, renewed emphasis on national accreditation, expanded systems of state program approval, and newly empowered professional standards boards were centralizing influences affecting teacher education. Accompanying the development of a national standards board offering advanced certification for teachers were refined means of assessing teacher competency for initial entry into the profession and seemingly contradictory state legislation limiting the amount of professional training that could be required of prospective teachers.

While these centralizing influences were occurring, decentralizing trends could also be seen as schools and universities created partnerships that generated professional development schools. States also appeared to be giving up some of their control as they authorized alternative routes to entry into the profession. Some of these efforts, such as Teach for America, seemed to parallel the privatization trend in P–12 education. The continued active presence of entrepreneurial colleges offering shortcut teacher preparation programs demonstrated that the market can not only affect costs but also have a negative effect on quality.

The simultaneous advance of centralizing and decentralizing programmatic efforts was accompanied by similar changes in funding. Federal and state categorical funds were sometimes targeted at certain student populations, as was the case of federal Title I funding for disadvantaged students. Sometimes state funds were aimed at specific programs, such as mathematics, science, AIDS education, or technology, or for reductions in primary class size. Higher education experienced similar funding directives in Texas, for example, where the state funding for professional development schools focused heavily on the use of technology in these settings.

As such centralization of categorical funding increased, new decentralizing legislation promoted site-based management of funds. Appropriations bypassed districts and went straight to schools and classrooms and, in the case of vouchers and charters, directly to parents. Conservatives urged that the marketplace drive schooling. Block grants (decentralist in theory and centralist in practice) took existing categorical funds and distributed parts of them to schools to decide how they should be spent. This change in funding methods and priorities affected higher education as well, as was most evident in federal funding policies that empowered local schools to determine what was needed in professional development and required institutions of higher education that wanted access to these funds to plan with the local schools that received the money. Although foundation funding was available for the development of reforms in teacher education in some instances, colleges that sought public funds through initiatives such as the federal Goals 2000 program found that they had to seek partnerships with local schools and obtain approval from professionally led councils.

As these reform elements have moved forward, the education of educators has continued in its historically underfunded condition. Various authors have noted that educating a teacher education candidate costs less than the average cost of educating other college students and about two-thirds of what it costs to educate a public school student.[21] For example, David Berliner noted in 1984 that it cost 13 percent less to educate a teacher at his institution than it cost to educate a liberal arts student.[22] Bruce Peseau, Carl Backman, and

Betty Fry concluded that the failure to recognize teacher preparation programs as clinical rather than classroom programs was a significant contributor to this historical underfunding.[23]

Richard Howard, Randy Hitz, and Larry Baker compared per-student expenditures for education with those in other disciplines and professions. They concluded: "In general, education programs are funded below the institutional average for all disciplines in all Carnegie Classifications [and] . . . in general, education programs are less well funded than other professional programs, with the exception of Social Work and Accounting, at research institutions."[24]

In considering the specific issue of finances for a professional development school, it is necessary to keep in mind that in light of the general resistance to increasing public expenditures for either P–12 or higher education and the historical tendency to underfund teacher education, the simple solution of adding funds is unlikely. Nor is the battle for equity likely to be a source of assistance in obtaining short-term financial support, although it identifies real societal needs. And the ambiguous and sometimes conflicting centralist and decentralist expectations of policymakers will probably continue. Still, there is cause for both hope and despair in Ralph Tyler's 1985 observations: "We learned that the education of teachers could be greatly improved without large additional expenditures, if the staffs of local teacher education institutions and school systems *worked together* to identify serious problems on which to focus their efforts and for which to develop solutions, i.e., programs that used local resources and that could be practicably implemented. What we learned more than 40 years ago seems to me to be worth careful consideration in improving the education of teachers today" [emphasis in original].[25]

The hope that comes from learning that efforts in the first half of the twentieth century demonstrated the efficacy of school-university collaboration is diminished but not eradicated when we realize that, even though the lesson has been learned, effective programmatic and financial collaboration still are not widespread.

As we turn from this review of reform and finances, we will identify some ways of thinking about how costs can be calculated and
funding can be identified for the PDSs of the future.

Costs of Professional Development Schools

Although there are numerous studies of the costs of P–12 education
and of professional education programs, one of the reasons for the
persistent difficulties in obtaining funds for PDSs may be that information about the specific costs of such schools is insufficient. Neil
Theobald speculated that PDSs would incur additional costs and
offered some models for student and staffing arrangements that
could be used in estimating costs.[26] He ultimately produced a sample PDS funding formula that takes into account school district and
university contributions toward expenses associated with preservice
preparation programs. The formula does not address costs for other
purposes for such schools that have emerged since his study was
completed: continuing education (professional development) for
educators in the school system, for example, or research and inquiry
work. In a later article, Theobald addressed in more detail the specific problems created when colleges of education are asked to consider reallocating funds to support the developmental costs of such
schools. As he discussed the economic implications of professional
development schools, Theobald gave considerable attention to costs
introduced by governance structures, issues of faculty (school and
college) load, and enrollment in terms of credit hours.[27] Although
his formulations are complex, there may be other significant variables that must be taken into account.

Varied approaches to creating and operating professional development schools lead to different costs for different schools. The discussion of costs that follows relies heavily on descriptions of four
PDSs. Once again, pseudonyms have been used, but for the most
part, three of the programs reflect actual practices of current PDSs.
The fourth model is hypothetical and is based on recommendations

being implemented to varying degrees by PDSs or partner schools in the National Network for Educational Renewal (NNER). The first three PDSs prepare elementary teachers: Sagebrush is affiliated with an undergraduate program in a research university; Bay is connected to a fifth-year program in a regional university (described in Chapter One); and Mountain works with a five-year program in a state university. The fourth school, Fairbrook, is the fictional high school PDS—a composite of various real programs—introduced in Chapter Five. It maintains ties to Brook State University, which has a five-year teacher preparation program. Each program was examined for the approach it takes to serving the four functions of a PDS—preservice education, professional development, research and inquiry, and school renewal—and then the costs associated with each of these functions were calculated. Overall costs are summarized in Table 6.1.

Accounting for Joint Funding and In-Kind Contributions

The four budgets reveal examples of components that either are jointly funded by the university and the PDS or represent in-kind contributions. In three of the four examples, the university and the school share the costs for university faculty time for preservice activities. Joint funding of positions creates particular problems for financial analysis because the determination of each party's share of the expenses is often based on an average cost per faculty member, which in turn is often based on an estimate of the average time

Table 6.1. Total Expenditures for Four Professional Development Schools, 1994–95

PDS	Paid by School	Paid by University	Total
Bay	$ 69,200	$ 75,800	$145,000
Mountain	$ 51,500	$111,500	$163,000
Sagebrush	$ 13,300	$172,550	$185,850
Fairbrook	$265,880	$192,400	$458,280

spent in providing service. This is clearly a reasonable way to proceed when forging partnership agreements regarding cost sharing, but the agreed-upon budget amounts will not exactly mirror the real costs that are incurred at each PDS site—a problem that exists in any effort to compare costs of programs in one setting with those in another. A similar difficulty arises when attempting to account for the value of in-kind contributions—of time and other resources—that are often part of PDS relationships.

Amortizing One-Time Contributions

A common type of funding for PDSs is one-time-only financial contributions. These one-time contributions are often called *start-up funds* or *seed money*. They are provided to PDSs at the beginning of their development for such expenditures as telecommunications equipment, computers, or initial training of professional participants.

There are at least two ways to account for one-time contributions. One is to devise a special budget category that contains all initial expenses. This method has the advantage of providing useful information to policymakers and funders who are interested in beginning or expanding PDSs. However, not all PDSs have access to these special contributions and consequently they absorb start-up costs through other means, such as in-kind contributions or spreading out start-up costs over several years of budgeting. Under this method, the only fair cost comparisons that could be attempted would be those that examined PDSs sharing the same level of in-kind contributions and start-up costs.

A second way to account for one-time contributions is to amortize their long-term value in order to arrive at a yearly expenditure amount. Consider the following simplified example. If a $10,000 contribution is made to provide computer equipment for the PDS and this equipment will be useful for five years, then this equipment could be reflected as an expenditure of $2,000 per year for five years. This method most accurately reflects the real value of the contribution.

However, it requires that some estimate be made of the annual net present value of the contribution. Doing this may be relatively simple for items such as equipment, but it is more problematic for other kinds of contributions—for example, professional training activities. Analytic problems arise no matter which method is employed to account for one-time contributions, and those conducting cost comparisons of these types of contributions should be alerted to the potential inaccuracies in accounting for costs.

Moreover, as we shall note later, there is a tendency to overestimate the extent to which something is a one-time developmental cost. For example, settings usually account for initial training costs but forget that as staffs turn over and program emphases shift, many of the elements of the initial training will have to be repeated.

These analytic differences are noted as a caution to those interested in conducting cost comparisons for PDSs. Although it may not be possible to resolve these challenges, we may be able to arrive at cost information that more accurately reflects the fiscal conditions under which PDSs currently operate if we acknowledge such characteristics clearly in cost documentation.

Building a General Model for Examining Costs

For the specialist in educational finance, the analysis of costs for PDSs, as for other areas of public education, is grounded in an examination of how various resources are allocated among competing interests and demands.

Economic cost analysis begins with the determination of *marginal costs*. Marginal costs represent the minimal level of resources necessary to provide services. Another way to think of them is as the costs that would disappear if the services were discontinued. For example, the marginal costs of operating a PDS are unlikely to include many of the facility costs because the school would continue to operate—to serve P–12 students—even if the functions directly associated with the operation of the PDS were eliminated. Obviously, institutions can provide services at a level that is greater than that supported by the marginal cost. However, in order to compare appropriately the costs of a variety of PDS models with a variety of traditional models of teacher education, it is important to make a determination of the marginal costs involved in each type of program.

Opportunity costs also need to be considered. Opportunity costs are the trade-offs made when a particular approach to providing services is selected. For example, decisions about the use of professional development time, the school curriculum, the responsibilities of the school principal, technological resources, faculty research and advising activities, and opportunities for school-university collaboration and school renewal often depend on the type of teacher education model used (for example, a PDS-based or a traditional four-year or five-year program). Consequently, policymakers should be made aware of both the marginal cost differences associated with PDSs and the opportunity cost differences. If a PDS aims to provide a different type of teacher preparation while at the same time providing benefits to all educators and students located in the PDS, then the cost of this expanded service must be compared with the costs of similar services provided by a school that does not experience these PDS-related benefits.

In addition, when we think about the allocation of resources we need to keep in mind that there are resources other than fiscal ones—*nonfiscal resources* also contribute value to the PDS. Nonfiscal resources include professional expertise and experience, nonmonetary incentives, individual commitment and motivation, articulation of curricular efforts, and collegiality and communication among professionals. Whereas fiscal resources are the dollar amounts displayed in budget categories such as those noted earlier for the four sample PDSs, nonfiscal resources are harder to quantify and compare from model to model.

Financial analysis of professional development schools requires a sequence of activities, beginning with being clear about what functions are to be pursued and proceeding to a determination of the sources of obtaining the needed funds. Unfortunately, listing these activities in this fashion implies that the process is a linear one. But in practice the process often requires advancing forward several steps and then, based on new information, returning and revising earlier conclusions. For example, when sources of funding are sought, it may be that funds sufficient to satisfying earlier thinking about the program cannot be obtained, requiring a restatement of the program-related variables from earlier stages. The intricacies of these relationships can be determined by using the matrix shown in Table 6.2. Each cell depicting cost variable interaction with a particular purpose will differ, depending on the sources of funding, the stability of funding, the amount of funding, and the stage of development of the PDS.

Variables

The four examples of PDSs make it clear that many variables fall within the general categories identified in Table 6.2. The following discussion offers some preliminary thoughts about the way in which these factors may influence eventual costs.

The first consideration is the *developmental stage* of the PDS. Available data do not permit analysis based on the five developmental stages discussed in Chapter Two (that is, getting organized, early success, waiting for results, major success and expansion, and mature partnership), but it is clear that there are added costs during the earliest stages of a PDS. Many of the other variables apply differentially depending on how mature a PDS is. Early develop-

Table 6.2. Relationships Between Cost Variables and Purposes of a PDS

	Variable		
Purpose	Context	Program	Economic
Preservice			
Professional development			
Inquiry/research			
School renewal			

mental or start-up efforts require more time from college and school faculty. They require extensive communication with community members served by the school and, often, with the power structure of the college. At Northern University, described in Chapter One, several years of conversations between college of education faculty and school-based faculty were essential in creating an extraordinarily integrated field-academy effort. The costs of such preparatory efforts might not be thought of as PDS costs, but without the benefit of such developmental efforts, Northern's PDSs, including Bay Elementary, would be much lesser places.

Trial operations during the early stages usually serve fewer preservice students than do more mature operations, making the per-student costs higher. School and university faculty members are hesitant to change habitual approaches to providing clinical experiences. This may mean that for a length of time old and new programs operate simultaneously, duplicating one another to some extent. Frequently, schools and colleges have sought private foundation support for this early phase. The Ford Foundation supported one such developmental effort,[28] and each of the three real PDSs discussed in this chapter had help during this stage: special state grants and private foundation funding helped Sagebrush, whereas regional foundations were the primary source of extra funding for the other two.

Except for amortization issues discussed earlier, developmental costs are relatively easy to estimate—partially because they are almost always added on to existing expenditures and include paying for discrete items. A $25,000 outlay for technology at Sagebrush and some of the professional development and school renewal activities there and at Mountain are examples of such items. Still, there are no reliable reports of what these costs have been across large numbers of PDSs, and it is reasonable to assume that these costs, even during the early stages, vary considerably depending on other conditions surrounding the PDS. It is also important to recognize that there are many ongoing developmental costs: as problems arise, new plans need to be made.

The following paragraphs consider other variables, with the caveat that eventually more detailed information will be needed on developmental costs. Three major categories of variables need attention: *context, program*, and *economic*. All three must be considered for each of the four functions generally ascribed to professional development schools, and all three must be considered in relation to contributions to be made by the schools and by the university.

Context Variables

The variables that would fall in the second column in the general model in Table 6.2 are *context variables*. Table 6.3 contains a general listing of these variables.

The setting. A professional development school's setting will influence costs. Factors such as staff and student travel costs between the university campus and the PDS vary considerably based on the population density. The magnitude of this issue may be most obvious in a rural state such as Wyoming where the university relocates significant numbers of preservice candidates to schools hundreds of miles from the main campus, raising costs of student housing, staff travel and lodging, and student support services. At Northern, one rural PDS setting is eighty miles from the main campus. Housing is provided for the full year for the cohort of

Table 6.3. Context Variables

Setting of PDS	Type of University	Grade Level/Scale
Urban	Regional	Elementary
Small urban/	Public/private	Middle school
Edge city	Research	High school
Suburban/rural	Public/private	
Regulatory	Liberal arts	
environment	Public/private	

students (at their expense). Faculty members have to be financially supported for the commute to teach classes at the site.

Costs also vary when students in urban settings are primarily commuters and find themselves assigned to PDSs some distance from the college campus or when students who usually live on or near the campus have to seek transportation to or housing near the PDS.

Ensuring safety for faculty and students, obtaining instructional materials, and gaining access to experts who may be desired to complement faculty may also require differential expenditures depending on the setting of a PDS.

The cost of living tends to vary with population density, a variation that affects PDS costs in several ways. Salaries and benefits are frequently (although not always) higher in urban and suburban than in rural or semirural areas. Per-student costs for P–12 education vary considerably among different states. For example, in the 1991–92 academic year the range of per-student costs for the fifty states ranged from a low of $2,827 in largely rural Utah to a high of $8,793 in predominantly urban New Jersey.[29] For the same year, there was a $1,412 difference in high and low per-pupil costs for the three states represented in the examples provided in this chapter. Salary costs are the largest element of this differential, and these salary differences mean that inevitably a PDS in New Jersey will be much more costly than one in Utah. Or in terms of the examples presented in this chapter, an expenditure of $5,000 at Sagebrush will buy more services than the same amount at Bay.

The regulatory environment in which each PDS exists also affects costs. Some states have specific requirements for ratios of supervisors to student teachers; faculty-student ratios are also sometimes spelled out in regulations. Various elements of state program approval processes may dictate some costs too.

University type. Among state-funded institutions of higher education, the major research universities are the most costly because of the added expenses associated with graduate programs and research work. Theobald described the difficult reallocation decisions facing such institutions if they are going to provide additional funding to PDSs.[30] Research institutions also tend to educate small numbers of teachers. Regional universities, which prepare the largest numbers of teachers, have some advantageous economies of scale in their operations.

Bruce Peseau and Roger Tudor began work on identifying peer program comparisons that could be used to help deans negotiate their fair share of university resources.[31] However, more investigation is needed into the relative costs of private and public institutions—not just from the standpoint of student tuition but in terms of per-student expenditures and general per-student costs of teacher education by institution type. Studies to date make it clear that cost differences inherent in the nature of these different institutional types also will affect the eventual costs of PDSs.

Each of the PDSs considered in this chapter is a public institution. Two identify themselves as research institutions. The faculty time spent in trying to determine the nature of a PDS in a setting where the primary mission is not perceived as being teacher education is extraordinary. People only indirectly involved with teacher education often dominate extended deliberations. Much of the unique cost of trying to operate PDSs in such settings is masked by annual budget figures included here. Theobald describes how priorities need to change to keep teacher education from being a cash cow within a college of education.[32] As indicated in Chapter Two, Goodlad has proposed the creation of centers of pedagogy to address such problems.[33]

Grade level. Generally speaking, increasing specialization at the secondary level has generated higher costs for secondary schools than for elementary schools. Costs for laboratory science and vocational programs have been the greatest contributor to this differential. In recent years, the push among local and state officials to reduce class size at the primary level has led to some changes in these historical relationships. In Washington State, for example, legislators mandated lower class sizes for primary grades, creating higher costs for that level of schooling. Similar action has been taken in Oregon, California, and other states.

The main effect of grade levels on preservice components of PDSs appears to be in the general size of schools at different levels. Because more preservice students can be assigned to larger schools, the tendency of high schools to be larger than elementary schools can lead to reduced costs for supervision of these preservice candidates. For example, one person providing general supervision for twenty preservice elementary students may have to work with two to four such schools, resulting in time lost in moving from school to school, whereas the same number of high school preservice candidates may all work in a single high school. Offsetting that apparent saving is the tendency to require external subject matter specialist supervisors for secondary schools and generalists for elementary schools. Thus, continuing to use the prior example, for the twenty high school preservice candidates, conventional practices may lead to the assignment of six or seven different supervisors because of the subject-matter specialization of the candidates. Differences in numbers of people served by PDSs are a financial consideration, but the decisions concerning how many are served turn on more than economic considerations. For example, the climate of trust between school and university faculty and the integration of preservice and professional development programs have significant effects.

The different PDSs described earlier not only reported different costs but also clearly serve different numbers of clients. Table 6.4 shows these differences.

The totals alone do not tell the whole story. Although 177 students from Plains University spend some time in learning activities other than internships at Sagebrush, 157 of them spend an average of two days per week at the school. The 60 who receive professional development assistance at Fairbrook not only participate in twelve workshop sessions but are also observed individually four times on the

Table 6.4. Numbers Served in Different Programs Shown in Relation to Total Expenditures

	Bay	Mountain	Sagebrush	Fairbrook
Total expenditures	$145,000	$163,000	$185,850	$458,280
Number Preservice				
Intern	12	8	12	10
Other		16	177	20
Number In-service	12	20	25	60
Number Inquiry	12	10	20	5
Number Renewal	20	20	25	60

job. In contrast, the 12 who participate in professional development classes at Bay simply sit in as added students with interns in methods classes and represent no additional marginal costs for Northern.

Program Variables

The second set of variables identified by the general model are *program variables*. Table 6.5 offers a general listing of these variables.

Training emphasis. Whether teachers, administrators, other educators, or some combination of these groups are going to be served by the PDS will obviously affect the cost of a school. Although it will cost more to serve more students, combining clinical programs at a single site for different programs may generate some savings. Establishing and maintaining relationships with a school has a cost associated with it for a college and a school district—the time to plan and coordinate efforts. Thus, if productive relationships have been established between a college, a school, and a school district, using a school to train administrators as well as teachers, for example, can generate savings.

As the program is considered, the way cost decisions blend with finding means of financing PDSs becomes evident. For example, if a PDS serves as a clinical setting for an administrative training program, interns assigned to work in the PDS may replace people who would have been assigned to the school at higher costs. Depending

Table 6.5. Program Variables

Training Emphasis	Program Component	Level
Teaching	Practicum	Undergraduate
Administration/	Clinical observations	Graduate/
leadership	Internship	undergraduate
Counseling	Workshops	Graduate
Other services	Seminars	Postdegree induction
	Mentorships	program
	Student/staff	Postdegree alternate
	continuity	certification
	Research/Inquiry	
	projects	

very much on how the program is designed, two such interns can replace an assistant principal at a high school—simultaneously increasing adult-to-student ratios and reducing costs.

In some instances, added services that may be provided for added program costs need to be carefully considered. Extensive inclusion of child-service interns in PDSs in several locations has proved to be an economical way for schools to extend more services to pupils. For example, the high number of school placements at Sagebrush is the result in part of the commitment by its affiliate, Plains, to integrate learning about professions serving young children. Candidates in counseling, social work, nursing, and other professions interact with people at the school and in the community served by the school. In another example, as many as 120 students have been assigned to one New England PDS in a single semester. Included among them are students ranging from juniors doing early practicums in education to graduate students doing doctoral research in social work.

Program component. This item is particularly related to determining opportunity costs. Costs at a PDS vary depending on the specific kinds of instructional activities carried out. Considerably more school and college staff time has to be devoted to support a student engaged in a practicum than one who is a member of a large class that uses the PDS to observe instruction. Research projects may entail more than just staffing costs; for example, they may call for computer support, extended communications with parents, and costs of preparing reports. However, the kind of activity selected may also help create a funding source. Preservice students working as tutors can be scheduled to replace staff paid for such activities; practitioners engaged in inquiry projects may replace hired investigators who would otherwise have been brought in to evaluate programs; and interns may (depending on program design) replace teachers (or provide low-cost improvements in teacher-pupil ratios). Although costs are associated with each activity, the extent to which these are added costs or marginal costs depends very much on the creativity of the people designing the program. For the student of finance (and, practically, for the operators of professional development schools), the question becomes this: What expenditures could disappear without altering the accomplishment of the identified goals? We will comment further on this in discussing means of financing PDSs.

Concurrent experiences—those occurring simultaneously with what is happening at a PDS but in a different location—were discussed in Chapter One. The four preservice programs whose costs are discussed in this chapter had similarities in that all paid more attention to foundations and learning methods related to disciplines than is often the case. In addition, they included extensive practical experiences and extended practice or internships. At Fairbrook and Bay, all methods instruction is conducted at the PDS so that field experiences and course content can be closely linked, while much of such instruction is conducted at the other two schools. The length and intensity of the internship also varied considerably among the four examples. Table 6.6 displays such differences in terms of credit hours allocated for work on or off the university campus.

Table 6.6. Preservice Credits for PDSs

Credits	Bay	Mountain	Sagebrush	Fairbrook
Total program	33	52	54	36
Earned at PDS	33	48	30	36
Internship credits*	6	12	13	18

*Included in "Earned at PDS" Totals.

Although PDS costs vary depending on how much instruction occurs, *total program costs* may not change merely because the location of some of the instruction changes. Significant cost variations at PDSs are also related to differences in program components other than preservice training. Fairbrook's focus on inquiry, professional development, and school renewal accounts for most of its cost differences with the other PDSs. Bay works through a general school-university partnership to accomplish much of its professional development, and the partnership, rather than the school, is the recognized cost unit.

Level at which teacher education is provided. Costs may also vary depending on whether a teacher preparation program is an undergraduate program, a postbaccalaureate program, or a five-year program. Several different kinds of postgraduate programs are emerging. In a number of colleges—particularly in large research universities, but in a scattering of institutions of all types—teacher education and other professional training for educators have been made postdegree programs. Whether or not a master's is associated with the program, proponents of such approaches claim that they have certain advantages. The application in Table 6.1 of a constant salary amount for full-time equivalent (FTE) faculty across the examples disguises this particular difference. Generally, graduate faculty members earn higher salaries than do those who teach only undergraduates.

True cost analysis of such efforts (those that account for all opportunity costs) would, of course, consider the added time students are enrolled in school. However, making the claim that there are added costs associated with this requirement of additional time is somewhat problematic given the tendency of students to require five to six years to complete existing "four-year" programs.[34]

Alternative certification programs that place degree-holding students in schools as interns with little prior training generally cost less than other types of teacher preparation efforts. Costs are reduced because there is limited instruction in professional courses provided, because preservice candidates often replace regularly certified teachers at a reduced wage, and because supervision of the work of the candidates is largely performed by adjunct faculty and low-paid or unpaid school faculty. However, if critiques such as those by Darling-Hammond apply generally to such programs, it would be difficult to justify them on a cost-benefit basis even if they are less expensive in the short run. Furthermore, such programs currently affect a very small proportion of all teacher candidates and have been in operation for a relatively short period of time. Both of these characteristics of alternative certification programs make cost-benefit analysis particularly difficult.

At least one state—Minnesota—is experimenting with placing degree-holding novices with initial certification in PDSs as part of an induction process not unlike the placement of interns and residents in teaching hospitals. It is not clear at this point what the role of colleges will be in working with such PDSs; nor is it clear how this induction year will be coordinated with other staff development efforts within the school district. Such an approach would add significant costs—if for no other reason than that it contradicts the common practice of assigning beginning teachers the heaviest loads in a school rather than easing them into the profession.

Attention needs to be given to the question of whether such well-designed clinical experiences—even if they have a higher initial cost—produce better student learning (thus making a greater return on investment). It is also possible that such experiences could generate teachers who are more likely to gain and retain employment. It is expensive to educate teachers who never teach or who leave after a few years of teaching, requiring expenditures in colleges and school districts to train replacements. Here, of course, one again becomes concerned with opportunity costs as well as the marginal cost and cost-benefit questions raised earlier.

On the surface, the least costly approach to the initial training of teachers is to ensure that all experiences, including clinical preparation, are completed prior to the awarding of a bachelor's degree. If the PDS is less willing to place significant responsibility in the hands of undergraduates, it will be harder to reduce costs at the school level. If undergraduate-only preparation leads to teachers who lack adequate academic and professional backgrounds, the cost-benefit returns of a bachelor's degree program might be lost. Also, the problem remains that the typical undergraduate is not able to complete the common requirements for an academic major and the requisite professional course work within four years.

Questions that might help with cost-benefit and opportunity cost analyses of teacher education in general and of teacher education as delivered using PDSs include these:

- Do teachers demonstrate increased desire to stay in the profession?

- Are teachers more committed to being advocates for children?

- Do teachers exhibit increased professional behaviors? (That is, within the profession is the turnover rate reduced, attendance increased, likelihood of pursuing graduate education increased, involvement in decision making expanded?)

- Do students attend and like the school (respond positively to school climate survey)?

- Do parents respond positively to the school?

- Do students "learn more?"

- Are there positive indicators of student participation and persistence in higher education?

Other questions that are more directly related to PDSs may also be asked, such as these:

- Are students from PDSs more apt to become teachers?
- Are school renewal activities more prevalent at PDS sites?
- Do PDS faculty report higher satisfaction with professional development activities?

Economic Variables

The third set of variables listed in the general model in Table 6.2 are *economic variables*. They overlap considerably with previous categories. Table 6.7 contains a general listing of economic variables.

Time. If a practicum is considered to be a thirteen-credit-hour course by the college, it will cost more than if it is considered a six-credit course. However, it is not as clear if students spending more time at a clinical setting than on campus will add expenses to the costs of a preservice program. It should generally follow that hav-

Table 6.7. Economic Variables

Time	Numbers of Students/ Clients	Faculty Loads	Compensation Levels for Staff and Students	Other
Credit hours	For each	School	Salary	Facility
Time on site	component	University	Benefits	Communications
	For each site		Tuition	Meetings
			waivers	Indirect
			Other	Fundraising

ing school employees spend time at a PDS site for staff development will be less expensive than conducting such training on a college campus, but in a specific situation even that condition could vary. This variable, as so many others, will depend on conditions at a particular setting and, therefore, it is a factor that each setting will need to consider. Table 6.6 displayed some of the differences on this variable among the four settings under discussion in this chapter.

There is another sense in which time is a costly variable. Both school and university faculty members must have sufficient time for collaboration and for the reflective practice of their art. University-based faculty members tend to find that the time consumed in this effort is even more demanding than their usual campus-based work. For educators in schools whose normal work schedule includes very little time for either reflection or collaboration, additional time free of direct interaction with students is essential.[35] Although some of this additional time could be acquired by restructuring both the instructional delivery system and the existing nonclassroom responsibilities of educators, providing time for reflection and collaboration represents significant opportunity and marginal costs.

Numbers of students/clients. Specific costs can be calculated only after determining how many students can be accommodated at each PDS site for each component (administration, teaching, other) of the program. Table 6.4 displayed such differences among the four examples being used in this chapter. Generally speaking, new PDSs seem to underestimate the number of students who can be assigned to a site, limiting the cohort to three or four preservice candidates on a particular site. Once faculty reach agreement on mission and sharing of governance, and the mutual benefits of engagement in the work are clear to school faculty in particular, many more can be assigned to a school. The New England high school PDS that served as many as 120 university students, for example, reached that level of involvement only after several years of collaboration had fostered mutual understanding among the high school and university educators.

Faculty loads. There are wide ranges in faculty loads depending, in part, on the type of university. Although NCATE and other accreditation agencies seek to ensure reasonable loads, variance between research and regional universities still means that using tenure-track faculty in the two settings will produce significantly different costs. In states with strong collective bargaining laws and histories, union contracts tend to specify loads for school faculty that will also determine costs of engaging them in the work of the PDS. Of course, the load issue is another way of stating the need for time for planning, collaboration, and reflection.

Compensation levels for staff and students. Lower pay for non-tenure-track student teaching supervisors has been a cost-cutting device used in teacher training for some time. Whether these supervisors continue to be hired, the extent to which tenure-track college faculty members are included (and then the extent to which senior faculty are used), and the compensation provided to school-teachers who serve in various ways in the PDS are all considerations when calculating compensation levels. Also, some colleges use tuition waivers as a form of compensation for school faculty participating in the program. In these instances, the true costs of such payments may be difficult to determine, but they need to be included.

When staff development and research activities are added to preservice work in a PDS, compensation for faculty for these activities often becomes complex. When are school faculty "double-dipping?" When should employees receiving training be paid for their participation?

Although it is obvious that employee pay rates are important determinants of cost, it should also be noted that in some instances there are compensation questions for students in the PDS. Some institutions provide compensation for student teachers who are postgraduate interns in somewhat the same way they provide graduate assistantships. Occasionally, such compensation takes the form of tuition waivers. As PDSs engage in providing induction experiences for new teachers and participate in alternative certification programs in which beginners replace regular teachers, compensation costs need to be considered. They may represent cost reductions from normal arrangements—but again depending on design, specific conditions present at the site may result in some unanticipated costs as well.

Other. Whether facility costs will increase as a result of working with a PDS is another question that needs to be examined. Although many such costs are not marginal, remodeling costs may be associated with the presence of the PDS on the school campus. In some cases, in order to provide an office and dedicated classroom space for PDS activities, portable classrooms or additions have been provided at a school. Such was the case at Mountain. It is also possible that there may be savings at a college as a result of increased use of school facilities. As with other variables, the question of whether this represents increased or decreased costs will depend on the specific local conditions.

There are also a variety of communication, meeting, and publicity costs that developers of PDSs need to consider. There does not seem to be any general report on the extent of such costs, but several authorities and a National Network for Educational Renewal group studying financing of PDSs offer testimony that attention needs to be given to such matters.[36]

In determining costs of any major effort such as a PDS, indirect costs must be taken into account—costs of administrative support, payroll, accounting, and purchasing. Calculating such costs is complicated by the presence of multiple agencies with different governance structures, sets of laws and regulations, and operating procedures. The bureaucracies of both school districts and colleges generate their own costs that must be considered in determining the costs of developing and operating PDSs.

Another set of considerations relates to valuable nonfiscal resources—as noted earlier, such as professional expertise and experiences—which are even more difficult to account for than many of the budgetable items discussed previously. From his study of five PDS sites, Jon Snyder reported that the resources required for a PDS have to be viewed more broadly than is possible through normal cost accounting. As he put it: "The visited sites collapsed the distinction between 'people' and 'money and policy' as resources, and to this mix of resources they added 'time.' Each educational community developed its own approach to blending these resources in support of PDS work."[37]

There are also volunteer services (possibly a cost-reducing measure), which are likely to be treated by parties as in-kind costs. To the extent that such resources and services exist, they have a significant impact on the amount of cash financing required to operate a PDS.

In addition to variables that determine the cost of an individual professional development school, institutions responsible for preservice and professional development are concerned about *multiple sites*. Indeed, if they simply have one "boutique" PDS and are continuing to operate the remainder of their preservice program in other ways, their costs for the isolated PDS will be excessive.

To determine costs for a setting consisting of multiple PDSs, it may be necessary to consider more than just the number of preservice students a setting will serve, the number of students to be placed at an individual PDS for various components, and the number of staff development students each PDS will serve. As the number at a particular location grows, the administrative support mechanism may also have to grow. At first, such growth may allow for greater efficiency: it may take about the same amount of administrative effort to support one PDS as to support four or five. No readily available data answer the question of whether there is a point at which the number of PDSs with which a particular college is working becomes so large that economies of scale do not pertain and bureaucratic inefficiency begins to set in.

With the closing comment that much of what has been said about these cost variables simply underlines the need for more study of PDSs to determine the specific effects of each of them, we turn next to how funds can be obtained to pay for such costs.

Financing Professional Development Schools

As is the case with costs, there is little information in the literature about financing operating professional development schools. Darling-Hammond observes that "despite substantial moral support, the PDS movement has been launched with remarkably little funding."[38] She suggests that generally there has been little external support from foundations or governmental agencies for initiating such schools and adds that the historical underfunding of teacher education within institutions of higher education suggests that it will be difficult to secure needed support from that source. Ishler confirms that there are difficulties in obtaining funds for professional development schools in his report of a survey done on behalf of the land-grant university deans of education: "The overwhelming majority of states have not established a funding structure nor provided legislated funds earmarked specifically for PDSs. By far the majority of respondents indicated that reallocated university and reallocated school/district funds along with moneys from private foundations were used to fund partnerships. The vast majority emphasized that funding of PDSs was indeed a problem."[39]

In more and more states, however, funding has been made available for PDSs. Darling-Hammond points to Michigan and Minnesota as two states in which some external funding has been provided on a limited basis.[40] As of 1995, West Virginia University had received nearly $3 million from the Claude Worthington Benedum Foundation to support its developmental efforts. Robinson and Darling-Hammond indicated that five-year funding of $1.7 million for a Kansas State project by the National Science Foundation made that project the best funded of a group of developmental projects they examined.[41] Ishler found that Texas has made substantial funding available to offset developmental costs associated with

PDSs and that legislation supporting partnerships for professional development has been passed in Missouri. His survey also revealed that various private foundations—Ford, Lily (Indiana), Winthrop Rockefeller (Arkansas), and Alabama Power—have helped local settings with start-up funding. Also, within the NNER, the University of Southern Maine has received assistance from the UNUM Charitable Trust and the Noyce Foundation for its efforts. Finally, several states (including Colorado and Hawaii) used Goals 2000 funds from the federal government to help with planning and development of such schools.

However, as noted at the outset of this chapter, "adding more" is not a likely means of funding PDSs. Instead, the most reliable means will be through reallocation of existing funds. This is accomplished most effectively when old programs are sunsetted and new programs instituted.[42] The three elementary school examples in this chapter provide some lessons concerning this approach.

As noted earlier, these three professional development schools relied on substantial external funding for start-up. During this phase at two of the settings, old programs were being sunsetted. Contributions from PDS districts and a few small grants (Atlas, state assessment project) provided support for continuing developmental efforts. Now Northern relies on PDSs such as Bay as it operates on funding comparable to that previously available. However, the university administration at Northern pressures the College of Education to make its program less costly because, with essentially the same outlay, it is now training fewer teachers than under the old approach. Although the graduate tuition charged Northern students is higher than that charged under the old undergraduate program, the tuition difference does not make up for the per-student cost difference. (Again, a cautionary note must be made regarding the calculation of per-student costs and benefits in a PDS program.) Also, the higher tuition may be keeping enrollment lower than is needed to offset current costs.

State University also experiences pressures as it tries to justify its considerably smaller new program. The old program, serving more than 1,000 students, has been sunsetted and replaced with the new focus on 350 students. As enrollment in their courses declines, arts and sciences faculty members have discovered that this change has had a significant financial impact on them, as it has had on the College of Education.

Sunsetting old programs and using the resources for new ones— and, in the process, reducing enrollment and trying to hold onto existing resources—represent two strategies for meeting the costs of PDSs. The first is essential; the second, although helpful, is politically problematic.

A third means of using existing resources is to shift those available within the college of education from other programs to teacher education or within a school district from one purpose to another. Whereas sunsetting of teacher education programs moves money from one approach to teacher education to another, shifting expenditures from graduate studies in such areas as educational psychology or school administration to teacher education represents a change in priorities for the college. Colleges have been reluctant to do this; some have refused even to consider the question. Still, policymakers in state legislatures and elsewhere indicate that they see professional training, not research, as the main mission of their universities—as the reason they are funding institutions of higher education in their state. Such views will keep pressure on colleges of education to find funds from within to pay for new costs. To make their case to the policymakers, professional development school advocates will need to be able to speak with more clarity than is presently possible about both opportunity costs and cost-benefit ratios. They will need to demonstrate that the results being obtained are greater than those achieved when similar expenditures are made for other approaches to preservice training, continuing education, inquiry, and school renewal. Similar concerns will have to be addressed in school districts to convince policymakers to shift funds from their traditional structures for professional development and school renewal to the PDSs.

There are a few examples emerging of programs that do not provide for alternative certification but instead deliberately reallocate school district funds to provide sufficient resources to support teacher training. Teachers for Chicago is a "break-even program" in which, ideally, "three interns fill three full-time teaching vacancies in sites hosting the program; the fourth intern covers the class that the mentor is assigned to. . . . The interns are paid the salary of provisional teachers, which is generally less than half the salary budgeted for each vacancy. Tuition costs for interns and partial overhead costs are recovered through this salary differential."[43]

Similar replacement strategies have been used for years at Brigham Young University in its Leadership Development Program and are found in programs affiliated with the University of Nebraska at Omaha, the University of Colorado at Denver, and the University of North Dakota.

Educators have long been interested in lessons that might be learned from the approaches taken by other professions when training their members. Marsha Levine suggests that there may be much to learn from the medical field's updating of the education of new doctors.[44] Indeed, an examination of the approaches to clinical experiences taken by other professions may help define how PDSs can be financed.

Preparation patterns for different professions vary. In medicine, campus-based undergraduate schooling usually requires four years and is followed by four years of postbaccalaureate study, sometimes referred to as "undergraduate" preparation by medical educators. Tuition, public funds, and endowments pay for this phase of the training. It is followed by another three to four years of graduate or clinical training involving internships and residencies in teaching hospitals. Young doctors are compensated during this phase of their training and the costs of it are paid from a combination of income from patients' fees (often covered by third-party providers),

Medicare and Medicaid, grants, and public support. Because the pay for interns and residents is generally quite low, the case can also be made that future doctors contribute to the financing of this stage of their professional training by deferring earnings.

Deferred earnings and low pay for professional training by the people receiving the training—these tend to be approaches that dominate in other professions. After accountants complete campus-based undergraduate programs, they will work at relatively low wage rates until they have passed qualifying exams. After engineers complete their campus-based undergraduate work (which may be supplemented by internships), they are employed with reduced responsibility at reduced wages. Only after they have worked under the mentorship of a licensed professional in their specialty for a set length of time can they take the examinations that qualify them as licensed professional engineers. Meanwhile, the clients of the firms for which they are working have paid the most significant part of this phase of their training. Architects follow a similar pattern.

Teachers likewise begin work at reduced wages, but they never reach the top earning brackets frequently associated with professionals. However, beginning teachers usually assume full loads and have only minimal guidance from mentors. Although school districts have expanded professional development activities, they do not usually assume significant responsibility for initial professional training comparable to that provided from the field for doctors, accountants, engineers, or architects.

It is also essential to recognize that the sheer number of teachers in the nation far exceeds the number of doctors, engineers, or accountants. This fact has tremendous cost implications. Along with less quantifiable variables—such as historical gender biases affecting compensation—the number of professional educators influences the content, scope, length, and compensation strategies for training teachers.

When he addressed the issue of financing PDSs, Neil Theobald echoed Tyler's 1985 comments about lessons learned in the first half of the century. Both recognized the need for added engagement by school systems in such training. Theobald observed that "professional development schools will necessarily wed public school districts, schools and colleges of education, teacher organizations, and state governments into an economic union which involves a significant reallocation of resources within and among the four sets of institutions."[45]

This returns us to our earlier review of the state of reform and finances for education in the nation. The partnership advocated here joins difficult issues of obtaining higher education funding with current troubles facing school systems as they seek support for their operations in an era that is generally resistant to maintaining the level of public expenditures, let alone increasing it. Odden has stated that "the future challenge for education will be to link improvements in school finance to local tax reform and, simultaneously, to produce high levels of achievement for all students, with school budgets that grow more slowly or even decline in some states over the rest of the 1990s."[46] He suggests that this will best be accomplished if policy initiatives designed to improve student learning are linked as a part of systemic reform and proposes that one such policy should lead to "substantially expanded professional staff development along with dramatically revised preservice teacher training."[47]

Odden also recognizes the limitations of "one-shot workshops"—which are typical of too many traditional staff-development efforts—but proposes using other traditional approaches, such as intensive summer workshops, rather than fundamentally revising training and school renewal as professional development schools do.[48]

Thus, there are a variety of possible sources of financing for professional development schools. Ultimately, they will require collaboration between the school districts and colleges engaged in systemic renewal efforts. However, for this collaboration to be successful, funds will have to be obtained during a time of limited public willingness to support education and during a time when the professional development school, although popular with advocates of reforming teacher education, still has not been accepted as a strategy that will produce better preservice, staff development, and school renewal than can be obtained through traditional approaches.

Case Examples

After briefly reviewing the state of educational reform and funding over the decade and a half following publication of A *Nation at Risk,* this chapter has examined programs and costs associated with four PDSs and observed that many variables affect these costs. The chapter has discussed some of the analytic issues involved in conducting cost comparisons and suggested that school district and university costs vary depending in part on whether the PDS is at a start-up stage or operational. Marginal costs, opportunity costs, and the relationship of costs to benefits need to be considered. Furthermore, context, program, and economic variables influence costs. Only by being very clear about such variables can one make accurate cost estimates.

To pay for these varying items, operators of professional development schools often turn to foundations and state grants to help with start-up costs, but they need to rely on reallocating funds through sunsetting old programs and shifting more money to teacher education. Ultimately, for PDSs to fulfill their four goals of school renewal, preservice education, inquiry, and professional development, school districts will have to invest significantly along with universities in paying for them. In order to secure support from policymakers for this investment, convince higher education faculty to reallocate funds to an institutional effort furthering school renewal, or persuade school policymakers to appropriate money to an institution with major responsibility for preservice education, some questions will need to be answered. The following questions, which have been derived from the previous discussion, are not necessarily answerable by information currently available.

- Beyond the question of the costs of developing and operating PDSs, are more benefits—such as better-prepared teachers, better-educated children, and more knowledge about schooling—obtained when PDSs are used than when they are not? In other words, what are the cost-benefit considerations of PDSs?

- How do school district and university costs of performing the services expected of professional development schools vary when performed in PDSs rather than through traditional means? In other words, what are the marginal and opportunity costs?

- What are the governance structures that can successfully blend the interests of the parties whose collaboration is needed in order to develop and operate PDSs?

- How does the proposed use of PDSs to improve induction processes for new teachers affect financing questions?

The case studies analyzed in this chapter help to explicate the foregoing generalizations about costs and the questions raised about financial support for PDSs. Northern University and Bay Elementary were described in Chapter One; Fairbrook High School and Brook University in Chapter Five. The following paragraphs discuss two additional schools and provide financial information for all four schools.[49]

State University and Mountain Elementary

State is a Research I university with a history as a major provider of teachers in a state with a surplus of teachers.

Preservice (Five-Year Program)

State University began with a program that enrolled more than 1,000 students a year in a four-year undergraduate sequence. With help from a multiple-year grant of several million dollars, the university developed its current five-year program intended to serve a more select group of about 350 students. Approximately 125 new students are admitted to the program each year—half to the elementary program of which Mountain is a part and half to the secondary program.

The new program requires students to complete fifty-two hours of professional education courses, thirty-two hours of which are graduate credits. Graduates earn B.A. and M.Ed. degrees simultaneously. Students are expected to complete various segments over the five years.

During years one and two, students complete a preeducation general education sequence. During this time they also participate in a seminar that familiarizes them with the program framework and are required to participate in volunteer activities with children outside of a school setting. These activities are not related directly to work at the PDS.

During year three, students are screened and prequalified for graduate school. Grade point average and Graduate Record Exam (GRE) requirements have been established for their admission to this stage of the program. Also during this year, students are assigned to Mountain or one of the twelve other PDSs and complete many of their experiences in these settings from then on. The first professional courses are identified as "Learning 1 and 2" and include field experiences (six credits each course for a total of twelve credits required).

Common themes—diversity, technology, and exceptionality—begin in the first course and continue in all professional education courses. Students work in three clusters to earn multidisciplinary degrees for elementary education. These courses have been jointly planned by the Mountain Elementary faculty (and other schools' faculties) and arts and sciences and College of Education faculty from State University. They include three semester blocks focused on literacy, science, math, and social studies (pedagogical content as well as pedagogy). Completion of the blocks carries into the fourth year.

During year four, students complete the study blocks, receive direct instruction in classroom organization and management, participate in school and society seminars, and engage in related field experiences.

In the fifth year (the ninth semester), students complete a twelve-credit internship at Mountain. They also participate in a teacher-as-researcher sequence, study issues of professional responsibility, complete a capstone course, and complete their portfolios.

The number of interns in a typical PDS such as Mountain depends on how large the school is. Generally, State University and the schools with which it works figure on eight in an elementary cohort, ten at the middle school level, and fifteen in high schools. In addition to housing the interns, each PDS serves as an instructional site for students in earlier phases of the program so, for example, at Mountain there might be twenty-four college students working at any given time.

Professional Development

Professional development for teachers at Mountain is ongoing as the school and university improve the school's service to its students and its readiness to serve the preservice program.

Target areas for staff development vary: at Mountain they have included technology and literacy. At Mountain and other schools they are also focusing on teams for leadership development. In this effort, faculty members from the State University College of Education collaborate with faculty from the business college.

Inquiry

State University and Mountain, along with other school sites, are engaged in a major effort to build teacher-as-researcher skills. In addition to the emphasis on this in the preservice program that was mentioned previously, a special course is taught at Mountain for teachers who are interested in such work.

School Renewal

Mountain Elementary competes with other PDSs for State University resources that can help with its restructuring, with strategic planning, and with areas identified by each school as needing particular attention. University faculty members receive no additional compensation for participating in the school renewal efforts, and promotion and compensation decision makers view that work as "service." There has been some reticence among university faculty to become involved because they are not sure the university will really value their work when it considers them for promotion or tenure.

Both school and college students experience a more challenging program as a result of the renewal processes ongoing at Mountain and State. A professional intern offers the following report about her program's ninth semester, spent at Mountain:

> This semester was great. I started school in the fall, and as far as the kids were concerned, I was just another teacher. I talked to parents and did report card write-ups and went to Faculty Senate and professional development like a regular teacher. My team was in charge of [an all school] program, and since I really like theater stuff, I was the director. I got nice letters about the program for my portfolio from the principal, the parent advisory council, and the special resource teacher. They were pleased with how I involved the teachers and parents in planning the program and with how I included the resource room students in the whole thing, too. Almost 500 people came to see it. We even got the newspaper to come, and they did an article about it.

My team's unit themes were exploration of the Western Hemisphere, American folk tales, and the development of technology. I worked with the team this summer to plan the core activities and objectives, and then I took the lead on the exploration unit. We integrated history, geography and world cultures, and a lot of mathematics and astronomy in the unit. When the kids realized how much math and astronomy were needed to navigate a ship, they were amazed. The journals they kept and the explorers' journals and logs we read led to the production of some neat plays too. I was able to plan so much astronomy work because I teamed with a science specialization student who had studied it. I think the kids really respected the way I deferred to her on that topic and the way she deferred to me on history and geography. Since we have worked together at Mountain for three years, it was easy to do. We also showed the field experience students how to plan a unit thematically. They helped us a lot with the journal writing as part of their writing process stuff in the reading course. Next semester I want to come back to Mountain and study how much the kids remember about the math in this unit compared to how much they remember from the math they did during the time it wasn't incorporated in the thematic unit.[50]

State University's dean of education estimated 1994–95 costs for Mountain Elementary's program as indicated in Exhibit 6.1.[51]

Plains University and Sagebrush Elementary

Plains University faculty designed their program so that undergraduates could complete the four semesters (fifty-four semester credits) of professional course work and receive certification at the time they graduated with a bachelor's degree.

Exhibit 6.1. Estimated Costs for Mountain Elementary PDS and State University's Program, 1994–95

Activity	Paid by School	Paid by University
Preservice (24 students —8 from each year of the program)		
Faculty FTE	.75	1
Other staff FTE		
Adjunct		.25
Stipends		$ 1,000
Supplies	$1,000	
Equipment		$10,000 (one-time grant)
Travel		$ 5,000 (local travel)
Professional development		$ 5,000 (payment for over-loads for faculty)
Inquiry	$ 500	$ 2,500 (research in PDS)
		$ 3,000 (support teacher-as-researcher project)
School renewal		
All faculty and administration at Mountain involved	$5,000 (substitute teachers' pay, etc.)	$10,000 (one-time grant-related assistance)

Preservice (Four-Year Program)

The Plains program graduates more than a thousand new teachers each year, only a small portion of whom are now enrolled in PDSs as part of their program.

Prospective teachers begin their study by completing a *preeducation* phase consisting of four three-credit courses. In these courses, students consider multicultural issues, learn about technology, examine basic information on literacy, and study child development. Associated with these courses are field experiences that include working with individual children and with other agencies. Also, students develop portfolios and prepare for admissions review during this preprofessional phase.

The second stage of preservice education at Plains is completion of the formal process of *admissions* to teacher education. This stage includes testing, a paper review to make sure prerequisite courses and grade point averages are satisfactory, a review of candidates' portfolios to learn about their prior experiences with children and their preeducation course achievements, and interviews in which final judgments are made about their appropriateness for entry into the program. In order to achieve greater diversity and a strong, talented pool of candidates, Plains actively recruits students from a variety of sources for its preservice programs.

After admission, students complete *professional semester 1*, which includes courses taught at PDS sites such as Sagebrush. These courses include study of reading and curriculum and an issues seminar. As part of the seven credits earned for this sequence, students also tutor children. At the same time students are completing the courses at their PDS, they are enrolled in social studies methods and health education courses for six credits. These courses are taught on campus.

In *professional semester 2*, preservice candidates complete ten credit hours of instruction at the PDS site. This includes attention to curriculum, methods, and a practicum that involves teaching individual lessons to whole classes of children. Students also complete six credit hours of other courses taught on campus; the content of these courses varies depending on the individuals' backgrounds.

Professional semester 3 consists of an integrated internship at a PDS such as Sagebrush for which candidates receive thirteen credits.

Professional Development

Professional development activities at Sagebrush include the following: workshops on technology for teachers and one-on-one help for teachers in using technology; opportunities for Sagebrush mentor teachers to learn about technology and other matters from student teachers; curriculum-planning efforts focused on integrated curriculum, including guided assistance from Plains faculty on curriculum development (integrated with courses provided for preservice candidates) and extended time for Sagebrush teachers during the summer for simultaneous planning of preservice and school curriculum; training in cooperative learning; and training in portfolio assessment.

Inquiry

Teachers develop their inquiry skills, and university faculty members engage in research activities culminating in published reports. The teacher-as-researcher is the focus of a course that prepares teachers to carry out research in their own classes. In a research program on the effectiveness of their overall school program, Sagebrush faculty members interact with university specialists in evaluation. This study is also used as part of an effort by Plains faculty to evaluate its program and PDS efforts and to publish their findings.

School Renewal

School renewal activities overlap with the professional development and inquiry efforts and include curriculum development activities; assistance to Sagebrush as the school develops participatory decision making; and focused assistance to help Sagebrush teachers solve problems they identify, such as low test scores in writing. Preservice and other students who come to school as volunteers work with initiatives such as the "writing buddies" program.

The associate dean for teacher education identified school and university costs at Sagebrush for 1994–95 as follows:

Exhibit 6.2. Cost of Program at Sagebrush Elementary PDS, 1994–95

Activity	Paid by School	Paid by University
Preservice (12 interns, 20 methods course students, and 157 other preservice students)		
Faculty FTE		1
Other staff FTE		
Adjunct		1 lecturer
		1 coordinator
Stipends		$10,800
Supplies		$ 3,000
Equipment	$4,500	$25,000 (one-time grant)
Travel	$5,000 (includes costs for substitute teachers)	$ 1,000 (local travel)
Professional development		
Summer planning		$ 3,000 (payment for overloads for faculty)
		$ 3,000 (payment for school substitute teachers)
		$ 1,500 (graduate student support)
Inquiry		
Faculty FTE		.2 (research in schools)
	$1,800	$ 4,250
School renewal		
All faculty and administration at Sagebrush involved	$2,000 (partnership membership prorated)	

The superintendent of the Fair District provided the following estimate of costs for the Fairbrook PDS, which operates in her district:

Exhibit 6.3. Cost of Program at Fairbrook High School PDS, 1994–95

Activity	Paid by School	Paid by University
Preservice (10 interns and 20 year-1 methods course students—10 per semester)		
Faculty FTE	.4 (Year 1)	2.1 (Year 1)
	.4 (Year 2)	.6 (Year 2)
Adjunct stipends	$ 5,760 (extended contract Year 1)	$ 6,000 (university extended time)
	$11,520 (extended contract Year 2)	
	$20,000 (stipends for interns)	
Supplies	$ 1,500	$ 1,500
Equipment	$ 0	$ 0
Travel	$ 1,000	$ 1,000 (includes local travel)
Professional development		
In-service for 60 teachers from 4 schools	$31,100 (staff mentoring of 60 workshop participants and assisting with workshops)	$14,400 (payment for overloads for faculty to conduct 4 workshops of 12 days each)
Inquiry		
Faculty FTE	1.5 (5 teachers at .3)	.1
School renewal		
All faculty and administration at Fairbrook involved	$57,000 (extended time for faculty)	$ 1,500 (payment for faculty overload)

The dean at Northern estimated the costs of the Bay PDS for 1994–95 as follows:

Exhibit 6.4. Estimated Costs for Bay Elementary PDS and Northern University's Program, 1994–95

Activity	Paid by School	Paid by University
Preservice (12 students)		
Faculty FTE	.5	.6
Other staff FTE		
Adjunct		.2 (8 different people)
Clerical and other		.3 (campus secretarial support for partnership and PDS)
Stipends		$7,800 (course leaders and master teachers)
Supplies	$ 500	$ 500
Equipment	$1,000	$ 500
Travel	$5,000 (substitutes and travel to professional meetings)	$1,000 (local travel)
Professional development	$2,500 (tuition, substitutes)	$3,000 (payment for overloads for faculty)
Inquiry		
Faculty FTE	.5	.2 (research in PDS)
Other costs		$ 500 (minigrants)
School renewal		
All faculty and administration at Bay involved	$ 200 (Bay share of district partnership dues)	$ 0 (all work done as "service" or as part of load as faculty assigned to site as supervisors)

If the emperor succeeds in keeping his britches up—and whether he really has any at all—are empirical questions whose answers will come only through continued observation, analysis, and synthesis. In the next chapter we turn to such questions—questions that are important for those trying to find answers about the benefits obtained through PDSs and for those whose task is the continual improvement of these institutions.

7

Ensuring That There Really Are Clothes
Evaluating a PDS

Had it not been for the insight of a child, the emperor might have persisted in flaunting his nonexistent new clothes before the public. Relying only on those who required his good will, he might have continued indefinitely to make a fool of himself. Such may also be the case for educational reforms like PDSs if those who create them fail to scrutinize their work carefully. Consider the following experiences described by an educator involved with PDSs:

In 1985 I participated in the process of creating four professional development schools. These PDSs were all middle schools affiliated with Truman University—a Research I IHE. The districts in which the schools were located were members of a school-university partnership formed to promote the simultaneous renewal of schools and the education of educators. The partner districts and the university invested substantial money in the promotion of the partnership. As it began the process of creating PDSs, it obtained outside private foundation support to help with start-up costs and

Note: Much of this chapter appeared previously in Richard W. Clark, "Evaluating Partner Schools," in Russell T. Osguthorpe et al. (eds.), *Partner Schools: Centers for Educational Renewal* (San Francisco: Jossey-Bass, 1995), pp. 229–262. It is reprinted here with revisions by permission.

obtained additional funding commitment from three of the four districts in which the new PDSs were housed.

For a year, principals and teachers from the schools met with faculty from the university and thrashed out some common understandings regarding what they were trying to accomplish and how they were going to proceed. At first, the middle school teachers were put off by university faculty who brought articles to the planning meetings—it seemed more like they were attending a class than participating as peers in a planning process. University faculty were also offended by school faculty who seemed to be telling them they knew nothing of value because of lack of daily contact with youngsters. However, by the end of the year a new culture had been born. School faculty were bringing articles and demanding more readings, and university professors were asking more and more questions about the day-to-day experiences at the school.

By the middle of the first year of operation, the faculty members from the school and university had begun to share their progress with others in the country. Over the next several years, articles and book chapters were published and presentations were made at national and regional conferences. Stories were shared about school faculty members who team-taught classes on the university campus and of tenured university faculty members who "did" short-term residencies in the schools to advance their knowledge about middle school children at the same time they facilitated teachers' professional growth. Plans were developed for an evaluation of the schools.

One of these schools, Horace Mann, is located in the neighborhood in which I live. A sign posted on one of the main arterials in the city identifies its location that is a block or so back from the busy street. As their work with the PDS progressed, the teachers at this school developed a great deal of pride in their new roles—pride they displayed by modifying the sign to indicate that their school was not just a *middle school*, it was also a *professional development school*.

One day, about ten years after the initiation of the PDS at Horace Mann, I was walking past the school's sign and noticed it had been modified again—boards had been placed over the words *professional development school*. Now, every time I pass the site, I am reminded of the enthusiasm in the early days of the PDS and wonder what happened. Unfortunately, I never saw the results of the planned evaluation. Unlike the articles extolling early success, the story of its demise, and the death of the other three initiated at the same time, is not being widely shared.

Did this emperor really have clothes? Were the teachers not justified in their pride? Were the PDSs ill-conceived or were there external interventions that led to the failure of these initiatives? Unfortunately, as is often the case with PDSs, we have little information to use to answer such questions about these schools, none of which continues as a PDS.

Careful evaluations of PDSs are important. Calvin Frazier and Joni Finney, following their survey of legislators and other state officials on behalf of the Education Commission of the States, reported that creation of professional development schools is one of the few things about which there appears to be universal agreement among policymakers.[1] The Holmes Group, the National Network for Educational Renewal, the American Association of Colleges for Teacher Education (AACTE) with support from the AT&T and Ford foundations, various states including Texas and Massachusetts, the American Federation of Teachers (AFT), the National Education

Association (NEA), the National Center for Restructuring Education, Schools, and Teaching (NCREST), and the National Council
for Accreditation of Teacher Education (NCATE)—these are just
some of the organizations seeking to stimulate the development of
professional development schools.

The preceding chapters demonstrated the complexity and difficulty of the task of creating and operating partner schools. For all
the different groups committed to creating something better than
present practice and the considerable good-faith efforts being made
to make these efforts successful, their evaluation appears to be an
afterthought. Frequently, sites developing such schools lament the
lack of money to provide for really thorough evaluations. Leaders
say, "We would really like to evaluate our partner school if only we
had the money to hire someone to do it." When evaluative activities are conducted, they are done gingerly, so as not to offend parties engaged in these fragile new collaborations.

How should those who seek to develop truly "stylish" PDSs gain
an accurate picture of whether, in fact, they have developed something that is real rather than imagined? How, as they engage in
their work, will they know if they are proceeding in a productive
way? How will those asked to fund PDSs know the benefits so they
can choose whether to spend their money on them rather than on
some other approach to improving schools and the education of
educators?

This chapter maintains that critical, collaborative inquiry must
be practiced by the developers of PDSs as a guide to their ongoing
work and as a means of determining whether they are accomplishing what they claim to be accomplishing—whether in fact they
have new clothes. As we address this issue, we will answer the following three questions:

- Will traditional approaches to research provide the
  necessary information?

- What is critical, collaborative inquiry?

- How should critical, collaborative inquiry be used to
  evaluate PDSs?

Will Traditional Approaches to Research Provide the Necessary Information?

Kenneth Sirotnik's chapter, "The Meaning and Conduct of Inquiry in School-University Partnerships," in *School-University Partnerships in Action: Concepts, Cases, and Concerns*, should be read by anyone interested in the question of evaluating professional development schools.[2] In this chapter and elsewhere, Sirotnik argues persuasively that the paradigm for evaluating educational programs (and for conducting much of what passes as research in education) is not useful for evaluating progress on school-university partnerships.[3]

If traditional approaches rooted in what Sirotnik calls *classical scientific methodology* were appropriate, one would expect evaluation of PDSs to be designed something like this:

Determine what the desired end is. For example, students in schools and educator preparation programs need to learn better than they now are: *learning* being measured by established instruments such as the Iowa Test of Basic Skills for school students and the National Teacher's Exam for preservice students; *better* being measured in terms of comparisons with previous school and college results on the same tests and usually further defined as being better to a degree that is statistically significant and not a product of chance.

Create an experimental design. Here the evaluator would seek to design the experiment so the effects of the PDS on student learning were isolated from other activities that may be influencing learning. PDSs would thus become the independent variable in the experiment. By use of various techniques, comparisons would be made that not only told the experimenter that learning was or was not better when students were involved with partner schools, but that also demonstrated that other, comparable students enrolled in schools and teacher preparation programs similar to the one being studied were not also making the same or greater improvements in learning. Like an agricultural expert studying the potential of a new hybrid of corn or the medical researcher testing a new drug, the focus would be on making sure that the "independent variable" (PDS) was the source of any improved learning and not something else. In the case of corn, a new fertilizer or beneficial weather conditions could be the sources of improvement, so the researcher attempts to hold such variables constant. In the case of professional development schools, new admission standards for college students, a change in school leadership, and changes in the district-specified curriculum are examples of other potential influences on outcomes.

Implement the design using an outside expert to ensure objectivity. Because outsiders are the only ones able to be unbiased, and because expertise is required to perform various experimental functions including the analysis of statistical data, such researchers are brought in to evaluate the PDS.

Report results to an external agency—frequently the funding source behind the independent variable (the PDS). The report may not be seen by the partner school at all or may arrive several months or years after critical decisions have been made without reference to the conclusions reached by the study.

This kind of approach has been highly successful in identifying new corn hybrids and in finding drugs that will effectively prevent or treat diseases. There are some issues of educational inquiry to which these techniques can usefully be applied. However, Sirotnik is only one of many who have pointed out its inability to provide answers to social policy questions. More than two decades ago, Lee Cronbach argued for "response-sensitive" research that would make continual adjustments on the basis of individual context-specific responses.[4] More recently, Michael Fullan and Matthew Miles stressed that a linear approach to the study of change simply would not work.[5] Generally speaking, the model does not seem useful in dealing with the "messy" nature of real-world social experiments such as the creation of new settings.[6]

Although researchers continue to argue about the applicability of traditional approaches to research, perhaps the most telling indictment of it in the area of educational policymaking is that (at least so far as this author knows) there is no significant instance of its having determined major policy.[7] Consider the following two examples. First, reasonably well-controlled experiments that demonstrate that retention in grade has a negative effect on students seem to have little influence on whether states, school districts, schools, or teachers flunk students as a means of "teaching them that the districts have to meet high standards." In fact, most urban districts seem to be rushing to convince their publics that they are putting an end to what is known as social promotion, as evidence that the districts are really improving. Second, studies that show *time* to be a significant variable in learning have had little effect in altering the regularities of schooling that provide the same length period and number of days for all students in all subjects. Even when secondary schools experiment with time by establishing various versions of block schedules, they manipulate time in such a way that all students experience common schedules of contact with different subjects.

Not all traditional inquiry is experimental in nature. Those who reject traditional experimental models may advocate another approach that they call *qualitative research*. Some of these scholars openly reject the idea of research that begins with any premise, arguing that the findings should emerge from the experience of the investigation. For them, "hypotheses are not stated in advance; rather, they emerge as the study progresses."[8] As an extension of this notion of emerging themes, some qualitative researchers stress their postmodern grounding, rejecting absolutes and emphasizing the socially constructed nature of all knowledge. They identify themselves as engaged in inductive reasoning, yet in their rejection of external standards they turn their backs on the scholar often credited with being the father of inductive reasoning: Francis Bacon.

Edward O. Wilson, a strong advocate of much associated with traditional scientific thought, calls our attention to some of Bacon's core beliefs: "Through light shed on the mental process, Bacon wished to reform reasoning across all the branches of learning. Beware, he said, of the *idols of the mind,* the fallacies into which undisciplined thinkers most easily fall. They are the real distorting prisms of human nature. Among them, idols of the *tribe* assume more order than exists in chaotic nature; those of the imprisoning *cave,* the idiosyncrasies of individual belief and passion; of the *marketplace,* the power of mere words to induce belief in nonexistent things; and of the *theater,* unquestioning acceptance of philosophical beliefs and misleading demonstrations. Stay clear of those idols, he urged, observe the world around you as it truly is, and reflect on the best means of transmitting reality as you have experienced it; put into it every fiber of your being."[9]

As contemporary qualitative research has increased in popularity, it seems to be particularly subject to the idols of the theater— for example, an unquestioning acceptance of relativism. For many who claim to be qualitative researchers, everything is relative— except one cannot question whether everything is relative. They also seem prey to those idols of the tribe that encourage them to believe that if something is quantified it is of little value, that they can make more sense of the world by examining a single case or a small number of cases than anyone can by studying a large population. As they proceed down these paths, they reject responsibility for answering causal questions, accepting only the task of dealing with "how" and "what" and shunning "why" as a question too complex to be examined. Leading qualitative scholars approach their task in a highly disciplined way and are not as prone to such errors, which are more evident in the work of graduate students and others who practice such research related to school issues with only a slight grasp of the theory and practice behind it.

Good qualitative scholars seek to understand connections among the many variables present in a particular situation, just as good experimental researchers seek to understand the causes of a particular phenomenon. Of course, just as learning about a new

hybrid of corn or a cure for AIDS may justify application of experimental methodology, qualitative case studies have their utility.
Questions of how and what are important, and the interviews, surveys, focus groups, observations, and document reviews that are
among the tools of qualitative scholars are useful for examining
many questions. Unfortunately, these tools lose much of their value
when employed with the objectivity urged by Bacon and those who
knowingly or unwittingly follow him in rejecting a role for emotion
as an idol of the cave. Researchers cannot remove themselves from
the inquiry, nor can social constructs be examined without recognizing the effect of the surroundings on the examination.

It is important to recognize that there is a difference between
evaluation and research. Evaluators may use many of the tools that
are employed by a researcher, but they have a different set of responsibilities. As Robert Stake has suggested, a researcher may be a
"noninterventionist,"[10] but an evaluator is engaged in work that is
very likely to affect the subject being studied.

As one proceeds with evaluation, both qualitative and quantitative research skills can contribute, but neither is sufficient. If one is
not likely to be able to evaluate partner schools effectively using only
the "classical scientific model" or "objective qualitative study," does
it mean that no approach can be taken? If policymakers frequently
seem to ignore the results of evaluations of various educational activities, does it mean that there is no use in evaluating partner schools?
The answer to both questions is no. There is, in fact, an approach to
evaluation that should be taken, and people making decisions about
partner schools do make judgments on their form and continuation
based on values that can be addressed through this approach. We
call this approach *critical, collaborative inquiry.*

What Is Critical, Collaborative Inquiry?

Collaborative inquiry has deep roots in American intellectual history. Emerson combined the notions of thought and action in his

early declarations of what American scholarship should be. In the twentieth century, Dewey provided grounding for much of the work to come later. Educators such as Robert Schaefer, Seymour Sarason, John Goodlad, and Donald Schön have continued the tradition.[11]

Related approaches go by many names: *scholarly activity, praxis, collaborative inquiry,* and *critical inquiry.* There are certain common elements to such research but, as we shall note later, critical inquiry also has some unique characteristics. This uniqueness lies in its connection with the concerns for fairness and justice that underlie the writing of critical theorists.

The first of these elements is the combining of action and study, as Ann Lieberman reminds us: "Some scholars, going beyond thinking or studying about improving schools, are taking action based on broad comprehensive conceptions for changes, conceptions that, in many cases, include new voices and ways of organizing work and understanding practice."[12]

Sirotnik observes that collaborative inquiry "rests on the notion of evaluation as the process of generating knowledge, by and for people who use it, enlightened by experiential data (both quantitative and qualitative), so long as a critical perspective is maintained throughout the process."[13] From the beginning, he insists, the process must include the formal incorporation of external parties—critical friends—who have the dual responsibility of encouraging the stakeholders to look carefully at themselves and of providing a mirror for the insiders to use in examining their own efforts.[14]

John Goodlad has worked for years to forge strong school-university partnerships that benefit both parties. To create an "ecology" for "continuous renewal," Goodlad insists on projects of mutual interest "organizationally linked to achieve shared purposes."[15] Traditional roles—professors as teachers of both teachers and scholars, public school educators as both students and subjects—have to be set aside without discrediting the unique strengths and skills of the participants. "Partnerships lacking this balance of selflessness and selfishness are short-lived."[16] Critical, collaborative inquiry also depends on the presence of critical friends of the kind that Sirotnik envisions.

Another pioneer in collaboration is Seymour Sarason. He created the Yale Psycho-Educational Clinic in 1962 to study and assist schools simultaneously. As a clinical psychologist, Sarason knew that "the understanding one gains of human behavior when one is in the helping role is extraordinarily difficult to obtain in any other way."[17] In his autobiography, Sarason recalled how he and his colleagues had to define and redefine their work as they moved into it. Starting the clinic made him feel as if he were flying "into a new fog with the most inadequate of radars."[18] There was no rule book to follow, no models close at hand to emulate. At times, he observed, "I knew exactly what we should do." Just as often, he admitted, "I felt like a snowflake in a storm."[19] But he persevered, and the clinic flourished for ten years.

As noted earlier, powerful arguments for collaborative inquiry and additional understanding of it emerge from the literature on critical inquiry by scholars such as Freire and Habermas. From them we learn that a praxis of critical inquiry should challenge groups to think together about their underlying interests and ideologies. Sirotnik elaborates on this connection as follows: "To be *critical*, an inquiry must also challenge directly underlying human interests and ideologies. This challenge is based explicitly on *normative* considerations. It is based upon a commitment to *social justice*—to the ideals of justice as *fairness*."[20] Educators who pursue critical inquiry do so as a continuing part of their professional responsibility. As Sirotnik states: "Critical inquiry is dialectical, dialogical, and deliberate. It is not something that happens serendipitously or casually. It has to be worked at with rigor and continuity. By its very nature, it is not something that comes to an end; rather, it is a way of professional life."[21] Such inquiry is a means by which those dominated by civic and academic hierarchies can become more self-reliant. Thus, these modern-day protesters reveal a link with Emerson, whose essays on self-reliance were a part of the original declaration of an American scholarship separate from its European heritage.

Sirotnik reminds us that such an activity requires participants to clarify values that are under consideration. He observes that "the 'teeth' of collaborative inquiry are the act of making it critical—that is, the act of . . . confronting descriptive information and the knowledge derived from it" through the values driving programmatic efforts. "This reservoir of values forms the basis for critique; moreover, the values are themselves subject to critique."[22]

Sirotnik observes that "given the root meaning of the term, it seems rather redundant to point out that evaluation is a *valuing* activity."[23] Evaluators and stakeholders need to be explicit about their values concerning professional development schools. Moreover, the extent to which values are commonly held becomes one of the most critical questions for evaluation. That is, any examination of the progress or accomplishments of professional development schools should incorporate a careful examination of the expectations of all involved concerning such schools. If there are significant differences in stakeholder expectations, there will likely be difficulties. For example, problems can be anticipated when school districts expect PDSs to produce teachers who are trained to follow their rules and when colleges expect them to produce teachers who are change agents. This is particularly important given the persistence of different views of the teacher's role in the classroom and in changing schools.[24]

Recently, the importance of agreement about values was demonstrated dramatically to me while I served on a panel that was evaluating the colleges of education in a state for the president of a state university there with three campuses. After a week of exhaustive document reviews and interviews with faculty and administration in schools and the university, the three panel members sat down to compose a report. Although we had a list of general questions that the president had posed, we had not talked among ourselves about the values we were going to use as we provided answers. As we talked, it became apparent that one of us had spent the week thinking of the schools in terms of NCATE accreditation standards because, as a dean, he had just finished his NCATE review. Another had used her position as a university provost to view the three colleges as a part of a university community. Having worked closely with John Goodlad, I used Goodlad's nineteen postulates and my own experiences with school-university relationships as my primary filter.[25] It took us an entire day to construct a framework from these separate views. One consequence of this was that the draft report for the president was not finished until three o'clock in the morning—just ahead of his arrival by plane at seven. As might be expected, work completed in this fashion had its rough spots. Each panel member was experienced as an evaluator, yet we allowed ourselves to be caught in the trap of unclear values.

It also took us a while to acknowledge the emotional loading that surrounds any set of values. Although some ideas may be considered in a relatively objective manner, people deal with their basic values emotionally as well as intellectually. In this instance, as in most instances of evaluation, two kinds of emotions needed to be thought through. First, many people had considerable emotional investment in the programs being studied. These were not simply the products of their rational planning but the visible indicators of dreams and struggles—in some cases, the key to their future lives. The second kind of emotional filters we had to recognize were our own. The views each of us brought to the table represented a combination of academic thought and successful and unsuccessful life and professional experiences. For example, our points of view on the relative value of an undergraduate or postgraduate teacher education program were not something we could expect to change easily in the face of compelling data offered by one of the others. The kinds of programs we had helped to nurture or had resolved to modify had left feelings within each of us that would influence our responses to whatever someone else said about this issue.

If values, both emotionally and rationally derived, are central to evaluative work, we are faced with some important questions. What are the values that are central to renewing schools and teacher education? Are the reformers trying to create schools that meet world-class standards? Do they want schools that ensure preservation of the culture as it is? Are they trying to create schools that will help to prepare students for a changing world—indeed, make them part of changing that world? Are the teachers being prepared to be skilled primarily at classroom management, control of students, and delivery of knowledge? To what extent should teachers being prepared by the program be committed to revolution, to radical changes in the schools where they will be teaching? What are the moral responsibilities of these teachers?

One set of answers to such questions is provided by the Center for Educational Renewal and the Institute for Educational Inquiry, which view their mission of renewing teacher education and the schools as being focused on four essential components:

- Enculturating the young in a social and political democracy;

- Ensuring access to knowledge for all students;

- Providing a nurturing pedagogy, developing the art and science of teaching that is needed to help all students learn; and

- Providing the stewardship needed to make schools renewing places.[26]

Each of these notions is complex and requires considerable dialogue before people understand them in the same way. Anyone seeking to evaluate a school-university partnership as represented by a PDS needs to look at the underlying mission for the partnership and engage in similar, extended conversation. Unless these underlying values are continuously examined, much of the agenda will mean many different things to different people. To make good use of an evaluation of PDS, the stakeholders for whom the evaluation is being prepared need to hold a common idea of what a PDS is and what it is trying to accomplish.

There is no shortage of descriptive statements about partner or professional development schools. The Holmes Group, NCATE, and the National Center for Restructuring Education, Schools, and Teaching (NCREST) have developed examples.

One of the Holmes Group deans, Frank Murray, suggested that PDSs must have ten necessary features. Those features are summarized briefly as follows:

1. The primary and overriding goal of the school is to have *all* its pupils use their minds well.
2. The curriculum must focus on important and essential knowledge.
3. The school must have high expectations for all of its pupils.
4. The mode of instruction in the school should be personal and fully responsive to the individual needs of all students.
5. The pupil must be actively engaged. His or her intellectual cooperation is a precondition of acquiring understanding.
6. Pupils should exhibit understanding in as direct and immediate fashions as possible, not by the indirect means employed by most school tests.
7. The school must be a model of the values of decency, honesty, integrity, democracy, [and] altruism it hopes its pupils will acquire.
8. The teacher in the school demonstrates professionalism by continually learning and continually inventing and discovering the means to respond to the diverse needs of students.
9. The PDS must be organized and financed in a manner allowing the foregoing. This includes support for teachers to engage in reflection and planning.

10. The school will team with other support services in
the community to provide a coordinated plan for
the welfare of the children enrolled.[27]

The ten attributes overlap considerably with the Common Principles that serve as the core value statements for the Coalition of
Essential Schools[28] and with similar statements advanced by other
reform efforts of the late 1980s.

Over a three-year period, settings in the National Network for
Educational Renewal worked on a statement that, in addition to
identifying characteristics of partner schools, sought to describe the
values on which the schools were to be constructed. The following
preamble to the NNER statement identifies values shared by its professional development schools:

> Partner schools in the National Network for Educa-
> tional Renewal (NNER) share a commitment to the
> nineteen postulates enumerated by John I. Goodlad in
> *Teachers for Our Nation's Schools* (1990). Each of these
> postulates has a bearing on the way partner schools are
> created and operated, with the fifteenth postulate speak-
> ing most directly to the subject: *Programs for the educa-
> tion of educators must assure for each candidate the
> availability of a wide array of laboratory settings for simula-
> tion, observation, hands-on experiences, and exemplary
> schools for internships and residencies; they must admit no
> more students to their programs than can be assured these
> quality experiences.*
>
> In addition to the nineteen postulates, NNER settings
> share common values that influence the ways in which
> they approach their overall mission of simultaneous
> renewal of schools and the education of educators. These
> beliefs include the following:

- Partner schools of the NNER ensure that all learners have equitable access to knowledge.

- Partner schools recognize and honor diversity, commit to multicultural curricula and culturally responsive practice, prepare individuals for active participation in a democratic society, and promote social justice.

- Partner schools contribute to the growth of students as citizens in a democratic society, as contributors to a healthy economy, and as fully human individuals versed in the arts and ideas that help them take advantage of their talents. In short, they are schools prepared to enculturate learners for participation in a democratic society.

- Partner schools enable educators to make educational decisions with students and other stakeholders.

- Partners in partner schools create educative communities that seek to develop a more just and sustainable society.

Whether they are called professional development schools, centers for teaching and learning, or something else, NNER partner schools are not an end but a means by which schools and universities seek to accomplish four purposes: educate children and youths, prepare educators, provide professional development, and conduct inquiry.[29]

This NNER statement then continues by spelling out definitions of the four purposes and providing examples of indicators that can be used to ascertain progress. Although statements by other professional and educational groups generally concur on the four purposes of PDSs, they are not as explicit as the NNER document or Murray's summary statement regarding other values. Also, in spite of the considerable overlap among such statements, stakeholders are reluctant to accept any statement as one that will be used as a standard for evaluating their progress, even if they will be the ones doing the evaluating. To some extent this reluctance reflects a general hesitancy among educators to accept external standards. Such concerns may be reflected in critiques of the value statements as "too linear" or "atomistic." External standards are also rejected by some undoubtedly because they are offered without clear indications about what needs to be done (or can be done) to satisfy them.

Other concerns may have their roots in very real differences in the ecologies of various partner schools. For example, those schools in rural areas that perceive a need to prepare educators for such settings may find that some of their values are not identical to those of schools serving urban populations. Schools with a religious base may perceive that they are seeking to develop different qualities in their graduates than those being sought by state schools.

The importance of values in evaluation and the relation of emotional stances to these values have many consequences for such work. Reluctance to engage in evaluation is one important consequence. During efforts by the Holmes Group to develop agreement around a set of conditions that could be used to evaluate PDSs, there was considerable resistance among member settings. As NCATE began the process of developing standards for PDSs, at least one setting that was asked to review an early draft refused to do so because those educators did not believe that external standards could be useful for their purpose. Similar concerns were expressed by educators at other IHEs who saw the draft standards published by the accrediting agency in 1997 and said that they considered them to be too restrictive to allow partners to develop PDSs that are responsive to local needs. Some within the NNER likewise voiced objections while the statements regarding common values were negotiated.

Whatever the reason for this resistance to acknowledging a common value base, it must be accomplished to some extent within any set of partner schools to be evaluated or the evaluation will be meaningless. Although it may be appropriate to use different values statements when conducting internal assessments of partner schools associated with separate institutions of higher education, comparisons across sites require agreement on the criteria to be used for the assessment. This presents a particular problem in efforts to conduct research that permits generalizations on benefits or costs of PDSs. If no common set of values or common definition is established, it is difficult to know whether one evaluation has any relationship to another. The evolving NCATE standards and the introductory section of the NNER statement, with its eleven general expectations and their accompanying indicators, may serve as the starting point for constructing a generally agreed-upon value statement.

How Should Critical, Collaborative Inquiry Be Used to Evaluate PDSs?

Few generalizations about collaborative inquiry hold true for all stages of the work. There are different considerations and challenges at every phase of the endeavor. It is important to take up each stage in order to understand the methodological pitfalls and potential.

Process: Formative and Summative

The eventual design and tools used in an evaluation may vary with the evaluation's purpose. However, the process used to create an evaluation for partner schools should be similar whether the intended purpose of the evaluation is to help shape the ongoing development of the school (a formative evaluation) or to stop at a particular point in time and assess how well the school is accomplishing its intended purposes (summative).

Identification of Stakeholders and Relationships

Evaluators of professional development schools need to start by identifying all of the stakeholders: the parties whose support is necessary to the successful functioning of the school. Evaluators need to know not only who these parties are but also what questions are critical to each of them. Answering questions raised by university-based participants in partner schools and ignoring those questions critical to school-based educators is likely to lead to dismissal of the evaluation as irrelevant by some of the individuals whose work is being evaluated. Similarly, tending only to the questions of professional stakeholders and ignoring those raised by parents and community members can lead to rejection of the evaluation by people whose support is critical to the continuation of the school.

Goodlad posits the need for a symbiotic relationship between school and university, with each succeeding in satisfying its own and the other's needs. Hampel reminds us of lessons from the history of relationships between higher education and public schools, which likewise suggest the need for these symbiotic partners to sustain their self-interests.[30] Schlechty and Whitford, in contrast, suggest that symbiosis is insufficient and that instead we need a truly organic relationship in which the partners become part of a common system and satisfy new common needs.[31] Such notions require a relationship between stakeholders that is substantially more advanced than has been achieved by most school-university partnerships. Still, evaluators need to be able to describe the nuances of the relationships among all the stakeholders.

Different groups generating partner schools encourage the engagement of different stakeholders. For instance, the sites involved with the NNER emphasize that the partnership should include participants from schools; one or more schools, colleges, or departments of education (SCDE); and one or more schools, colleges, or departments of the arts and sciences (SCDAS). But the stakeholders whose questions must be answered by evaluation activities are broader than this partnership, including at least the local

parent and business communities, the state and its various legisla-
tive and regulatory bodies, and faculty professional organizations.

Collaborative inquiry used for evaluation should engage the
stakeholders in valuing activities. Again quoting Sirotnik, such a
process "rests on the notion of evaluation as the process of generating knowledge, by and for people who use it, enlightened by experiential data (both quantitative and qualitative), so long as critical
perspective is maintained throughout the process."[32]

Exhortations to stakeholders to engage in critical, collaborative
inquiry are not enough. From the beginning, as Sirotnik has noted,
the process must include the formal incorporation of external parties.
They should be critical friends who have the dual responsibility of
goading the stakeholders to look carefully at themselves and of providing a mirror for the insiders to use in examining their own efforts.
Once the stakeholders have been identified and their commitment
to the evaluation effort obtained, the next steps can be taken.

A Basic Process

Sirotnik outlines those steps in the following description of the
process of critical inquiry.

> The process of making inquiry critical can be conve-
> niently represented by a set of interdependent generic
> questions that guide the discourse between the stake-
> holders of a collaborative inquiry. These questions are:
>
> - What is going on in the name of X? [where "X is a
>   placeholder for the issue(s) in question"]
> - How did it come to be that way?
> - Whose interests are (and are not) being served by
>   the way things are?
> - What information and knowledge do we have—or
>   need to get—that bear upon the issues? (Get it and
>   continue the discourse.)

- Is this the way we want things to be?
- What are we going to do about all this? (Get on with it.)[33]

To answer these questions, stakeholders must have considerable communication and observational skills. They must be prepared to gather "thick descriptions" of the ongoing activities of the partner school. It is not possible to answer questions about "what is going on" by waiting until several years into the life of a partner school and then trying to "remember" what happened at the beginning.

Recently I worked as part of a group that was creating a set of partner schools. Although some efforts were made to identify an evaluation design at the beginning, and those of us connected with the effort knew that we should be documenting progress, two years after we had initiated the effort we discovered that among us there were very different versions of its origin.

Unfortunately, each of us had only partial files and thus each was unable to answer questions about who had made what commitments at the beginning. As a result, it was difficult to accomplish the formative evaluation goal of assessing whether what we had been doing was consistent with original intentions and thus on track. It was also difficult to answer some stakeholders' summative questions, such as "Are we getting what we wanted from the professional development schools?" Failure to gather complete records on all aspects of the partner schools becomes problematic when leaders change within the school or university in the partnership. Frequently, those are the times when summative evaluations are needed, but a lack of information often makes such analyses superficial.

Tools for Evaluation

Minutes of meetings of collaborative groups, calendars of major events, course descriptions, records of student performance on various kinds of assessments, portfolios, videotapes, operating budgets, newspaper clippings, and journal articles are among the items that should be included in the information collections. However, records of deliberately planned inquiry are also essential. Materials such as pre- and postexperience interviews of preservice teachers, periodic interviews of school- and university-based administration and faculty, and interviews and surveys of students and parents in the PDS need to be included. Focus groups composed either of people who play different roles (for example, mixed groups of teachers, preservice teachers, and students) or people who are in the same roles (for example, groups composed only of parents or teachers or students) can provide multiple perspectives on what is happening in the partner school.

In addition to such sources, specific data concerning the classroom life in the school need to be obtained. Although teacher and student reports of what happens (from surveys or interviews) can be helpful, ultimately there is no substitute for extended, critical observation of the classrooms. Jianping Shen provides an example of what can be learned from a relatively simple inquiry into the opinions of participants in partner schools.[34] Classroom observations can take a variety of forms. Members of the PDS community may engage in collegial observations of one another's teaching. In one setting in the BYU-Public School Partnership, school-based and university faculty observe preservice teachers and are in turn observed by these prospective teachers. Classroom observations can include single sessions, but the more extended the observation period the more productive the information obtained. Observers may also choose to shadow students for a day (or some other period of time) in order to experience the partner school from the eyes of students. There should be careful documentation, including a review by the observer with the person or persons observed to negotiate meaning from the observations.

It is essential that the stakeholders in the PDS conduct their own information gathering and communicate with one another on the basic questions identified earlier. This kind of work enables them to understand where they are making progress and to modify their work as appropriate. This activity is unlikely to occur unless the stakeholders identify what Goodlad calls a "chief worrier" to oversee the gathering and analysis of information.

Examples of Evaluations

The University of Texas at El Paso (UTEP), one of the NNER sites, secured state funding in the summer of 1993 for work related to its new Center for Professional Development and Technology. Its proposal included a commitment to collaboration in the design and management of the center by public school personnel, university faculty, education service center staff, and community members. Although clearly identifying these parties as stakeholders, it unambiguously placed responsibility for evaluation of the effort in the hands of the project director. He noted at the outset: "The evaluation approach followed will be holistic and humanistic. It will examine a range of abilities in preservice and in-service teachers, and it will verify the degree to which these abilities are integrated and employed. Individualizing the evaluation tools in accordance with the culturally diverse nature of the program will be a priority and will provide an equitable process. In order to validate this approach, evaluation will be ongoing as well as internal and external in character."[35]

The UTEP proposal called for three types of evaluation approaches: internal evaluation by a full-time staff person (the evaluation specialist), informal case-study examination of each of the five partner school or PDS sites involved in the proposal, and external evaluation by a consultant retained to provide information to UTEP and the funding agency. Forty-two outcome listings were identified and listed in relation to the objectives of the project. These outcomes will be reflected in numerous documents of various kinds as enumerated in the design. Such advance planning should ensure the "thick descriptions" that will allow the participants to use the evaluation activities to help them refine or redirect their effort.

The planners at UTEP also recognized that it is essential that stakeholders encourage outsiders to examine their work and share the results of these observations with them. Negotiating meaning with outside observers can be one of the most useful ways of understanding progress that is being made at a professional development school. Such observers need to understand fully the values and beliefs that are driving the partner school, and they have to be clear regarding the questions that are of value to the stakeholders. Given such understandings, they can play an effective role as "critical friends."

Much of the evaluation in education, unfortunately, is assessment by outsiders who report to third-party funding sources and share little or nothing with the participants in the effort being evaluated. Although reports to funding sources (one significant group of stakeholders) are inevitable, they should be designed to be useful to as many of the varied stakeholder groups as possible. This use of evaluation must be planned from the beginning.

Terry Deniston provides an example of an evaluation of a PDS from which we all can learn. She tells the following story about the origin of her study: "Shortly after assuming the responsibility for this non-traditional PDS in the fall of 1994, I was asked in a hurried manner by a colleague, 'How do you think the PDS at Michener is going?' I shared a few self-effacing remarks, having been caught off-guard by the question. What followed, however, really took me aback. 'I have to go to a Teacher Licensure meeting and report on PDSs, do you think we should just close this one?' Shocked and confused, I replied, 'No . . . (disoriented pause) . . . we just started.' I do not remember the rest of the conversation because I went numb."[36]

Determined to provide an evaluation that answered the questions of such critics, Deniston also wanted her study to demonstrate the collaboration and partnership that were central elements in the formulation of the school. She attempted to adopt a research strategy that operationalized the concept of authentic inquiry and collaboration. She wanted her evaluation to be one that would report on the "ideas, feelings, motives, and beliefs behind people's actions with respect to a nontraditional PDS."[37] Toward those ends, she initially created a two-stage process. The first stage was to involve asking key school and university stakeholders, "What do we want to know about this particular PDS?" The second stage would then employ cooperative inquiry to answer these questions. It was, in other words, to be an example of doing research *with* people rather than *on* them.

As Deniston continued her planning, two questions emerged: What is the nature of a PDS at an alternative high school setting? What is the experience of authentic inquiry and collaboration at a nontraditional PDS?[38]

Although these questions did not come out of the kind of rich, collaborative thought originally sought, they did permit Deniston to advance to the stage of gathering information seen as valuable by the faculty as well as herself, the researcher-evaluator. These questions were then used to begin the process of identifying the samples of individuals connected with the school from whom data could be sought. Interviews, document review, participant observation, and reflexive journals were chosen as the tools to be used in the study. As she proceeded, Deniston realized that she was imposing a research agenda on a setting that, in spite of its expressed commitment to the four functions that characterize NNER partner schools, really did not value or practice inquiry as a central part of its activity.

Deniston closes her report on the study with a metaphor based on pizza lunches. This metaphor was useful to her as an analytical tool in examining the data she gathered, and it is helpful as a descriptive device in illuminating the themes (reported in italics in the following excerpt) that emerged from the study.

In the early stages of the work involving the PDS Deniston was studying, faculty from the university and high school got together over pizza to discuss their work. These lunches were later discontinued because of conflicting work schedules. The following excerpt from her report provides a cryptic but clear picture of what she found as she looked closely at the PDS. Although many stakeholders probably would not be satisfied with information reported in this way, those who had been engaged in the work of trying to make Michener a successful PDS undoubtedly found in it much food for thought (no pun intended):

Initiation: The administrators at CSU and MHS decide to have pizza luncheons.

Definition: The administrators at CSU decide whom to call to order the pizza.

Uniqueness of Site: The administrators ordered a variety of different kinds of pizza to accommodate the tastes of the CSU administrators, faculty and future teachers, as well as the administrator, teachers, and students at MHS. Everyone (vegetarians, carnivores, vegans, onion-haters) gets at least one slice of the pizza they love the most.

Impact: At the end of the luncheon everyone leaves happy, full, and having met and spent time with lots of other interesting people.

Renewal: Several of the individuals from the luncheons have looked around at other people's pizza slices, and decide that next time there is a pizza luncheon, they want to try what some of the other people were eating.

Inquiry: MHS wonders why CSU is not having pizza luncheons anymore.

Collaboration: MHS tells CSU that it also knows of some great pizza places in town and would love to have some input into choosing the vendor for the next event.

System constraints: CSU tells MHS they think it is a great idea for MHS to start helping to choose the pizza vendor, because they are tired of having all that

responsibility when there are so many other things
they are supposed to be doing. And, by the way, who's
going to pay for the next luncheon?[39]

This study and the authentic voice in which it is written fills the
need for formative examination of PDS work at Michener. The
pizza metaphor undoubtedly helped the individuals who worked
with the PDS, because it recognizes in an indirect way some of the
difficult value questions that need to be confronted. At the end of
her report, Deniston also provided a more conventional list of
actions recommended as a result of her study. Chances are good that
these recommendations were given greater attention than might
otherwise have been the case because of the way in which the evaluator acknowledged the legitimate role of each party in the school.

However, often the evaluation needed is summative information as well as formative data. The policymaker wants to know
whether the PDS should be closed, the legislator does not understand why funding should be provided, the superintendent and principal have to explain why the school is being used by so many
college students. In each of the situations, people are seeking information on the benefits of a PDS, not just trying to get an understanding of how it functions and what things helped or failed to
help it function.

The Colorado Partnership for Educational Renewal (COPER)
prepared an evaluation designed to serve both formative and summative functions. The evaluation was needed in part to help PDSs
within the partnership respond to demands for data from state and
local funding sources.[40] Therefore, some of the stakeholders were
immediately evident. However, the school- and university-based
educators who conducted this evaluation wanted to do more than
provide information that would be useful to their funders.

Accordingly, their evaluation was designed to inform PDS educators about how well they were doing based on previously agreed-
upon benchmarks (see Chapter Four) and other criteria, to

empower these educators to identify skills and activities they needed to attain their desired outcomes, and to help these educators engage in reflection about their work. At the same time, the evaluators sought to examine the process of transformation at the school from the perspective of a particular theory of change. As they moved into the second year of their evaluation, they expanded their overarching question beyond what was happening at an individual PDS to how they were progressing on their overall agenda of simultaneous renewal of schools and the education of educators.

To accomplish these complex ends—ends that are clearly interventionist—the evaluators decided to use focus groups, surveys, logs, and classroom observations. As they analyzed data, they anticipated using qualitative analysis of the transcripts from focus group discussions and examination of descriptive statistics regarding the PDSs as well as a cross-case analysis.

Their basic evaluation questions were these:

- What changes are occurring at partner school sites?

- Is there a generalizable developmental progression of changes?

- Do partner schools make a positive difference in results for participants?

- What impact has COPER had on the simultaneous renewal of university schools of education and their P–12 sites?[41]

With these questions and the aforementioned tools, the partnership team embarked on a three-year evaluation that was clear about the values on which it was grounded and that sought to address *why* as well as *how* and *what*. Although connected to the partnership, many of those involved in the evaluation were external to the specific PDSs being examined.

There are many examples of external evaluation that fail to contribute to the critical examination of practice by insiders, but there are also too many examples of insiders failing to examine their own work critically. Such inquiry sometimes needs external priming—from a funding source or from a party such as a university scholar who is interested in understanding more about professional development schools. Designs such as those from UTEP and COPER address both issues.

The University of Wyoming initiated an evaluation project that also serves as an example. This evaluation effort is one of several initiated as part of the National Education Association's Teacher Education Initiative (TEI). Each of these evaluations used nine guiding principles for the project as well as whatever set of value statements may have guided the original work of the settings. Wyoming's work with its PDSs—which are called Centers for Teaching and Learning—had roots in the Holmes Partnership and in the National Network for Educational Renewal.[42]

Wyoming faced a complex set of stakeholders in preparing this evaluation. It had to satisfy external demands for process established by the NEA project that provided some of the funding for the study. There were also other funders who supported the evaluation through grants to the Institute for Educational Inquiry (IEI). The Wyoming program was under scrutiny by the university, the legislature, and the state department of education, all of whom had differing concerns about changes that had been made. Faculty within both arts and sciences and education had raised questions about the new approach being evaluated, and the educators in the schools had their own set of questions. In other words, as is often the case, these evaluators had to serve many masters.

The investigators made extensive use of surveys and focus-group interviews involving preservice teachers, mentor teachers, building principals, district administrators, College of Education faculty, and administration. Reactions to near-final drafts of the report were sought from key stakeholders who read for accuracy as well as to assess interpretations made by the evaluators.

The evaluation continues as of this writing. However, three broad answers were obtained in early findings: "(a) the partnership is educating a better-prepared preservice teacher, (b) communication problems challenge partnership work, and (c) partnership roles must be examined for clarity and equity."[43]

The first of these answers was well received by most of the critical stakeholders. Because many had been involved in the inquiry, they were ready to accept the preliminary findings. However, one may expect that they will demand more data than were provided by the original surveys before they are ready to accept the causal link between the new program and the better-prepared teachers being claimed by the evaluators. Although scholars involved in a research study might be able to pursue questions with little regard to the field's reactions to the questions, evaluators engaged in projects such as the assessment of a PDS do not have that luxury. In fact, they have the added burden of contributing to action. Remember that Sirotnik's final question in his description of the collaborative inquiry process calls for action.

Action, Feedback, and Collaborative Analysis

Too often, assessment becomes an end rather than a basis for action. By integrating the action step with the inquiry steps, Sirotnik follows a line of scholars including Dewey who urge what elsewhere I have called *reflaction*—a combining of reflection and action.[44] Unless an evaluator takes this final step, asking all the other questions has little effect on professional development schools. The following discussion draws on information in the Study of School Change, a critical, collaborative inquiry conducted with high schools in the Coalition of Essential Schools.[45] The example treats a number of issues that must be considered in the final stages of the process.

To initiate action, a crucial aspect of collaborative inquiry is setting norms for feedback and analysis of the findings of the study. In the Study of School Change, Pat Wasley, Robert Hampel, and I set the following ground rules. Of course each study requires its own set, but these serve as a useful example of conditions that must be established at the outset if the final stages of a study are to be successful.

- Nobody can quit—neither researchers nor practitioners—no matter how tough it gets. (This flies in the face of the American Educational Research Association [AERA] ethics statement, which indicates that a participant should always be able to withdraw. In reality, it was intended as a statement of commitment to the project not as an unbreakable rule.)

- Everyone must raise concerns as soon as they emerge so they can be discussed.

- First drafts of written work will be reviewed and discussed with a substantial number of people from the school.

- In case of an impasse on the correctness and accuracy of written work, a mutually acceptable arbitrator will be called on, and if we still cannot agree, minority opinions will be included in the written work.

- Final drafts will be distributed to those parties with whom the faculty and administration of the school wish to share.

- After data gathering has ended, the researchers have no obligation to negotiate the final products of the study. However, we promise to visit and discuss the final products with the schools before releasing them to the general public.

- We will submit ourselves to the same kind of critical review we are using in studying the schools by asking faculty and administration in the schools to provide an annual critical analysis of our work to the members of our senior advisory board.

Although we never had to call an arbitrator, we did in all five schools negotiate differences between our perceptions and the teachers' views. We also found that the visits of the advisory board facilitated increased mutual understanding in several instances.

The main source of feedback was a paper written after each visit, a twenty- to sixty-page "snapshot" that encompassed the perspectives of teachers, students, administrators, and parents, and included several classroom vignettes. Twenty-four of these snapshots were prepared and are available from the Coalition of Essential Schools. Taken as a group, each school set provides a comprehensive view of two to three years of school change efforts. Initially, they served as mirrors for the people in the schools. Just as many of us are not pleased with what we see when we look in the mirror, there were times when people at the schools were uncomfortable with the images reflected in their snapshots. The study advisers were able in several instances to help teachers and administrators in the schools deal with anxieties generated by interpretations of their work. As the study progressed and trust grew, it became easier to negotiate such differences directly.

The educators in the schools rarely asked for rewrites of the snapshots to cast them in a more favorable light. Instead, they usually pointed out what was too simple or misleading. They knew that there was more to the situation that had to be mentioned in order to explain it fully. An example that illustrates this point deals with the turnover among principals and other school leaders, which occurred at each school. One snapshot reported that a principal left because he felt exhausted by the constant demands of the job at the same time the faculty felt he was too timid. He suggested that more information was necessary. He had been willing to let the staff run faculty meetings and set the agenda each time. After years of service elsewhere as a rather authoritarian principal who always set the agenda, he welcomed a lighter touch, and preferred quiet work focused on individual teachers' instruction. Yet, to his disappointment, that style had not inspired enough confidence in his leadership. Clarifications like that provide different perspectives and illuminate the genuine confusion that arises when longstanding roles suddenly change.

Efforts to provide feedback sometimes produce unanticipated results. For instance, the design called for teachers to take the snapshot they were provided and use it to engage in reflection about their practices. Thoughtful group conversation about the snapshot's implications for the whole school proved harder to generate than imagined. It was apparent from the start that individual teachers found the feedback they received productive, but responses were scattershot and uncoordinated. Teachers had no history of seminarstyle analysis of the evidence in the papers and no experience in acting on information provided by a study—no matter how collaboratively it had been conducted. To obtain this action, the study team began to devise exercises and activities to help the schools make use of the snapshots. Sometimes they included questions in the papers, at other times teachers were asked to share their reactions with another teacher, and periodically individual members of the study team went to the schools to facilitate workshops and retreats built on the feedback provided from the study. It became clear that if researchers could not build habits of reflection among the faculty members who were participating in the study and if the school leaders merely handed out the snapshots, they would be scanned quickly and then shelved, in the same way that research reports and academic studies often are. *In planning the studies, there must be from the beginning a plan for using the information or there is no sense developing it.*

Let us summarize what was said in this chapter. Evaluators should continually seek to be clear about their values and beliefs as represented in the partner school. Moreover, they should keep in mind the principles of fairness and justice that are central to the notion of critical inquiry. Early in the process, evaluators should identify their stakeholders, what these stakeholders' values and beliefs are, and how such values and beliefs may affect the outcome of the evaluation. Throughout the evaluation process they must work *with*— not *on*—these stakeholders.

Because evaluation has several purposes, evaluators need to ensure that they are clear about the purposes at the outset. That clarity must be maintained throughout the course of their work as they join with participants in the school and other stakeholders to identify the questions requiring answers to satisfy those purposes.

Similarly, from the beginning of the evaluation and throughout the process, evaluators and participants in the setting that is being evaluated should agree about how information will be collected and analyzed and what information developed in the normal course of the partner school efforts needs to be preserved. Of equal importance is early and continuing determination of what new information needs to be acquired. As a part of the design work, evaluators need to determine who will collect and analyze information, making sure that one individual is designated as the lead person for the assessment effort. The people involved in this process must include those stakeholders most closely associated with the work. In a PDS, this means that both university- and school-based faculty need to play key roles in gathering and analyzing information rather than be mere passive receivers of the results. Similarly, also important are the evaluators' selecting and refining the tools to be used and being knowledgeable about the power of those tools to answer the critical questions they and their stakeholders have.

Again, from the beginning of the evaluation design and throughout the process, evaluators need to be specific about how the assessment will culminate in feedback, analysis, and action. People who create PDSs, convinced as they are about the efficacy of their new settings, owe it to themselves and the people who populate these settings to examine their progress and use this examination to renew their efforts continually. Traditional forms of evaluation are unlikely to satisfy the needs of these settings, but by using collaborative, critical inquiry, PDS stakeholders can use evaluation to act in knowledgeable ways to enhance the quality of their efforts. As a result, their school is likely to have real clothes, not the emperor's false garments.

8

Lead On

The Leadership Imperative

Imagine our emperor all dressed up in his new clothes. He positions himself at a prominent spot in the parade—just behind a team of six motorcycles and the band that plays mightily to announce the coming of the parade. The time arrives for the start of the parade. One motorcyclist decides to get a drink of water and abandons his bike in the middle of the street. Another one heads south on First Avenue, while two others head north on First. The remaining two move out straight down Main Street, paying no attention to their colleagues. The drum major blows his whistle and points his baton to the right while marching rapidly to the left, following the cyclist who went south. The drum majorette on the right side of the band throws her baton in the air and steps out with a smile—until she trips over the abandoned bike, at which point the trombones run into her. Meanwhile, the drum majorette on the left side of the band—a smile fixed firmly on her face—cries big tears and the bandleader throws up her arms in utter frustration.

Without effective leaders, the PDS emperor has no clothes. Leaders are essential to creating an effective PDS. Each of the steps discussed in the preceding chapters depends on effective leadership for realization. That is, the leaders in a PDS cultivate the fabric, select the first layers of clothes, make sure that the PDS is stylish and not just another fad, acquire the support mechanisms to keep the britches up, and oversee the evaluation that ensures that the emperor is worth seeing.

This chapter addresses three broad questions:

- Who are the leaders that are necessary for successful PDSs?

- What do these leaders need to know and be able to do?

- How can the required leaders be developed and sustained?

Who Are the Leaders That Are Necessary for Successful PDSs?

First, it is important to recognize that we are talking about leaders and not *a* leader. Although a single charismatic individual may have considerable influence on a PDSs, the presence of one leader, no matter how effective, is insufficient in the long run. Leaders are required in various roles in higher education and the schools.

The first leader needed is the initiator. For a PDS, that person often comes from the university community, but in some instances school-based educators have been the force behind the initiation of a PDS. Ideally, this person has charismatic qualities and considerable credibility in both the school and the university communities.

Boundary-spanners—individuals who understand the culture of higher education and schools—are the next group of leaders needed. This critical group is hard to find. One would assume that because most school-based educators have spent considerable time in higher education they would be able to understand the culture of both types of institutions, but that is hardly the case. The effective boundary-spanner not only has credibility in both arenas but also possesses the skills needed to energize workers from both.

Within the PDS, as in any school, the principal plays a critical role. The principal's ability to engage others from the school and community in leadership is even more important than the vision and direction he or she provides to the school. It is also important that there are teacher leaders from both the university and the school who can enlist their peers in the work and communicate effectively with their counterparts. People who are in traditional leadership positions such as department heads should be included in this group, but new faculty leadership roles should also emerge.

There also must be leaders among parent groups and community school advisory groups who understand and support the PDS's adoption of an expanded mission.

Finally, system support from leaders in the university and school district administration is critical to successful operation of a PDS. Steven Baugh, superintendent of the Alpine School District in Utah, expressed this need as it relates to school district central administration when he said, "As we enter into this process, there are mistakes. There is confusion. There are questions. Occasionally there is anger and frustration; faculty member to faculty member, parent to school. The district office, central administration, provides support, provides in some ways protection. Provides a framework—a setting—wherein a school can embark on this renewal process. . . . If, at the first cloud on the horizon, the district pulls the support, we set the agenda back twenty years. It's not fair."[1]

Similar observations can be made regarding the role of administration in higher education.

What Do These Leaders Need to Know and Be Able to Do?

Regardless of their roles, leaders in effective PDSs need certain characteristics.

Common Characteristics

One trait a leader obviously needs is what Postman and Weingartner have called a built-in "crap detector."[2] Regarding this virtue that he sees as necessary for leaders who accept their moral responsibilities,

Goodlad said, "Good crap detecting is, thankfully, much more the science and art of knowing and addressing the essence of worthy human endeavor than it is the analyzing of taxonomies of crap. For crap is infinite in its production and rendered virtually ubiquitous in its presence by today's ease and rapidity of communications. The control of its tarnishing influence through raising the social self-consciousness of our entire society is an educational task of mammoth proportions . . . it is one of focusing on the essence of education in schools and protecting that essence from harmful intrusions."[3]

Leaders need to apply their "crap-detecting" skills particularly vigorously to those pronouncements on the purpose of public schooling that trivialize it by downplaying its centrality to a social and political democracy. They also need to exercise these skills when snake-oil purveyors approach their PDS with the latest panacea for curriculum, instruction, or assessment. Crap detecting is also particularly important when that panacea is developed with the assumption that the teacher is a mechanical instrument to be directed by higher, more knowledgeable authorities.

The second necessary ingredient for all leaders is one that is a vital precondition to the development of good crap detectors. Leaders require the kind of sound intellectual grounding that gets its start in a good liberal education and continues to develop throughout a person's life and career by the pursuit of both broad and specialized knowledge. Chapter Two addressed the issue of the general education required for all teachers. The learnings that characterize such study become particularly important for leaders, helping them to understand the work of others in their PDS and to develop an integrated view of the various disciplines.

Communication skill is an element of a good liberal education that leaders need to continue to perfect. Written and oral communications are the means by which leaders understand the needs of their constituents (listening and reading) and provide direction, persuasion, explanation, and encouragement (speaking and writing). Too many would-be leaders rely on skills in this area developed early in their academic experiences instead of seeking formal and informal opportunities to refine them.

Communication is the means by which relationships are maintained, and maintaining relationships is one of the key responsibilities of a leader. Leaders who are sensitive to relationship issues listen and observe carefully. For example, leaders need to understand how school- and university-based educators perceive one another and what university students' needs are as they seek new relationships with the younger students with whom they are working.

A fundamental aspect of leaders' communication ability and wise dealing with relationships is their capacity to work with the broader community in which the PDS is located. One sense in which schools are public is that they are the public's schools. A leader must understand this and, if working with a public school PDS or a public institution of higher education, must understand and respect what the public wants from its schools. At the same time, leaders must work to make sure that public understanding is based on good information. Leaders obtain and share good information through careful evaluation, as discussed in Chapter Seven. They also keep abreast of pertinent research and help serve as "crap detectors" for the public when others begin to advocate the adoption of faulty innovations. Leaders need to exhibit special skill in helping the community to see the fallaciousness of solutions like exorbitant testing or aggressive use of grade retention simply to demonstrate that high standards are being maintained.

Leaders need to understand the change process. Wasley and Linnon describe fourteen change theories that have been used to describe how outside innovation can be brought into schools and how schools can be helped to carry out their own changes. They distill these processes, which have evolved over the last forty years, into *research*, *action*, and *reflection*—a series of events that parallels those described in Chapter Seven as essential for critical, collaborative inquiry.[4] Leaders should understand a variety of change models and be able to use those that are appropriate for a particular situation.

Leaders who work with PDSs must be particularly knowledgeable about curriculum, instruction, and assessment. Moreover, they have to know how to help teachers strengthen their grasp of these fundamental elements of their professional life. This means that they have to know good teaching when they see it and know how to help teachers build on strengths and eliminate weaknesses.

Leaders understand the resources that are needed for a PDS. Chapter Six treats this topic at length. In this instance, some leaders may need to have greater understanding than others. That is, individuals in formal leadership positions such as dean or principal may need more knowledge than faculty members. However, all need to have a general understanding of this issue.

Uncommon Knowledge

All leaders require those skills and understandings described in the previous section. But as is the case with understanding resources, some leaders have additional needs. For instance, the boundary-spanners who are critical to the success of a PDS must know the cultures of both institutions well enough to be accepted by both. They must be comfortable in the highly egalitarian school setting and in the university structures where individual achievement is rewarded ahead of group attainment. They need to value the unique contributions that representatives of each setting can make and understand the time demands on participants. But they need not only to understand the different cultures and be able to function in each but also to be able to bring parties together across cultures in a mutually respectful manner.

Much of what leaders need to do in developing and refining PDSs is spelled out in Chapters Two and Four. Leaders who initiate PDSs need to have particular sensitivity to the past relationships and a commitment to building on positive elements of those relationships.

Leaders who have responsibility as "chief worriers" for evaluation need to be well informed about the quantitative and qualitative research skills required of an evaluator as discussed in Chapter Seven.

Doing as Well as Knowing

Communicating with the public and the professionals involved, teaching those with less knowledge about matters such as evaluation and funding, and selecting and implementing appropriate change strategies are examples of general activities that PDS leaders must carry out well in an uncommon PDS. There are also specific actions they should take that grow out of these general roles.

School-based leaders need to set policies and goals that make teacher education a priority within their school and school district. Similarly, university-based leaders need to contribute to a commitment by their institution to engage in the renewal of schools. As suggested in Chapter Two, these efforts may be best carried out if coordinated through a formal school-university partnership.

Leaders in both schools and universities need to participate actively in recruiting and selecting students for preservice education. It is particularly important, for example, that leaders act to increase the number of minority teachers prepared to function in renewing schools. Programs such as those developed by former national superintendent of the year Ken Moffet in Lennox, California, help to identify aides and others who move on to college and return to the district to increase the number of minority and second-language teachers available for the classroom.[5] Instead of waiting to see who self-selects for programs, educational leaders who create such programs encourage good candidates to make early decisions and place them in cohorts that enable these preservice candidates to move through programs learning from one another.

Leaders from both the university and the schools need to work together to insist on higher-quality teacher preparation programs by collaborating in shaping these programs and being selective in field placements during teacher preparation programs. Also, by hiring selectively—requiring that those they select come from good preparation programs—school-based leaders can eradicate inferior programs more quickly than by any other action they can take.

Leaders' primary responsibility is to secure the resources that are required for successful operation of their PDSs. This requires the application of many of the general skills mentioned previously. It means that good evaluative data will have to be available. They will need to be persuasive with policymakers—be they university regents, legislators, school boards, or the public at large.

How Can Leaders Be Developed and Sustained?

A common observation made when looking at the job description for a new dean or a new principal is, "Oh yes, and she has to walk on water, too!" A lot is asked of those who would be leaders in a PDS. How can such people be found and, once found, how can strong leadership be sustained?

Initial Preparation

The first step toward strong leaders for effective PDSs is ensuring that their initial education is sound. In other words, just as Goodlad has suggested that better teachers and better schools are linked,[6] so are better schools and better leaders for schools. These better preparation programs need to focus on developing the kinds of understandings and skills described earlier. Their ability to provide leadership to the educational enterprise will not be satisfied by a preparation program focused on generic management skills. PDSs such as Northglenn High School and others working with the University of Colorado at Denver recognize the connection between leadership preparation and success and build leadership development in as a key element to their program.

Good leadership preparation programs have strong clinical components. For example, new preparation programs for principals, such as those developed by the University of Washington, call for a minimum yearlong half-time internship in approved schools, and several districts working with the program support interns full time for a year. These programs also emphasize the development of reflective behavior for leaders and of expanding their understanding of the role of education in a democratic society.

Attention must be given to providing programs for prospective leaders in higher education as well as for future principals and teacher leaders. Smith and Fenstermacher report on one such effort. The IEI Leadership Associates Program was developed initially for a small cohort selected from rising leaders on faculties in education, the arts and sciences, and schools in the NNER. The program has been replicated in nearly all NNER settings.[7]

Professional Development

The continuing education of leaders is at least as important as their initial preparation. Programs such as the IEI Leadership Associates Program provide opportunities for some leaders to continue their growth once they enter into positions of leadership. However, the exigencies of their roles often conspire to interfere with continued learning. Opportunities available through professional organizations are too often short and superficial examinations of topics—particularly for school-based leaders. It is this area of continued professional growth for leaders that the school-university partnerships discussed in Chapters Two and Three serve particularly well. The potential of such partnerships for this role is also well described by contributors to *School-University Partnerships in Action*, edited by Sirotnik and Goodlad.[8] These partnerships enable university faculty to grow in learning about new teaching methods and issues related to learning in the classroom. For example, at Columbia College in South Carolina, school-based teachers conducted training in new approaches to cooperative learning for their college colleagues. Experiences facilitated by higher education faculty and partnership staff in Colorado helped school and university people grapple with issues related to building seamless curricula for grades kindergarten through sixteen. In PDSs across the country, university- and school-based faculty join with preservice candidates to promote continuing learning. At the Center of Inquiry, operated by the University of South Carolina and the Richland One School District, these groups come together several times a week to critique one another's work. In these reflective sessions there is a give-and-take that helps all grow.

Succession Planning

It is not enough to prepare new leaders and provide them with professional growth opportunities. It is also necessary to make provisions for replacements as leaders move on to other positions or retire from the profession. Each leader must accept responsibility for developing future leaders. Too often leaders are focused on the next rung of their own career ladders and lose sight of the need to help others. Good succession planning not only involves identifying prospective leaders and helping them secure the formal training required for a position but also means creating opportunities for these prospective leaders and carefully mentoring them in these roles.

A leader who tends to this responsibility is unlikely to take credit for work performed by an assistant. Rather, leaders thinking of the future go out of their way to make sure that developing leaders are recognized for their work. They are given full credit for contributions toward publications—not mentioned as an afterthought in an endnote. They are introduced to key decision makers as the persons responsible for successes—but not held up for blame during tough times.

Leaders working to ensure that succession is handled well always have several potential candidates to replace them. They avoid promising promotions they cannot make, but they encourage prospective leaders to seek advancement—even if it means losing their services. There is nothing worse for a leader than to have only followers no one else wants.

Rewards

Closely tied to the issue of succession is the matter of the rewards leaders receive for their efforts. There are traditional issues related to this, such as the processes established in higher education that lead to advancement and tenure. One kind of leader found in some institutions of higher education advises young professors to make sure that they focus on the traditional writing activities that will ensure their promotion. Good leaders make sure that their aspiring leaders advance as they work with PDSs by arranging publication opportunities for them and arguing the case for their scholarship with the appropriate reviewing bodies.

Rewards are just as important for school-based leaders as for those in higher education. Rewards in the form of different career opportunities, recognition by the institution of higher education for service, opportunities to participate in professional meetings, and increased compensation—all help build a strong commitment among school leaders to the PDS work.

———————

The emperor's new clothes will be real if care is taken in determining the nature of the garments, cultivating the fabric, putting on the first layer of clothing, ensuring that the clothes are stylish and not just faddish, providing support to keep the britches up, and evaluating critically and collaboratively. PDSs will be effective if strong leaders—leaders who understand what PDSs are and how to develop, support, and evaluate them—are prepared, nurtured, retained, and rewarded.

This chapter began with what may well have been an overdone metaphor, but the chaos experienced by the cyclists and bandleaders heading in different directions is really not unlike that experienced by some PDSs. Strong leaders and effective PDSs can accomplish much for the renewing schools needed by our social and political democracy and for the children whose education they will enrich.

Notes

Series Foreword

1. Theodore Roosevelt, "The Manly Virtues and Practical Politics," *Forum* 17 (July 1894): 551.

2. I explored this relationship in *Morality, Efficiency, and Reform: An Interpretation of the History of American Education*, Work in Progress Series no. 5 (Seattle: Institute for Educational Inquiry, 1995).

3. Neil Postman, *The End of Education: Redefining the Value of School* (New York: Vintage, 1996, orig. Knopf, 1995), pp. 5–6.

4. John I. Goodlad, *Educational Renewal: Better Teachers, Better Schools* (San Francisco: Jossey-Bass, 1994), pp. 4–6.

5. John I. Goodlad, *A Place Called School: Prospects for the Future* (New York: McGraw-Hill, 1984); John I. Goodlad, Roger Soder, and Kenneth A. Sirotnik (eds.), *The Moral Dimensions of Teaching* (San Francisco: Jossey-Bass, 1990); John I. Goodlad, Roger Soder, and Kenneth A. Sirotnik (eds.), *Places Where Teachers Are Taught* (San Francisco: Jossey-Bass, 1990); John I. Goodlad, *Teachers for Our Nation's Schools* (San Francisco: Jossey-Bass, 1990); and John I. Goodlad and Pamela Keating (eds.), *Access to Knowledge: An Agenda for Our Nation's Schools* (New York: College Entrance Examination Board, 1990).

   By 1997, four more books contributed to the growing literature associated with the Agenda: Goodlad, *Educational Renewal*; Roger Soder (ed.), *Democracy, Education, and the Schools* (San Francisco: Jossey-

Bass, 1996); John I. Goodlad and Timothy J. McMannon (eds.), *The Public Purpose of Education and Schooling* (San Francisco: Jossey-Bass, 1997); and John I. Goodlad, *In Praise of Education* (New York: Teachers College Press, 1997).

6. The postulates were first defined in Goodlad, *Teachers for Our Nation's Schools*, pp. 54–64, and later refined in Goodlad, *Educational Renewal*, pp. 70–94.

Prologue

1. Mary Diez, Program Notes for Critical Issues Forum (annual meeting of the American Association of Colleges for Teacher Education, Phoenix, February 1997).

2. John I. Goodlad, *Educational Renewal: Better Teachers, Better Schools* (San Francisco: Jossey-Bass, 1994), p. 100.

3. National Commission on Teaching & America's Future, *What Matters Most: Teaching for America's Future* (New York: National Commission on Teaching & America's Future, 1996).

Chapter One

1. National Commission on Teaching & America's Future, *What Matters Most: Teaching for America's Future* (New York: National Commission on Teaching & America's Future, 1996), p. 11.

2. Much of the following section is reprinted, with permission, from Richard W. Clark, *What School Leaders Can Do to Help Change Teacher Education*, 2nd ed. (Washington, D.C.: American Association of Colleges for Teacher Education, 1996).

3. National Commission on Teaching & America's Future, *What Matters Most*, p. 5.

4. National Commission on Teaching & America's Future, *What Matters Most*, p. 6.

5. Quoted in Clark, *What School Leaders Can Do to Help Change Teacher Education*, p. 3.

6. John I. Goodlad, *Teachers for Our Nation's Schools* (San Francisco: Jossey-Bass, 1990); and John I. Goodlad, *Educational Renewal: Better Teachers, Better Schools* (San Francisco: Jossey-Bass, 1994).

7. Goodlad, *Teachers for Our Nation's Schools*, Chapters Seven and Eight, and *Educational Renewal*. See also Robert S. Patterson, Nicholas M. Michelli, and Arturo Pacheco, *Centers of Pedagogy: New Structures for Educational Renewal* (San Francisco: Jossey-Bass, 1999).

8. Goodlad, *Teachers for Our Nation's Schools*, p. 63.

9. See, for example, Boyer Commission on Educating Undergraduates in the Research University, *Reinventing Undergraduate Education: A Blueprint for America's Research Universities* (Stony Brook: State University of New York at Stony Brook, 1998); and Christopher J. Lucas, *Crisis in the Academy: Rethinking Higher Education in America* (New York: St. Martin's, 1996).

10. See, for example, Richard W. Clark and Donna M. Hughes, *Partner Schools: Definitions and Expectations* (Seattle: Center for Educational Renewal, College of Education, University of Washington, 1995); Holmes Group, *Tomorrow's Schools: Principles for the Design of Professional Development Schools* (East Lansing, Mich.: Holmes Group, 1990); and National Council for Accreditation of Teacher Education, "Draft Standards for Identifying and Supporting Quality Professional Development Schools" (Washington, D.C.: National Council for Accreditation of Teacher Education, 1997).

11. Ismat Abdal-Haqq, *Professional Development Schools: Weighing the Evidence* (Thousand Oaks, Calif.: Corwin, 1998); and Richard W. Clark, *Professional Development Schools: Policy and Financing, A Guide for Policymakers* (Washington, D.C.: American Association of Colleges for Teacher Education, 1997).

12. National Council for Accreditation of Teacher Education, "Draft Standards."

13. Lynne Miller, "Partnership: Getting Broader, Getting Deeper," *NCREST Resources for Restructuring* (New York: National Center

for Restructuring Education, Schools, and Teaching, Teachers College, Columbia University, Winter 1995), pp. 1–2, 4–6.

14. Slightly modified from Clark, *Professional Development Schools: Policy and Financing,* pp. 6–7. The benefits listed here were identified in 1996 by an NNER work group consisting of school and university educators directly involved in PDS work. Evaluative data exist to support most of the claims, but they clearly do not apply to all PDSs.

Chapter Two

1. Marsha Levine, "Information Item," memorandum prepared for meeting of National Advisory Group Meeting, Professional Development Schools Standards Project (Washington, D.C.: National Council for Accreditation of Teacher Education, June 1997), p. 1.

2. John I. Goodlad, *A Place Called School: Prospects for the Future* (New York: McGraw-Hill, 1984).

3. "Fillmore" is a pseudonym that has been used by other researchers; because Temple University is identified in the chapter that serves as a reference for much of the following material, its name is retained here.

4. Morris J. Vogel and Essie Abrahams-Goldberg, "The Professional Development School as a Strategy for School Restructuring: The Millard Fillmore High School–Temple University Connection," in Michelle Fine (ed.), *Chartering Urban School Reform: Reflections on Public High Schools in the Midst of Change* (New York: Teachers College Press, 1994), p. 50.

5. Vogel and Abrahams-Goldberg, "Professional Development School as a Strategy for School Restructuring," p. 62.

6. Richard W. Clark, *Community-School-University Partnerships: Literature Review* (Washington, D.C.: Hamilton Fish National Institute on School and Community Violence, The George Washington University, May 1998). Much of the discussion that follows is taken from this review and is reprinted with permission from the Hamilton Fish Institute.

7. Robert Hutchison et al., "School University Collaboration: A Case Study" (paper presented at the meeting of the Mid-South Educational Research Association, Biloxi, Miss., 1995). Available through ERIC Document Reproduction Service, no. ED 393340.

8. Mitzi Lewison and Sue Holliday, "Control, Trust, and Rethinking Traditional Roles: Critical Elements in Creating a Mutually Beneficial University-School Partnership," *Teacher Education Quarterly* 24 (Winter 1997): 123–124.

9. Barbara A. Beyerbach et al., "A School/Business/University Partnership for Professional Development," *School Community Journal* 6 (Spring/Summer 1996): 102.

10. Philip Nyden et al. (eds.), *Building Community: Social Science in Action* (Thousand Oaks, Calif.: Pine Forge Press, 1997).

11. Nyden et al. (eds.), *Building Community*, p. 21.

12. John Silber, "The Partnership: The Vision," *Journal of Education* 176:1 (1994): 3–7; Anthony DiGregorio et al., "Influence of the Partnership on Education in Chelsea: A Conversation with Principals," *Journal of Education* 176:1 (1994): 121–125; and Edwin J. Delattre, "The Future in Chelsea," *Journal of Education* 176:1 (1994): 137–143.

13. Delattre, "Future in Chelsea," p. 138.

14. Richard Barnes and Lynne Miller, "Universities and Schools: The Two Sides of the Street and in Between," *Metropolitan Universities* 2 (Summer 1991): 51–60; and Lynne Miller and David L. Silvernail, "Wells Junior High School: Evolution of a Professional Development School," in Linda Darling-Hammond (ed.), *Professional Development Schools: Schools for Developing a Profession* (New York: Teachers College Press, 1994), pp. 28–49.

15. "El Paso, Texas: Overcoming Cultural and Economic Barriers," *Strategies for School System Leaders on District-Level Change* (Panasonic Foundation in collaboration with the American Association of School Administrators) 5 (January 1998): 7–11; Dolores DeAvila, "Parent & Community Engagement in Partner Schools," *Center Correspondent* (Center for Educational Renewal and the Institute for

Educational Inquiry) no. 13 (Fall/Winter 1997): 5–7; Arturo Pacheco, "University Commitment to Simultaneous Renewal," *Record in Educational Leadership* 15 (Spring/Summer 1995): 42–44; and Elizabeth R. Reisner, "High Standards for Reform: Final Report on the First Round of Implementation Grants to Community Compacts for Student Success" (Washington, D.C.: Policy Studies Associates, 1997).

16. Such linkages can create positive results or lead to the activist group's seeking to exert the same kind of influence in relation to the partnership as they do with other elements of the community.

17. "El Paso, Texas: Overcoming Cultural and Economic Barriers," p. 9.

18. Paul E. Heckman and Francine Peterman, "Indigenous Invention: New Promise for School Reform," *Teachers College Record* 98 (Winter 1996): 307–327; Paul E. Heckman, Christine B. Confer, and Jean Peacock, "Democracy in a Multicultural School and Community," in Jeannie Oakes and Karen Hunter Quartz (eds.), *Creating New Educational Communities: Ninety-Fourth Yearbook of the National Society for the Study of Education*, part I (Chicago: National Society for the Study of Education, 1995), pp. 187–201; and "ECC Creates a New Kind of Teacher Education Program," *Educational & Community Change Projector* 3 (Spring 1997): 1, 3–4, 6.

19. Brent Wilson, *The Quiet Evolution: Changing the Face of Arts Education* (Los Angeles: Getty Education Institute for the Arts, 1997).

20. See Theodore R. Sizer, *Horace's Compromise: The Dilemma of the American High School* (Boston: Houghton Mifflin, 1984); Theodore R. Sizer, *Horace's School: Redesigning the American High School* (Boston: Houghton Mifflin, 1992); and Theodore R. Sizer, *Horace's Hope: What Works for the American High School* (Boston: Houghton Mifflin, 1996).

21. See Olatokunbo S. Fashola and Robert E. Slavin, "Schoolwide Reform Models: What Works?" *Phi Delta Kappan* 79 (January 1998): 370–379.

22. Education Commission of the States, *A Policymakers' Guide to Education Reform Networks* (Denver: Education Commission of the States, 1997).

23. Fashola and Slavin, "Schoolwide Reform Models," p. 371.

24. Fashola and Slavin, "Schoolwide Reform Models," p. 376.

25. Carol Wilson, Richard Clark, and Paul Heckman, "Breaking New Ground: Reflections on the School-University Partnerships in the National Network for Educational Renewal," Occasional Paper no. 8. (Seattle: Center for Educational Renewal, College of Education, University of Washington, 1989).

26. For example, Ethne Erskine-Cullen examines the work of the Learning Consortium in Toronto in terms of these five stages of development in "School-University Partnerships as Change Agents: One Success Story," *School Effectiveness and School Improvement* 6 (1995): 192–204; and Jana R. Noel found this schema accurate in her analysis of a school partnership involving the Bozeman, Montana, school district and Montana State University. See her "Collaborative Inquiry into a Partnership Community," *School Community Journal* 6 (Fall/Winter 1996): 61–69.

27. Erskine-Cullen, "School-University Partnerships as Change Agents," p. 197.

28. Wilma F. Smith and Gary D Fenstermacher, *Leadership for Educational Renewal: Developing a Cadre of Leaders* (San Francisco: Jossey-Bass, 1999).

29. Sidney Trubowitz, "Stages in the Development of School-College Collaboration," *Educational Leadership* 43 (February 1986): 18–21.

30. Richard W. Clark and Wilma F. Smith, "Partnerships, Centers, and Schools," in Kenneth A. Sirotnik and Roger Soder (eds.), *The Beat of a Different Drummer: Essays on Educational Renewal in Honor of John I. Goodlad* (New York: Peter Lang, 1999).

31. Russell T. Osguthorpe et al. (eds.), *Partner Schools: Centers for Educational Renewal* (San Francisco: Jossey-Bass, 1995); and Robert S. Patterson, Nicholas M. Michelli, and Arturo Pacheco, "Brigham Young University, Utah," in *Centers of Pedagogy: New Structures for Educational Renewal* (San Francisco: Jossey-Bass, 1999).

32. Clark and Smith, "Partnerships, Centers, and Schools."

33. John I. Goodlad, *Educational Renewal: Better Teachers, Better Schools* (San Francisco: Jossey-Bass, 1994), p. 96.

34. Goodlad, *Educational Renewal*, p. 98.

35. Seymour B. Sarason, *You Are Thinking of Teaching? Opportunities, Problems, Realities* (San Francisco: Jossey-Bass, 1993), p. 32.

36. James B. Conant, *The Education of American Teachers* (New York: McGraw-Hill, 1963), pp. 92–93.

37. Conant, *Education of American Teachers*, pp. 93–94.

38. Conant, *Education of American Teachers*, p. 98.

39. Goodlad, *Educational Renewal*, p. 142.

40. Goodlad, *Educational Renewal*, p. 143.

41. Lee S. Shulman, "Knowledge and Teaching: Foundations of the New Reform," *Harvard Educational Review* 57 (February 1987): 8.

42. Conant, *Education of American Teachers*, pp. 94–95.

43. In addition to those set forth by Goodlad and colleagues working with the NNER, recent recommendations have come from many places, including the National Commission on Teaching & America's Future, *What Matters Most: Teaching for America's Future* (New York: National Commission on Teaching & America's Future, 1996); and the Holmes Group, *Tomorrow's Schools: Principles for the Design of Professional Development Schools* (East Lansing, Mich.: Holmes Group, 1990). Other school-renewal initiatives, such as Project 30 and the Renaissance Group, have also advocated changed approaches.

44. A case argued well by Linda Darling-Hammond in "Who Will Speak for the Children? How 'Teach for America' Hurts Urban Schools and Students," *Phi Delta Kappan* 76 (September 1994): 21–34.

45. Goodlad, *Educational Renewal*, pp. 155–156.

46. Slightly modified from Richard W. Clark, *Professional Development Schools: Policy and Financing, A Guide for Policymakers* (Washington, D.C.: American Association of Colleges for Teacher Education, 1997), pp. 15–16. Used with permission.

Chapter Three

1. Bruce C. Hafen and Jonathan O. Hafen, "The Courts: Order in the Classroom," *First Things* 65 (August/September 1996): 19.

2. Hafen and Hafen, "The Courts: Order in the Classroom," p. 19.

3. For an analysis based on both concepts and early experiences with school-university partnerships, see Kenneth A. Sirotnik and John I. Goodlad (eds.), *School-University Partnerships in Action: Concepts, Cases, and Concerns* (New York: Teachers College Press, 1988).

4. Barry L. Bull argues the case for both teachers' limits of authority and their freedom to teach effectively from the perspective of teaching as a risk-laden freedom. See his "The Limits of Teacher Professionalization" in John I. Goodlad, Roger Soder, and Kenneth A. Sirotnik (eds.), *The Moral Dimensions of Teaching* (San Francisco: Jossey-Bass, 1990), pp. 87–129.

5. Benjamin R. Barber expresses deep concern over the degree to which what goes on around and beyond schools undoes each workday what the school tries to do each school day. See his "America Skips School," *Harper's Magazine* 286 (November 1993): 39–46.

6. During this period of almost a century, reports on school reform virtually omitted reference to the role of teacher education, and reports on teacher education reform similarly omitted the connection to school reform. See Zhixin Su, "Teacher Education Reform in the United States (1890–1986)," Occasional Paper no. 3 (Seattle: Center for Educational Renewal, College of Education, University of Washington, 1986).

7. James B. Conant, *The American High School Today* (New York: McGraw-Hill, 1959), and *The Education of American Teachers* (New York: McGraw-Hill, 1963).

8. See, in particular, National Commission on Teaching & America's Future, *What Matters Most: Teaching for America's Future* (New York: National Commission on Teaching & America's Future, 1996).

9. For elaboration of what I mean by "education" and of the conditions education needs in order to flourish, see John I. Goodlad, *In Praise of Education* (New York: Teachers College Press, 1997).

10. For example, parents and other segments of the public have expectations that extend far beyond academic standards. See Jean Johnson and John Immerwahr, *First Things First: What Americans Expect from the Public Schools* (New York: Public Agenda, 1994).

11. Sheldon Richman, *Separating School and State: How to Liberate America's Families* (Fairfax, Va.: Future of Freedom Foundation, 1994).

12. Robert M. Hutchins, *The Higher Learning in America* (New Haven, Conn.: Yale University Press, 1936).

13. Neil Postman, *The End of Education: Redefining the Value of School* (New York: Vintage, 1996), pp. 27–28.

14. I have used the word *reform* on preceding pages only to align with popular parlance. However, I regard the word as having dysfunctional connotations that poorly fit educational improvement initiatives. *Renewal* fits much better my conception of education as an enterprise of the self, whether that self be individual or collective as, for example, in the case of institutions.

15. The reasons for both schools and universities to have reservations about joining in symbiotic partnerships put forward in this and the succeeding three paragraphs became evident in the inquiry that colleagues and I conducted in the late 1980s and that was reported in John I. Goodlad, *Teachers for Our Nation's Schools* (San Francisco: Jossey-Bass, 1990).

16. For further understanding of the influence of yesterday on teacher education today, see Jurgen Herbst, *And Sadly Teach: Teacher Education and Professionalization in American Culture* (Madison: University of Wisconsin Press, 1989); and Donald Warren (ed.), *American Teachers: Histories of a Profession at Work* (New York: Macmillan, 1989).

17. Timothy J. McMannon, *Morality, Efficiency, and Reform: An Interpretation of the History of American Education*, Work in Progress Series no. 5 (Seattle: Institute for Educational Inquiry, 1995).

18. Postman, *End of Education*, p. 197.

19. Encyclopaedia Britannica Educational Corporation has produced a series of short videotapes focused on major components of schooling in the context of the garden metaphor for educational renewal: John I. Goodlad, *Renewing a Place Called School*, series of six fifteen-minute videocassettes (Chicago: Frank Frost Productions for Encyclopaedia Britannica Educational Corporation in cooperation with the Southern Association of Colleges and Schools, 1988).

20. The founders are, in alphabetical order, John I. Goodlad, Kenneth A. Sirotnik, and Roger Soder.

21. John I. Goodlad, "Linking Schools and Universities: Symbiotic Partnerships," Occasional Paper no. 1 (Seattle: Center for Educational Renewal, College of Education, University of Washington, 1986, rev. 1987).

22. See, for example, Sirotnik and Goodlad (eds.), *School-University Partnerships in Action*; Richard W. Clark, "School/University Relations: Partnerships and Networks," Occasional Paper no. 2 (Seattle: Center for Educational Renewal, College of Education, University of Washington, 1986); Calvin M. Frazier, "An Analysis of a Social Experiment: School-University Partnerships in 1988," Occasional Paper no. 6 (Seattle: Center for Educational Renewal, College of Education, University of Washington, 1988); Carol Wilson, Richard Clark, and Paul Heckman, "Breaking New Ground: Reflections on School-University Partnerships in the NNER," Occasional Paper no. 8 (Seattle: Center for Educational Renewal, College of Education, University of Washington, 1989); and John I. Goodlad and Roger Soder, "School-University Partnerships: An Appraisal of an Idea," Occasional Paper no. 14 (Seattle: Center for Educational Renewal, College of Education, University of Washington, 1992).

23. John I. Goodlad, "Reflections on Agendas," *Center Correspondent* (Center for Educational Renewal, College of Education, University of Washington) no. 5 (October 1993): 1, 23–25.

24. For a detailed description and analysis of this agenda, see John I. Goodlad, *Educational Renewal: Better Teachers, Better Schools* (San Francisco: Jossey-Bass, 1994). For elaboration of the public purpose component of the agenda, see John I. Goodlad and Timothy J.

McMannon (eds.), *The Public Purpose of Education and Schooling* (San Francisco: Jossey-Bass, 1997).

25. For more information about and understanding of these partner schools and the concepts guiding their work, see Russell T. Osguthorpe et al. (eds.), *Partner Schools: Centers for Educational Renewal* (San Francisco: Jossey-Bass, 1995).

26. Goodlad, Soder, and Sirotnik (eds.), *Moral Dimensions of Teaching*. A later book enlarges this vision; see Roger Soder (ed.), *Democracy, Education, and the Schools* (San Francisco: Jossey-Bass, 1996).

27. Gary D Fenstermacher, "Where Are We Going? Who Will Lead Us There?" (presidential address at annual meeting of the American Association of Colleges for Teacher Education, San Antonio, Tex., February 25, 1992).

28. Israel Scheffler, "Basic Mathematical Skills: Some Philosophical and Practical Remarks," *Teachers College Record* 78 (December 1976): 206.

29. Edward Tenner, *Why Things Bite Back: Technology and the Revenge of Unintended Consequences* (New York: Knopf, 1996), p. x.

Chapter Four

1. Theodore R. Sizer, *Horace's Compromise: The Dilemma of the American High School* (Boston: Houghton Mifflin, 1984). See also Sizer's *Horace's School: Redesigning the American High School* (Boston: Houghton Mifflin, 1992); and *Horace's Hope: What Works for the American High School* (Boston: Houghton Mifflin, 1996).

2. Elizabeth Kozleski, William R. Munsel, and Carol Wilson, "Benchmarks for Partner Schools" (Denver: Colorado Partnership for Educational Renewal, 1996). Reprinted here with minor revisions by permission.

3. Colorado Partnership for Educational Renewal, "Response Rubrics: Potential Partner School Site Identification Process" (Denver: Colorado Partnership for Educational Renewal, 1996). Reprinted here with minor revisions by permission.

4. National Council for Accreditation of Teacher Education, "Draft Standards for Identifying and Supporting Quality Professional Development Schools" (Washington, D.C.: National Council for Accreditation of Teacher Education, September 1997), p. 2.

5. National Council for Accreditation of Teacher Education, "Draft Standards," pp. 11–18.

6. The outline for the agreement is not intended to be an offer of legal advice. The components suggested relate to those matters that are important to the partners, but they may not constitute all elements that are required legally. Partners should obtain legal assistance from appropriate sources regarding such agreements.

7. Reprinted in Susan Jackman Breck, "Implementing Professional Development Schools: Seeking a Shared Vision" (Ph.D. diss., University of Kansas, 1994), pp. 216–221. Reprinted here with minor revisions with permission from the School of Education, University of Kansas.

Chapter Five

1. John I. Goodlad and Timothy J. McMannon (eds.), *The Public Purpose of Education and Schooling* (San Francisco: Jossey-Bass, 1997); and John I. Goodlad, *In Praise of Education* (New York: Teachers College Press, 1997).

2. See, for example, Karen W. Arenson, "CUNY to Tighten Admissions Policy at 4-Year Schools," *New York Times,* 27 May 1998, late ed. East Coast), p. A1.

3. Erma Bombeck, "The Politicians Elude the Credibility Factor," *Seattle Times,* 17 April 1988, p. K5.

4. Seymour Sarason, *The Predictable Failure of Educational Reform* (San Francisco: Jossey-Bass, 1990).

5. Joel Spring, *The Sorting Machine Revisited: National Education Policy Since 1945,* rev. ed. (New York: Longman, 1989).

6. Mary Ann Glendon, *Rights Talk: The Impoverishment of Political Discourse* (New York: Free Press, 1991), p. 129.

7. Two overviews that include references providing detailed information about such efforts are Education Commission of the States, *A Policymakers' Guide to Education Reform Networks* (Denver: Education Commission of the States, 1997), and Kathleen Florio, *Twenty-One Initiatives for Educational Renewal* (Seattle: Institute for Educational Inquiry, forthcoming).

8. Theodore R. Sizer, *Horace's School: Redesigning the American High School* (Boston: Houghton Mifflin, 1992); and Theodore R. Sizer, *Horace's Hope: What Works for the American High School* (Boston: Houghton Mifflin, 1996).

9. Patricia Wasley, Robert Hampel, and Richard W. Clark, *Kids and School Reform* (San Francisco: Jossey-Bass, 1998); and Patricia Wasley, Robert Hampel, and Richard W. Clark, "The Puzzle of Whole-School Change," *Phi Delta Kappan* 78 (May 1997): 690–697.

10. M. Scott Peck, *The Different Drum: Community-Making and Peace* (New York: Simon & Schuster, 1987).

11. Mary Ann Raywid, *Taking Stock: The Movement to Create Mini-Schools, Schools-within-Schools, and Separate Small Schools* (ERIC Clearing House on Urban Education, Urban Diversity Series no. 108, 1996); Deborah Meier, "The Big Benefits of Smallness," *Educational Leadership* 54 (September 1996): 12–15; and Thomas J. Sergiovanni, *Leadership for the Schoolhouse* (San Francisco: Jossey-Bass, 1996), Chapter Six.

12. Robert L. Fried, *The Passionate Teacher* (Boston: Beacon Press, 1995).

13. The district receives as well as gives in this relationship. As noted in Chapter Four, the Colorado Partnership benchmarks identify a number of ways in which professional development schools are useful to school districts.

14. National Council for Accreditation of Teacher Education, "Draft Standards for Identifying and Supporting Quality Professional Development Schools" (Washington, D.C.: National Council for Accreditation of Teacher Education, September 1997), pp. 11–18.

15. Mary McDonnell Harris and J. Sharon Gates, "Using Standards in Simultaneous Renewal," *Action in Teacher Education* 19 (Summer 1997): 29.

16. Harris and Gates, "Using Standards in Simultaneous Renewal," p. 30.

17. Mary McDonnell Harris, JoNell Bakke, and Sandy Johnson, "Professional Development Schools Standards Project, Pilot PDS Partner Site Application, University of North Dakota and Grand Forks Public Schools," unpublished manuscript (Grand Forks: College of Education, University of North Dakota, May 1998). Reprinted here with minor revisions by permission.

18. Agnes Hamerlik and Mary McDonnell Harris, "Inside and Outside: Working Together at a Professional Development School," *Insights into Open Education* 27 (October 1995): 8–9.

19. Hamerlik and Harris, "Inside and Outside," p. 9.

20. Among the schools drawn on for material in this composite profile are Bulkeley High School in Hartford, Connecticut, as described in Kay Norlander, Charles W. Case, and Timothy Reagan "Bulkeley High School in Partnership with the University of Connecticut: A Profile of Simultaneous Renewal," unpublished draft (Storrs: School of Education, University of Connecticut, November 1995); Richland Northeast in Columbia, South Carolina, as described in Lucy Snead, "A Portrait of the Partnership between Richland Northeast High School and Columbia College," *Portraits of Twelve High School Partner Schools in the National Network for Educational Renewal,* Reflections on Practice Series no. 3 (Seattle: Center for Educational Renewal, University of Washington, November 1997); Orem (Utah) High School as described in John Childs et al., "Secondary Partner School Portrait: Orem High School," *Portraits of Twelve High School Partner Schools in the National Network for Educational Renewal,* Reflections on Practice Series no. 3 (Seattle: Center for Educational Renewal, University of Washington, November 1997); and Madeira Junior/Senior High School in Cincinnati, Ohio, as reported in D. J. Hammond, Robert Larbes, and Bernard Badiali,

"Experiencing the Promise of Simultaneous Renewal: A Portrait of Madeira Junior/Senior High School," *Portraits of Twelve High School Partner Schools in the National Network for Educational Renewal*, Reflections on Practice Series no. 3 (Seattle: Center for Educational Renewal, University of Washington, November 1997).

21. Enculturating the young in a democracy, providing access to knowledge, and serving as stewards of the schools are, along with providing a nurturing pedagogy, the moral mission of schooling and teaching as outlined by John I. Goodlad. See his *Educational Renewal: Better Teachers, Better Schools* (San Francisco: Jossey-Bass, 1994), pp. 4–5.

22. Childs et al., "Secondary Partner School Portrait: Orem High School," p. 6.

23. After Snead, "Portrait of the Partnership between Richland Northeast High School and Columbia College," p. 6.

24. After Hammond, Larbes, and Badiali, "Experiencing the Promise of Simultaneous Renewal," p. 5.

25. Norlander, Case, and Reagan, "Bulkeley High School in Partnership with the University of Connecticut," p. 16.

Chapter Six

1. Substantial portions of this chapter have been reprinted with permission from Richard W. Clark and Margaret L. Plecki, "Professional Development Schools: Their Costs and Financing," in Marsha Levine and Roberta Trachtman (eds.), *Making Professional Development Schools Work: Politics, Practice, and Policy* (New York: Teachers College Press, 1997), pp. 134–158.

2. Richard W. Clark, "Who Decides? The Basic Policy Issue," in Laurel N. Tanner (ed.), *Critical Issues in Curriculum: Eighty-Seventh Yearbook of the National Society for the Study of Education*, part I (Chicago: National Society for the Study of Education, 1988), pp. 175–204.

3. Evans Clinchy, "Higher Education: The Albatross around the Neck of Our Public Schools," *Phi Delta Kappan* 75 (June 1994): 744–751.

4. National Commission on Excellence in Education, *A Nation at Risk: The Imperative for Educational Reform* (Washington, D.C.: U.S. Government Printing Office, 1983).

5. Allan Odden, "Sources of Funding for Education Reform," *Phi Delta Kappan* 67 (January 1986): 335.

6. John I. Goodlad, *Teachers for Our Nation's Schools* (San Francisco: Jossey-Bass, 1990), p. 238.

7. Linda Darling-Hammond and Milbrey W. McLaughlin, "Policies That Support Professional Development in an Era of Reform," *Phi Delta Kappan* 76 (April 1995): 597–604.

8. Although the master's requirement was repealed in Washington, an even more demanding professional certification requirement was established. This requirement calls for an individualized professional growth program for all new teachers during their first five years of teaching (regardless of the advanced degrees they may hold). The costs of this added requirement have not yet been fully recognized or calculated.

9. Darrell R. Lewis, "Estimating the Economic Worth of a Fifth-Year Licensure Program for Teachers," *Educational Evaluation and Policy Analysis* 12 (Spring 1990): 25–39; and Deborah A. Verstegen, "Education Fiscal Policy in the Reagan Administration," *Educational Evaluation and Policy Analysis* 12 (Winter 1990): 355–373.

10. Allan Odden, "Including School Finance in Systemic Reform Strategies: A Commentary," *CPRE Finance Briefs* (New Brunswick, N.J.: CPRE Rutgers, The State University of New Jersey [A publication of the CPRE Finance Center, University of Wisconsin at Madison], May 1994), p. 1.

11. William S. McKersie, "Philanthropy's Paradox: Chicago School Reform," *Educational Evaluation and Policy Analysis* 15 (Summer 1993): 109–128.

12. Mary Beth Marklein, "Economics 101: Why College Costs So Much," *USA Today*, 5 February 1997, p. D2.

13. Chris Pipho, "Stateline: Getting a Return on the Education Dollar," *Phi Delta Kappan* 76 (April 1995): 582–583.

14. Odden, "Including School Finance in Systemic Reform Strategies," p. 1.

15. For an example of the polemic continuing to come from the political and academic communities on the reasons why more money should not be spent on public education, see Lewis C. Solmon and Michael Fox, "Fatally Flawed School Funding Formulas," *Education Week*, 17 June 1998, pp. 60, 48–49.

16. Marklein, "Economics 101," p. D2.

17. Kerry A. White, "As Tuition Climbs, More States Ponder College-Aid Plans," *Education Week*, 18 March 1998, p. 26.

18. William A. Firestone et al., "Where Did the $800 Million Go? The First Year of New Jersey's Quality Education Act," *Educational Evaluation and Policy Analysis* 16 (Winter 1994): 359–373; and Kerry A. White, "Finance Battles Show Solutions Remain Elusive," *Education Week*, 11 June 1997, pp. 1, 32–33.

19. Jacob E. Adams Jr., "Spending School Reform Dollars in Kentucky: Familiar Patterns and New Programs, But Is This Reform?" *Educational Evaluation and Policy Analysis* 16 (Winter 1994): 375–390.

20. Lawrence O. Picus, "The Local Impact of School Finance Reform in Four Texas School Districts," *Educational Evaluation and Policy Analysis* 16 (Winter 1994): 391–404; Firestone et al., "Where Did the $800 Million Go?"; Adams, "Spending School Reform Dollars in Kentucky"; and White, "Finance Battles."

21. See, for example, Bruce A. Peseau, "Developing an Adequate Resource Base for Teacher Education," *Journal of Teacher Education* 32 (July-August 1982): 13–15; Bruce A. Peseau and Paul Orr, "The Outrageous Underfunding of Teacher Education," *Phi Delta Kappan* 62 (October 1980): 100–102; Goodlad, *Teachers for Our Nation's Schools*, p. 85; and John I. Goodlad, *Educational Renewal: Better Teachers, Better Schools* (San Francisco: Jossey-Bass, 1994), p. 50.

22. David C. Berliner, "Making the Right Changes in Preservice Teacher Education," *Phi Delta Kappan* 66 (October 1984): 96.

23. Bruce A. Peseau, Carl Backman, and Betty Fry, "A Cost Model for Clinical Teacher Education," *Action in Teacher Education* 9 (Spring 1987): 21–34.

24. Richard Howard, Randy Hitz, and Larry Baker, "Comparative Study of Expenditures Per Student Credit Hour of Education Programs to Programs of Other Disciplines and Professions," prepared for the Government Relations Committee of the American Association of Colleges for Teacher Education, the Association of Colleges and Schools of Education in State Universities and Land Grant Colleges and Affiliated Private Universities, and the Teacher Education Council for State Colleges and Universities (Bozeman: Montana State University, Fall 1997).

25. Ralph W. Tyler, "What We've Learned from Past Studies of Teacher Education," *Phi Delta Kappan* 66 (June 1985): 684.

26. Neil D. Theobald, "The Financing and Governance of Professional Development or Partner Schools," Occasional Paper no. 10 (Seattle: Center for Educational Renewal, College of Education, University of Washington, 1990).

27. Neil D. Theobald, "Staffing, Financing, and Governing Professional Development Schools," *Educational Evaluation and Policy Analysis* 13 (Spring 1991): 87–101; Neil D. Theobald, "Allocating Resources to Renew Teacher Education," Occasional Paper no. 14 (Seattle: Center for Educational Renewal, College of Education, University of Washington, 1991).

28. C. Raymond Anderson (ed.), *Voices of Change: A Report of the Clinical Schools Project* (Washington, D.C.: American Association of Colleges for Teacher Education, 1993).

29. *Education Daily*, 12 March 1992, p. 1.

30. Theobald, "Staffing, Financing, and Governing Professional Development Schools."

31. Bruce A. Peseau and Roger L. Tudor, "Exploring and Testing Cluster Analysis," *Research in Higher Education* 29 (September 1988): 60–78.

32. Theobald, "Staffing, Financing and Governing Professional Development Schools," pp. 94–95.

33. Goodlad, *Teachers for Our Nation's Schools*, Chapters Six and Seven; and *Educational Renewal*.

34. Goodlad, *Teachers for Our Nation's Schools*, p. 238.

35. Among those making this observation are Anderson, *Voices of Change*; Sharon P. Robinson and Linda Darling-Hammond, "Change for Collaboration and Collaboration for Change: Transforming Teaching through School-University Partnerships," in Linda Darling-Hammond (ed.), *Professional Development Schools: Schools for Developing a Profession* (New York: Teachers College Press, 1994), pp. 203–219; and Marsha Levine, "21st Century Professional Education: How Education Could Learn from Medicine, Business, and Engineering," *Education Week*, 1 February 1995, pp. 33–36.

36. Levine, "21st Century Professional Education"; Clark and Plecki, "Professional Development Schools: Their Costs and Financing," pp. 134–158; and Richard W. Clark, *Professional Development Schools: Policy and Financing, A Guide forPolicymakers* (Washington, D.C.:·American Association of Colleges for Teacher Education, 1997).

37. Jon Snyder, "Finance and Policy Conditions that Grow and Sustain Professional Development Schools," unpublished paper (Washington, D.C.: NCATE Professional Development Schools Standards Project National Advisory Group Meeting, 4–5 June 1997), p. 2.

38. Linda Darling-Hammond, "Developing Professional Development Schools: Early Lessons, Challenge, and Promise," in Darling-Hammond (ed.), *Professional Development Schools*, p. 23.

39. Richard Ishler, "Professional Development Schools: What Are They? How Are They Funded? How Should They Be Evaluated?" draft copy (Monterey, Calif.: Report of Task Force on Professional Development Schools, Association of Colleges and Schools of Education in State Universities and Land-Grant Colleges and Affiliated Private Universities, 16 October 1994), p. 10.

40. Darling-Hammond, "Developing Professional Development Schools," p. 23.

41. Robinson and Darling-Hammond, "Change for Collaboration," p. 215.

42. Goodlad, *Teachers for Our Nation's Schools*, p. 374.

43. Bart Gallegos, "Teachers for Chicago: Ensuring Urban Teachers with Class," *Phi Delta Kappan* 76 (June 1995): 784.

44. Levine, "21st Century Professional Education," pp. 33–36.

45. Theobald, "Staffing, Financing, and Governing Professional Development Schools," p. 89.

46. Odden, "Including School Finance in Systemic Reform Strategies," p. 4.

47. Odden, "Including School Finance in Systemic Reform Strategies," p. 5.

48. Odden, "Including School Finance in Systemic Reform Strategies," pp. 7–8.

49. In order to examine the costs of these four different approaches to PDSs more completely, the following assumptions were made concerning compensation. Salary and benefits for a full-time faculty member at the school or university: $60,000; salary and benefits for an adjunct faculty member (lecturer, coordinator): $30,000; salary and benefits of clerical personnel: $25,000. In Table 6.1 these common dollar figures were used to report the summary of total costs for the four schools.

50. Jane H. Applegate, "A New Vision for Teacher Education at West Virginia University: Report of the Participants of Partners for Progress: A Collaborative Project for Educational Improvement in West Virginia," 2nd rev. (Morgantown: Center for Renewal of Professional Preparation and Practice, College of Human Resources and Education, University of West Virginia, 30 August 1994), p. 42.

51. Costs reported for schools include all items for which school district checks are written *regardless of original source* of the funds; similarly, the items classified as costs for the university are those for which the university writes the checks. For example, if a university is the fiscal agent for a school-university partnership, minigrants written for assessment inquiry projects conducted by teachers as part of the partnership effort are listed under the university even though the funds came originally from the districts in the partnership. The PDS's por-

tion of a school district's contribution to a partnership shows as an item paid by the district. Faculty members are listed as full-time equivalents rather than as salary amounts to avoid distortion because of regional and other factors that determine salary variances among schools and universities. The costs listed are those associated with the school's serving its mission as a PDS and do not include the underlying costs of educating the elementary or secondary children enrolled or those aspects of professional education of preservice students that takes place at locations other than the PDS.

Chapter Seven

1. Joni E. Finney, "At the Crossroads: Linking Teacher Education to School Reform" (Denver: Education Commission of the States, October 1992); and Calvin M. Frazier, "A Shared Vision: Policy Recommendations for Linking Teacher Education to School Reform" (Denver: Education Commission of the States, July 1993).

2. Kenneth A. Sirotnik, "The Meaning and Conduct of Inquiry in School-University Partnerships," in Kenneth A. Sirotnik and John I. Goodlad (eds.), *School-University Partnerships in Action: Concepts, Cases, and Concerns* (New York: Teachers College Press, 1988), pp. 169–190.

3. For a contrary view, see Francis Schrag, "In Defense of Positivist Research Paradigms," *Educational Researcher* 21 (June-July 1992): 5–7.

4. Lee Cronbach, "Beyond the Two Disciplines of Scientific Psychology," *American Psychologist* 30 (February 1975): 119.

5. Michael G. Fullan and Matthew B. Miles, "Getting Reform Right: What Works and What Doesn't," *Phi Delta Kappan* 73 (June 1992): 744–752.

6. Seymour B. Sarason, *The Creation of Settings and the Future Societies* (San Francisco: Jossey-Bass, 1972); Seymour B. Sarason, *The Culture of the School and the Problem of Change* (Boston: Allyn & Bacon, 1982).

7. This statement is offered in part based on thirty-eight years of personal observations of public school and higher education policy-

making. For more "scholarly" support of the statement, see Amitai Etzioni, *The Active Society: Theory of Societal and Political Processes* (New York: Free Press, 1968).

8. Barbara Feezell, "One Site's Beginnings: Developing a University-Partner School Relationship as a Member of the Nebraska Network for Educational Renewal" (Ph.D. diss., University of Nebraska, Lincoln, 1997), p. 63.

9. Edward O. Wilson, *Consilience: The Unity of Knowledge* (New York: Knopf, 1998), p. 27.

10. Robert E. Stake, *The Art of Case Study Research* (Thousand Oaks, Calif.: Sage, 1995).

11. Robert Schaefer, *The School as the Center of Inquiry* (New York: Harper & Row, 1967); Sarason, *Culture of the School and the Problem of Change*; John I. Goodlad, *The Dynamics of Educational Change* (New York: McGraw-Hill, 1975); Donald A. Schön, *The Reflective Practitioner: How Professionals Think in Action* (New York: Basic Books, 1983).

12. Ann Lieberman, "The Meaning of Scholarly Activity and the Building of Community," *Educational Researcher* 21 (August-September 1992): 5–12.

13. Sirotnik, "Meaning and Conduct of Inquiry," p. 175.

14. For examples of reports based on such inquiry, see Patricia Wasley, Robert L. Hampel, and Richard W. Clark, "The Puzzle of Whole-School Change," *Phi Delta Kappan* 78 (May 1997): 690–697; and Patricia Wasley, Robert Hampel, and Richard W. Clark, *Kids and School Reform* (San Francisco: Jossey-Bass, 1998).

15. John I. Goodlad, "School-University Partnerships for Educational Renewal: Rationale and Concepts," in Sirotnik and Goodlad (eds.), *School-University Partnerships in Action*, p. 12.

16. Goodlad, "School-University Partnerships for Educational Renewal," p. 24.

17. Sarason, *Culture of the School and the Problem of Change*, p. 121.

18. Seymour B. Sarason, *The Making of an American Psychologist: An Autobiography* (San Francisco: Jossey-Bass, 1988), p. 354.

19. Sarason, *Making of an American Psychologist,* p. 367.

20. Kenneth A. Sirotnik, "Critical Inquiry: A Paradigm for Praxis," in Edmund C. Short (ed.), *Forms of Curriculum Inquiry* (New York: State University of New York Press, 1991), p. 245. For this passage Sirotnik cites John Rawls, *A Theory of Justice* (Cambridge, Mass.: Harvard University Press, 1971); and "Justice as Fairness: Political Not Metaphysical," *Philosophy and Public Affairs* 14 (Summer 1985): 223–251. Roots of critical theory are found in works of Paolo Freire, *Pedagogy of the Oppressed* (New York: Seabury Press, 1973); and Henry A. Giroux, *Theory and Resistance in Education: A Pedagogy for the Opposition* (South Hadley, Mass.: Bergin and Garvey, 1983).

21. Sirotnik, "Critical Inquiry: A Paradigm for Praxis," p. 247.

22. Sirotnik, "Meaning and Conduct of Inquiry," p. 175.

23. Sirotnik, "Meaning and Conduct of Inquiry," p. 174.

24. Linda Darling-Hammond, "Reframing the School Reform Agenda: Developing Capacity for School Transformation," *Phi Delta Kappan* 74 (June 1993): 753–761.

25. For listings and descriptions of the postulates, see John I. Goodlad, *Teachers for Our Nation's Schools* (San Francisco: Jossey-Bass, 1990), pp. 53–65; and John I. Goodlad, *Educational Renewal: Better Teachers, Better Schools* (San Francisco: Jossey-Bass, 1994), pp. 67–95.

26. Goodlad, *Educational Renewal,* p. 4.

27. Frank B. Murray, "'All or None' Criteria for Professional Development Schools," *Educational Policy* 7 (March 1993): 63–67.

28. Theodore R. Sizer, *Horace's Compromise: The Dilemma of the American High School* (Boston: Houghton Mifflin, 1984), pp. 225–227; and Theodore R. Sizer, *Horace's School: Redesigning the American High School* (Boston: Houghton Mifflin, 1992), pp. 207–209.

29. Richard W. Clark and Donna M. Hughes, *Partner Schools: Definitions and Expectations* (Seattle: Center for Educational Renewal, College of Education, University of Washington, January 1995), pp. 1–2.

30. Robert L. Hampel, "Apart-nerships," *Record in Educational Administration and Supervision* 13 (Spring/Summer 1993): pp. 27–31.

31. Phillip C. Schlechty and Betty Lou Whitford, "Shared Problems and Shared Vision: Organic Collaboration," in Sirotnik and Goodlad (eds.), *School-University Partnerships in Action*, pp. 191–204.

32. Sirotnik, "Meaning and Conduct of Inquiry," p. 175.

33. Sirotnik, "Meaning and Conduct of Inquiry," pp. 175–176.

34. Jianping Shen, "Voices from the Field: School-Based Faculty Members' Vision of Preservice Teacher Education in the Context of a Professional Development School," Occasional Paper no. 16 (Seattle: Center for Educational Renewal, College of Education, University of Washington, April 1993).

35. Jorge Descamps, "Evaluation Design, University of Texas, El Paso, Schedule #4C—Program Evaluation Design," part of grant application to Texas State Board for Educator Certification, prepared at College of Education, University of Texas at El Paso, 1993, and reprinted in Clark, "Evaluating Partner Schools," pp. 257–260.

36. Terry L. Deniston, "Authentic Inquiry and Collaboration at a Non-Traditional Professional Development High School," (Ph.D. diss., Colorado State University, 1997), pp. 29–30.

37. Deniston, "Authentic Inquiry and Collaboration," p. 32.

38. Deniston, "Authentic Inquiry and Collaboration," p. 35.

39. Deniston, "Authentic Inquiry and Collaboration," pp. 105–106.

40. Elizabeth Kozleski et al., "Studying Partnership through Empowerment Evaluation: A Statewide View" (paper presented at annual meeting of the American Educational Research Association, Chicago, March 1997).

41. Kozleski et al., "Studying Partnership through Empowerment Evaluation," p. 2.

42. Edward E. Paradis, Audrey M. Kleinsasser, and T. A. Grindrod, "Wyoming Teacher Education Program NEA/TEI Evaluation Report: 1996–97" (Laramie: College of Education, University of Wyoming, November 1997).

43. Paradis, Kleinsasser, and Grindrod, "Wyoming Teacher Education Program," p. 3.

44. See Richard W. Clark, "The Development of Schools That Practice Reflaction," in Michelle Fine (ed.), *Chartering Urban School Reform: Reflections on Public High Schools in the Midst of Change* (New York: Teachers College Press, 1994) pp. 31–46; and Lieberman, "Meaning of Scholarly Activity."

45. Wasley, Hampel, and Clark, "Puzzle of Whole-School Change," pp. 690–697; and Wasley, Hampel, and Clark, *Kids and School Reform*.

Chapter Eight

1. Quoted in Richard W. Clark, *What School Leaders Can Do to Help Change Teacher Education*, 2nd ed. (Washington, D.C.: American Association of Colleges for Teacher Education, 1996), p. 25.

2. Neil Postman and Charles Weingartner, *Teaching as a Subversive Activity* (New York: Delacorte, 1969), p. 1.

3. John I. Goodlad, "Teachers as Moral Stewards of Our Schools," commencement address, University of Victoria, Victoria, British Columbia, 6 June 1998, pp. 2–3.

4. Patricia A. Wasley and Nancy Linnon, *Making Change* (San Francisco: Jossey-Bass, forthcoming).

5. Clark, *What School Leaders Can Do*, p. 15.

6. John I. Goodlad, *Educational Renewal: Better Teachers, Better Schools* (San Francisco: Jossey-Bass, 1994).

7. Wilma F. Smith and Gary D Fenstermacher (eds.), *Leadership for Educational Renewal: Developing a Cadre of Leaders* (San Francisco: Jossey-Bass, 1999).

8. Kenneth A. Sirotnik and John I. Goodlad (eds.), *School-University Partnerships in Action: Concepts, Cases, and Concerns* (New York: Teachers College Press, 1988).

Index

University of Kansas School of Education, sample partnership agreement of, 113–118

University of Nebraska, Omaha, 186

University of North Dakota (UND)-Lake Agassiz Elementary partnership: assessment at, 139, 140; background on, 136–137; curriculum of, 139; full-service school of, 139–140; funding of, 186; resident teacher program of, 138; steering committee of, 137; support to pre-service teachers in, 137–138

University of North Dakota (UND)-Lake Agassiz Elementary School partnership, 136–141

University of South Carolina (USC), 107; Center for Inquiry, 132, 247–248

University of Southern Maine Partnership, 37, 184

University of Texas, El Paso (UTEP), 43; Center for Professional Development and Technology evaluation of, 226–227

University of Washington, 55; Center for Educational Renewal (CER), 41–42, 85–86; Extended Teacher Education Program (ETEP), 41–42; principal preparation program of, 246–247

University of Wyoming evaluation project, 232–233

UNUM Charitable Trust, 184

Urban settings, 169

USA Today, 155, 156

Utah, 169, 241

V

Valéry, P., 89

Values: clarification of, for professional development schools, 216–221; clarification of, for school renewal and teacher education, 215–216; clarification of, in critical, collaborative inquiry, 213–221,

236–237; emotional filters and, 215; resistance to clarifying, 220–221; stakeholders' clarification of, 216, 223; summary statements of, 217–221

Volunteer services, 182, 193, 197

Vouchers, 158

W

Waiting for results stage, 49

Washington State: affirmative action demise in, 157; lowered primary class size in, 170–171; teacher certification legislation of, 154–155

Wasley, P. A., 233–236, 243

Weingartner, C., 241

West Virginia University, 183

West Virginia University PDS Collaborative, 37, 46

Wheelock College partnerships, 54

Whitford, B. L., 222

Wiggins, G., 140

Wilson, B., 45

Wilson, C., 47–50

Wilson, E. O., 209–210

Winthrop Rockefeller, 184

Workplace preparation, as goal of schooling, 77, 80–81

Workshops, professional development, 146, 188

Wyoming, 168

Y

Yale Psycho-Educational Clinic, 212

Ysleta Elementary, 43

Substantial portions of Chapter 7 were originally published in *Partner Schools: Centers For Educational Renewal* edited by Russell T. Osguthorpe, R. Carl Harris, Melanie F. Harris, and Sharon Black. San Francisco: Jossey-Bass, 1995.

Portions throughout the book originally appeared in several occasional papers and items in the *Correspondent* from the Center for Educational Renewal of the College of Education at the University of Washington.